PRAISE FOR

Maria's Scarf

"Sometimes, we need to see how someone overcomes the obstacles in their life to muster up the courage necessary to meet our own. *Maria's Scarf* is a portrait of courage that will inspire dreamers, both young and old. A timely immigrant story of a family pursuing the American dream. You'll be thinking about these heartbreaking, hilarious, and harrowing adventures long after you put the book down!"

—JOYCE MEYER, *New York Times* bestselling author

"Both Zoro and I were blessed to live our dreams. *Maria's Scarf* will inspire you to never give up on yours."

—FRANKIE VALLI,
lead vocalist of Frankie Valli and the Four Seasons
and cocreator of *Jersey Boys*, the Broadway musical

"I can't recall ever reading a book when I just wanted to stand up and cheer again and again, but that's how Zoro's memoir affected me. If I could, I would give this book to every young person in the world."

—HOMER HICKAM,
New York Times bestselling author of *October Sky*

"Zoro's beautiful and touching memoir, *Maria's Scarf*, is a testament to the strength and tenacity of the human spirit."

—COUNTESS LUANN DE LESSEPS,
original cast member of *The Real Housewives of New York City*

"Captivating ... exhilarating ... inspiring ... riveting ... An eight-course meal with dessert! Bravo, Zoro!"

—DYAN CANNON,
three-time Academy Award–nominated actress

"Much like his drumming, Zoro's memoir is filled with heart and soul and captures the rhythm of a life filled with adversity, adventure, and ascension. Through his unforgettable journey, he shows us all how to become a shining star. A deeply affecting book about overcoming the odds that will make your heart sing."

—VERDINE WHITE,
founding member and bassist of Earth, Wind & Fire

"One of the best books I've read in years. Uplifting, hilarious, heartbreaking, and heartwarming, *Maria's Scarf* is a revelation. A love letter to those who love us unconditionally."

—TOSCA LEE,
New York Times bestselling author

"*Maria's Scarf* is an overcoming family saga of epic proportions, brimming with heart and soul, joy and pain, tribulation and triumph. The book is real at every level."

—JAY SEKULOW,
Chief Counsel for the American Center for Law & Justice

"This book had me laughing and crying, sometimes on the same page, but is more than a memoir. With its cinematic splendor, *Maria's Scarf* is a movie that calls to be made—one that will inspire millions."

—JIMMY STEINFELDT, legendary rock photographer

"You quickly fall in love with these characters. All the elements of a visual story leap off the page at you with every turn. It's *Whiplash* meets *Rocky* meets *The Blindside* . . . with the heart of *Forrest Gump*. A must-read . . . and hopefully soon a must-see as well."

—RICK ELDRIDGE,
CEO/producer, ReelWorks Studios

"Although I make my living with words, I find myself at a loss for words to express how amazing Zoro's story is. At times, it is hilarious; at other times, heartbreaking; at all times, deeply and beautifully human. I have never read anything like it."

—KEN GIRE, author of *Windows of the Soul*

"*Maria's Scarf* is emotional and inspiring. I couldn't put it down!"

—GARY BRYAN,
K-EARTH 101 Radio, Los Angeles

"If you have ever doubted the power to become what you dream despite your circumstances, then read *Maria's Scarf*. The American dream comes alive in this wonderfully poignant and exquisitely written account of how an immigrant mother's faith and fortitude transforms the lives of her children. You'll be singing the Hallelujah chorus at the end!"

—JOE BATTAGLIA,
president of Renaissance Communications
and author of *Make America Good Again*

"A must-read for anyone who has lived, loved, lost, and knew there was something greater waiting for them."

—CATHY RICH,
vocalist, producer, and daughter of Buddy Rich,
the world's greatest drummer

"This story is for all who dream. It's for all who have felt shut out and let down; it's for all who have been buoyed up by someone who unrelentingly kept a candle of faith and hope lit."

—KIM DORR-TILLEY,
Hollywood agent

"These pages aren't just about how to live a beautiful life when it's easy, but how to press forward with tenacity and courage and love when life is hard. If you've got a pulse, you are going to be touched by this book."

"Zoro's memoir portrays a boy who is rich with faith, tenacity, resiliency, and drive! He reminds us that sometimes we just have to fake it 'til we make it! My whole-hearted applause for *Maria's Scarf*."

"*Maria's Scarf* proves how becoming one of the world's greatest drummers is not only about technique, but it's also about the forging of a man's soul so that each time he lays down a beat, you can feel the pain, joy, and love of Zoro's improbable and incredible story."

"The rich and colorful details that are woven into every story make his book come alive. If ever there was a story about God making way for one of His own, this is it. Highly recommended!"

"Belief is powerful. It can cause us to persevere against all odds and do great things . . . An extraordinary example of how a mother's faith in God and steadfast belief in her son can make all the difference. It will restore your hope even in the hardest of times."

MARIA'S
SCARF

BOOKS BY ZORO

*Maria's Scarf: A Memoir of a Mother's Love, a Son's
Perseverance, and Dreaming Big*

*SOAR! 9 Proven Keys for
Unlocking Your Limitless Potential*

The Big Gig: Big-Picture Thinking for Success

*The Commandments of R&B Drumming:
A Comprehensive Guide to Soul, Funk, and Hip-Hop*

*The Commandments of R&B Drumming Play-Along:
A Play-Along Guide to Soul, Funk, and Hip-Hop*

The Commandments of Early Rhythm and Blues Drumming
(with Daniel Glass)

The Commandments of the Half-Time Shuffle

MARIA'S SCARF

A Memoir of a Mother's Love, a Son's Perseverance, and Dreaming Big

ZORO

BLACK STONE

PUBLISHING

Printed in the United States of America

First edition: 2024
ISBN 979-8-212-41733-4
Biography & Autobiography / Personal Memoirs

Version 1

Blackstone Publishing
31 Mistletoe Rd.
Ashland, OR 97520

www.BlackstonePublishing.com

My Dedication in Three Acts

ACT I: THE PAST

This memoir represents a past but not forgotten life. To those who lived it with me, I salute, beginning with my mother, Maria, a resolute woman of boundless love and vision who made me the man I am today. It is to her I owe my greatest debt. And to my six siblings with whom I shared the journey: Armando, Mary, Ricardo, Patricia, Bobby, and Lisa. Together we were the "magnificent seven," and what an unforgettable ride it was. Our belief in one another made it possible for us to defy the odds. Thank you for your resilience and the unconditional love you have shown me throughout my life!

ACT II: THE PRESENT

This book would not be possible without the love, support, and understanding of my wife, Renée, and our children, Jarod and Jordan. You are the sun, the moon, and the stars to me. Thank you for enduring my endless banter about this vision and believing in me with faith and patience. My chief aim was to make you proud and, through this book, learn more about what makes me who I am.

ACT III: THE FUTURE

My motivation for completing this book was to inspire all the dreamers of the world to keep dreaming and reaching for the stars. My charge to you: Believe that all things are possible, do the work, be brave, walk by faith, and never give up!

Mothers hold their children's hands for a while . . .
their hearts forever.

—Author unknown

Contents

Scan this code to listen to the official *Maria's Scarf* playlist on Spotify, featuring all the songs mentioned in this book.

Prologue

Every great dream begins with a dreamer. Always
remember, you have within you the strength, the
patience, and the passion to reach for the stars, to
change the world.

—Author unknown

Maria was my mother, and the scarf around my neck was hers. Here is
the story behind it.

I remember the day before my second-grade school pictures were
to be taken, when I asked if I could wear her orange scarf. She tried to
dissuade me, certain that my classmates would make fun of me. I persisted; she relented. The next morning, she knelt down to tie the scarf
around my neck and whispered something in my ear that I will never
forget. Something that would change the trajectory of my life.

She had been the daughter of a supreme court justice in Mexico
City. Their house was graced with diplomats, aristocrats, politicians,
and a steady flow of people from the film industry—producers and directors, actors and actresses. Mesmerized by the magic of the movies,
my mother dreamed of becoming a star on the silver screen. And she
was on the road to becoming one.

As fate would have it, though, her dream was shattered by a sudden
reversal of her family's fortunes. So she left her dream behind in Mexico
and immigrated to America. There, she dedicated herself instead to nurturing the dreams of her children.

She was a woman. A single mother. Now with seven children. And she was a Mexican immigrant. You can imagine how hard that was. But she had an indomitable spirit.

She saw America as an adventure, like when the eight of us piled onto a city bus destined for the beach. Afterward, we'd shower the sand off and change clothes for a trip to the grand Crest Theatre. And it was grand indeed, built during Hollywood's golden era. Sinking into the plush seats, we'd watch as larger-than-life characters flickered across the screen and found their way into our imaginations. When the movie was over, we'd take up a row of spinning stools at the diner, where my mother would order a couple of grilled cheese sandwiches and a chocolate malt to be split between us.

She had a phonograph, and music always filled whatever tenement we were living in. Albums by Frank Sinatra, Elvis, and music from her beloved homeland formed much of the soundtrack of our lives. We all danced, not just with her but with each other.

I've always loved a good story, especially one where the underdog goes on to victory. I was that underdog, and I found great hope in those stories, which helped to fuel my dreams. Given the difficult circumstances of my childhood, however, it would have been easy to give up. But I discovered a voice—a voice that was superior to circumstance. It was my mother's voice. *Maria's Scarf* tells how I followed that voice through the darkness and into the light.

In a world filled with turmoil and despair, finding significance can seem impossible, pointless even. This book is a ticket. A ticket to a fantazmical excursion that I hope will lift your spirits, inspire you to reach for the stars, and remind you that, even in the face of great travails, we must never abandon hope. As a young boy, I took my name from a masked hero. My life story is about the hero that lives in all of us—a hero with the power to dream, believe, and overcome. You have a stage waiting for you to command, but there are obstacles you'll need to conquer before you can take your place on it. These pages can revive your resolve to fight through them. Dreams are important, and I was rescued by mine. This memoir is yet another dream come true, and I've poured my heart and soul into every word.

My true-life tale is filled with twists and turns—trauma and triumph, love and hate, adventures and misadventures, and great acts of sacrifice. It is a story for both the young and the old—the sinner and the saint—the dreamer and the schemer. I was blessed to live it. I hope it blesses you to read it.

INTRODUCTION:
Wind beneath
My Wings

From backstage, I peered out at nearly a million concertgoers on the National Mall in Washington, DC. People of all ages filled every inch of space between Constitution and Independence Avenues. I was about to play for the masses that had gathered to celebrate our nation's founding principles—the very principles that enabled me to dream the impossible dream I was now living, and the same principles that had enabled my mother, Maria Islas-Bravo, to come to the United States from Mexico to rear her family here in the land of opportunity.

As the Stars and Stripes swept across my view, I thought of the many sacrifices my mother had made so I could perform on this stage. This was no small moment for either of us. In fact, it was everything.

Hoping to slow my pulse, I focused on the Lincoln Memorial Reflecting Pool stretching out behind me. In front, a sea of red, white, and blue flags waved in the wind. My nerves were getting the best of me, and I had to keep reminding myself: *breathe.*

The heat had formed a thick haze as the noon sun beat down on us. I wiped sweat from my brow and pulled a pair of worn drumsticks from my bag. Hands clammy and shaking, I paced the side of the stage, rolling my fingers around the familiar wooden sticks like a baseball player swinging his favorite bat. This was the biggest concert I had ever played, and I couldn't afford to miss a beat. But it wasn't just the crowd that was making me nervous. The Sea to Shining Sea concert was airing live on national television, and Mama would be watching from home in Los Angeles.

As the starting time neared, the teeming crowd began to clap as one, coaxing us to take the stage. From somewhere near the back, a chant began: "New E-di-tion! New E-di-tion!"

Even the more seasoned band members looked wide-eyed at one another, amazed by the magnitude of what was taking place around us. Our stage manager gave us the go-ahead to take our positions. As we entered, the droning chants turned to deafening cheers. My heart raced.

Perched at the top of my drum riser, I peered through my cymbals. With the sun glaring off the golden disks, I squinted toward the crowd, remembering the words my mother had whispered to me as a young boy when she had leaned close and tied her orange silk scarf around my neck: "One day, my precious son, you will do something *fantazmical* with your life." It was her own word—a mix of *fantastic* and *amazing*—one she coined to indicate the level of success she hoped all her children would achieve. Something so enormous it would be too wonderful for any ordinary superlative.

The musical director gave the green light, pulling me back to the moment. I took one last deep breath, signaled a thumbs-up to my fellow musicians, and started counting us in. It proved impossible for them to hear my count over the screams of teenage girls, so at the last second, I gave a visual cue instead, clicking my sticks four times loudly above my head. Away we went into our hit single, "Mr. Telephone Man."

The five vocalists of New Edition strode single file to the front of the stage, microphones in hand. Dressed in matching amethyst lamé jackets, bow ties, and cummerbunds, the dynamic showmen dazzled the audience with their perfectly choreographed moves. In crisp white pants and patent leather loafers, Bobby Brown and Ralph Tresvant took front and center. Behind them, Ricky Bell, Michael Bivins, and Ronnie

DeVoe provided harmony as Bobby and Ralph slid and shimmied across the stage, sharing the lead.

Sitting high on my drum throne, I was adorned with as much bling as an ancient prince. Wearing my signature black gaucho hat, silver sequined vest, and rhinestone tie, I laid down the groove as beads of sweat trickled down my back. The entire song became a blur as adrenaline surged and my body took over, working instinctively after countless hours of intense practice.

As the song neared its end, it was my time to shine. The rest of the band stopped, and I threw myself into a rousing drum solo, imagining my mother sitting in her living room with tears in her eyes as she smiled at the TV. I glanced toward the crowd, hoping to give a nod to the camera, showing Mama I had made it and it was all because of her.

That's when the audience began to sway hypnotically, waving their arms in tandem and moving in sync to the beat. People in every direction were clapping to the rhythm. The sight overwhelmed me. The crowd could not have been more diverse. Different races and religions, different educational and economic backgrounds, different genders, different dreams, different heartaches. Countless factors could have divided us, but when they all joined with the beat of my drums, the many became one. At that moment of synchronicity, I experienced an epiphany. Deep in my soul I could feel what Mama had always told me. I had been given the gift of bringing happiness to others through the power of rhythm. And here was proof! Music really could overcome the many fears, prejudices, and tensions that divide us. Music—*my* music—had the power to unite.

I also realized, once and for all, that Mama had been right about something else too: "Anything is possible when we refuse to give up."

Against all odds, my wishes had come true. Amid the backdrop of that musical splendor, I forgot that I had scrounged through Salvation Army donation bins as a kid, that my family was once homeless, reduced to living in our dilapidated 1962 Chevy Nova, and that my father had deserted me when I was six months old, leaving me nothing but a set of bongos. No one here could have guessed my true identity, not even my bandmates. They had never heard of a Mexican Irish American kid named Danny Donnelly. They knew me only as Zoro, their enthusiastic twenty-three-year-old drummer.

I had worked so hard to conceal the shame and brokenness of my past, and now I was doing something truly fantazmical with my life, exactly as Mama had predicted. That's when I knew. This was just the beginning!

The world said I would never amount to anything.

My mother said that all things are possible to those who believe.

I believed my mother.

This is our story.

CHAPTER 1

Straight Outta Compton

In the summer of 1969, my life revolved around the notorious South-Central Los Angeles neighborhood known the world over as Compton, an area made up of mostly Black and brown folks, particularly those with little money. While some kids in our "hood" were full-blooded Mexican, like my two older siblings, only a few, like me, had white fathers. Or so I had been told. I had never met the man. For that matter, I couldn't remember meeting many white people at all.

Recognized as the most crime-ridden zone of California, our ten-square-mile hub of concrete, overshadowed by smoggy skies and surrounded with gang graffiti, was crisscrossed by the 405, 605, 105, 110, 710, and the 91—the dangerous freeways that hemmed us in. Adding the Alameda Corridor, a freight rail expressway that ran directly through Compton all hours of the day and night, the city had an audible pulse to it. Between the horns of aggravated drivers, the sirens of police cars, the rattling of freight cars over tracks, the squealing of railcar brakes, and the harsh sounds of violence from all directions, silence was nowhere to be found.

That summer, I was seven and champing at the bit to do something exciting, especially after watching Apollo 11 blast into space and seeing

Neil Armstrong walk on the moon. Anything seemed possible after that, and I wanted to do something to raise the stakes. Thus far, my posse and I had ridden our bikes down the dangerously steep concrete ravine at the LA River, thrown dirt clods at unsuspecting cars from a ditch, and flown a fleet of paper kites into the power lines just to see if we could cause an outage. By the end of July, even traumatizing younger kids on the monkey bars at Lueders Park had lost its thrill.

One sizzling-hot day, when we were bored out of our minds, my five-year-old little brother Bobby and I were sitting on the sagging wooden steps of Sparks' corner store. Marvin Gaye's "I Heard It through the Grapevine" played from my transistor radio, an older model that emitted as much static as music. Through the open screen door, a steady stream of dust particles floated down the sunlit aisles, drawing my attention to the red Coca-Cola machine with the words "Ice Cold" embossed on its front. I craved a thirst-quenching bottle of Coke while wondering what to do with the rest of our day.

The song ended, and Elvis took over with his new hit single, "In the Ghetto." That's when our older brother Ricardo joined us, along with our friends Tyrone and Darnell. With the five of us crowding the stoop, customers had to step around us to enter the store. Mrs. Sparks, an old woman with scraggly gray hair, a pronounced limp, and a cigarette dangling from her lips, bellowed from behind the register, "You boys stop blocking the doorway!" Then she puffed out a ring of smoke and added, "I mean it. If ya ain't gonna buy nuttin', then scram!"

We just sat there and laughed.

With a fierce squint in her eyes, her brows furrowing into one, the old crone hobbled toward us across the creaky wood floor as her tattered muumuu rippled around her like a tent in a storm. "Now go on, now. *Git!*" She shooed us away as if we were strays, slamming the door behind us.

"What now?" Bobby asked as we sauntered down the street in search of adventure elsewhere.

With no trees big enough to climb, we relied on the tall, bristly junipers for shade. But the trees were skinny, and the shade scant.

"We could go up on a roof," I suggested. Our neighborhood had been built after World War II, with small stucco homes and a vast array of apartment buildings packed tight between industrial structures and corner shops. We would often climb to the rooftops, where white gravel had been spread across the flat, tarry surfaces, but even from the highest points, we could look all around us and still not find any lakes, rivers, or lush green landscapes. Just cement, broken glass, and steel power-line towers stretching as far as the eye could see.

"Too hot," Ricardo said, pretending to be in a boxing match with a tree before raising his arms in victory.

As the minutes dragged on, we drifted farther out of our neighborhood, skipping down buckled sidewalks and stepping over the cracks where dry weeds and overgrown dandelions battled for space. We tossed rocks at telephone poles and kicked empty cans between potholes until we finally came up with a scheme.

We weren't hardened criminals, mind you, but like most of the kids we'd grown up with, we'd all been tangled up in petty crimes for a while. We snitched candy and gum mostly. Sometimes a soda. Sometimes a toy.

Feeling confident in our skills, we hatched a plan and worked together to compile a shopping list. Well, I suppose a better name for it would have been a *shoplifting* list.

We were a motley bunch. My older brother, Ricardo, who had an annoying habit of flipping his sandy brown hair out of his face, was the decisive one. At age eleven, he was dead set on a model airplane, glue, and paint. Next was our crafty ringleader, Tyrone. Twice my age with ten times the muscle, he looked more man than teen with his short Afro and James Brown T-shirt. For him, it was all about the Duncan yo-yos he'd seen on TV, but he also wanted a set of wax lips and a handful of Zotz.

Moving down the hooligan hall of fame was Darnell, Tyrone's twelve-year-old brother. He was the kid we didn't want sitting on the other end of a teeter-totter for fear of being launched into orbit. Darnell had his heart set on some Cracker Jack, a cap gun, and a box of Fudgsicles that he had no intention of sharing.

Next in the rogues' gallery was my squeaky-voiced younger brother

Bobby. He shifted his almond-shaped eyes. "I'm gettin' one of those Hi-Flier paper kites, a Slinky, a G.I. Joe, and some Bazooka," he said, smacking his lips on a wad of worn-out gum he'd been chewing for two days straight.

Then there was scrawny, seven-year-old me, two front teeth missing, a protruding cowlick, and bright hazel eyes, tying up my Converse high tops with double knots in preparation for a quick getaway. What I wanted was a box of sixty-four Crayola crayons and, most important of all, a carton of mint chip ice cream.

But where could we find all that loot in one place? The Rexall Drug Store! We knew of a huge one about two miles away—a safe bet because the manager wouldn't recognize us.

The plan was simple. Each of us would grab what we wanted and skedaddle. How hard could that be?

But then our fearless leader, Tyrone, changed the plan at the last minute and appointed *me* to confiscate all the merchandise. I was excited about the idea, but Ricardo had reservations.

"I thought each of us was gonna get our own stuff," he argued.

"Yo, man," said Tyrone, with his usual tone of certainty. "I know what I'm talkin' 'bout. It won't look right if we're all in there scoutin' the aisles. They'll know sumpem's up. One person goes in, grabs the stuff. The rest of us wait in the alley."

"So why Danny?" Bobby asked, trying to blow a bubble with his gum.

"Ricardo's too big and slow. You're too small to carry it all. But Danny . . . well, no one will suspect a kid who looks like Alfalfa."

The gang burst out laughing.

"Hey, I have an idea," I said. "What if you guys go in and start a fight near the cash register? Then while the grown-ups are trying to break it up, I'll grab everything and sneak out the back."

Tyrone slowly stroked his chin. "Too much could go wrong. But I like how you think, and you're quick on your feet, which is why I chose you for the job."

I was thrilled to be chosen. For me it was a rite of passage: my first big heist. I felt like Robin Hood, robbing from the rich to give to the poor, and somehow that emboldened me.

I only had one question: "How am I gonna carry all that stuff?"

"I got you, little brother." Tyrone slowly pulled a faded green military jacket out of his backpack. "See? I know what I'm doing." He explained that the coat had belonged to his big brother, Jefferson, an army cadet. He went on to show off the many compartments and zippers. "Plus it's big, so you can stuff everything we want in there without getting caught."

"Cool," I said, slipping it on and testing all the hidden pockets.

"Now remember, Danny," Tyrone said, "you're doing the right thing. Robbing from 'the Man.' Trust me, those rich white folks have so much stuff they'll never miss it."

I was a spy about to go behind enemy lines. I didn't know who "the Man" was or why he was our enemy. I just knew he was white and rich, and we weren't. I also knew he had all the things we wanted. If I could pull this off, I would be the group's new hero.

As we walked toward the store, I said to my crew, "Whatever happens, don't ditch me."

"Never!" Tyrone assured. "We'll be waiting in the alley. We'll split the stash and all go our separate ways. Then, mum's the word."

Although none of us really knew what "mum" meant or why it was "the word," we agreed to Tyrone's plan and gave each other our secret handshake to seal the deal.

As we approached the back door, I wiped the sweat from my forehead and gave my amigos one last look. They nodded back, keeping eye contact as if to say, "You got this." To conceal my identity and further my persona as a bona fide hero, I pulled out my Zorro mask from my back pocket, a disguise I'd been using for lesser capers since Halloween.

When the door opened, a blast of chilly air swept over me, a reminder to play it cool. My hands fidgeted around in my pockets as I covertly glanced around the store. After getting a glimpse of the burly, bald-headed manager, I gulped and averted my gaze from his suspicious eyes. Browsing the aisles, I pocketed goodies from the shelves, one by one. The G.I. Joe was the first to come down. From there, I walked innocently over to the aisle with the models and picked out an airplane for Ricardo, settling on the Boeing 707. I continued stuffing items from our list into my oversized jacket, adding a few bonus objects. I planned to wow the guys at the victory party, pulling out these extra surprises while they hailed me as their hero.

Within minutes, that army jacket was stuffed with treasures:

- A jar of Tang instant breakfast drink
- A G.I. Joe
- A model airplane, paint, and glue
- One box of Cracker Jack
- A set of wax lips
- A handful of Bazooka bubble gum
- A Fudgsicle
- A Duncan yo-yo
- A small lawn sprinkler (I was hoping we could find a way to set it up and cool off)
- And, most importantly, a pint of mint chip ice cream

In the last aisle, I stumbled upon the only thing I couldn't imagine leaving without: a box of sixty-four Crayola crayons with all those exotic colors like crimson, indigo, chartreuse, and burnt sienna. Suddenly the box was staring me in the face, complete with its built-in sharpener, seducing me to take it. So I did. With pockets bulging, I waddled toward the exit.

Then I walked out. Simple as that. A clean getaway.

Or so I thought.

I had barely reached the alley when the manager burst through the door, yelling, "Hold it right there, kid!"

I froze, cold and stiff as a Popsicle. When I raised my hands in the air, half my loot fell to the ground. My crew scattered. So much for Robin Hood's merry men.

When the manager stormed toward me, my survival instincts kicked in, and I beat feet to make my getaway. The middle-aged man ran in hot pursuit. More than a little overweight, he was no match for the speed of a frightened kid who didn't want to do time.

As I bolted, the jar of Tang fell and shattered all over the sidewalk, slowing the angry manager but not stopping him. I zipped through the streets, outrunning barking dogs that gave chase and blasting past three kids on the corner who were doing the Double Dutch. At the next intersection, I blazed past a group of thugs running a drug deal from their cars. Beads of sweat dripped from under my Zorro mask as police sirens sounded in the distance.

Following every step, the man hollered words at me I had never heard before. (Well, that wasn't exactly true. I had *heard* them many times, just not shouted at me.) "Why, you good for nothin' *blankety-blank*! You're dead, kid. You hear me? Dead!"

He didn't give up until I threw the lawn sprinkler at him. Thank goodness I'd had the sense to grab it.

Finally free of him, I fell to the ground and hugged my knees tight. My heart was in my throat, my chest about to explode.

It took a while, but eventually my pulse slowed, and the only remaining trace of my brazen heist was ice cream dripping down my shirt. I was bummed that I'd dropped the two things I wanted most: the crayons and the carton of ice cream. What bothered me more was getting caught and the possibility that Mama would somehow find out. She believed I was her little angel, and I didn't want to disappoint her.

Of all the dreams I'd had as a boy, I had certainly never dreamed of prison. Not until that shiftless day in the summer of 1969. *What was I thinking? A Rexall Drug Store heist?* I knew crime didn't pay. It didn't pay for Warren Beatty in *Bonnie and Clyde*, and if it didn't pay for him, then who was I to think it would pay for me? I would regret this. Maybe not today, but someday, and probably for the rest of my life.

The rest of my life . . .

As the sirens grew closer, my overactive imagination kicked in, and I saw my tragic future unfolding before my very eyes. Two policemen ushering me into a packed courtroom, one on each arm. Me wearing a loose-fitting, county-issued jumpsuit with my hands cuffed and ankles

shackled. My court-appointed lawyer in a burnt-orange leisure suit digging wax out of his ear with his little finger as if it were a seller's market
in wax futures. The courtroom gasping as the judge reads my sentence:
life without music.

Luckily this courtroom scene never happened. But it *could* have,
at least in the far-flung galaxy of my daydreams. What was not in my
imagination on that hot summer day was what awaited me at home.

CHAPTER 2

Living for the City

Shortly after catching my breath and licking the ice cream from my shirt, I tucked my mask in one of the army jacket pockets and left Lueders Park, eager to get back to the safety of my own room. As I turned the corner and approached my block, I saw only one thing—my mother. A warning flag that I was in trouble if ever I knew one. She was standing at the bottom of the apartment stairs, wearing her checkered, short-sleeved vest and a purple scarf around her hair.

With each step, my heart pounded faster. "What's wrong, Mama?"

She remained eerily silent, waving a letter above her forehead as if to cool herself down from the news it contained. She placed it on the step beside her and clutched my hand.

I inched my way to her, swallowing hard. "What does it say?"

She gazed into my eyes. "*¡Ay, Dios mío!* We have to be out of this apartment. Today." She fought back tears. I sat and listened. "I thought this place would work out for us. Seems the landlord wasn't happy to find out I've got seven kids."

My stomach knotted. I didn't know what to do.

"I'm sorry we have to live like this, *mijo*," she said. "I'm so sorry."

With a sigh, I pushed my mother's scarf farther back on her head, then gently ran my fingers through her jet-black hair and said, "Don't worry, Mama. Everything will be all right."

She hugged me so tightly I could hardly breathe.

According to the eviction notice, we didn't have much time to leave. This had happened more times than I could count. We all knew the drill.

On the brink of twenty years old, Armando, the oldest and therefore self-appointed man of the house, hurried off with Mama, and with dogged determination they succeeded in finding a new apartment to call home. She threw her hair up in a bun, slipped on a pair of black rubber gloves, and spent the rest of the day on her knees scrubbing the floor of our new digs while Armando cleaned out the dirty cupboards. Eleven-year-old Ricardo took charge of orchestrating the move as seventeen-year-old Mary and ten-year-old Patricia feverishly packed boxes, little Lisa toddling at their feet.

With no money to rent a moving truck or car, we loaded up my red Radio Flyer wagon as if playing a round of Jenga. Only this was no game. It was survival, and we had to find a way to pull it off. First, we loaded Mama's twin mattress and box spring on their sides across the bed of the wagon, then bookended them with her small dresser and nightstand. Ricardo pulled the handle while Bobby and I buttressed each side, trying to keep the cargo from teetering as we moved it down the street.

Crowning this unwieldy pile of stuff was the most important item we owned—a box of record albums that I guarded with my life. Together, we wiggled and wobbled our way through the city blocks, trying to navigate one unnerving jolt after another. The temperature had risen, and vapors rose from the sidewalk as the fronds of brown-tinged palm trees hung limply in the sweltering heat. We maneuvered past a local butcher shop that always smelled of ground beef, a few shadowy bars with flickering neon signs and the stench of stale beer and cigarettes, and our family favorite: the immaculate Sears and Roebuck, an oasis of polished linoleum floors, ceiling fans, and the heady aroma of freshly roasted cashews we could never afford.

About a mile into the journey, we came to a major intersection with a steep incline. Working in tandem, we carefully lowered the front of the wagon from the edge of the sidewalk to street level, preparing to cross. But then we lost control.

"Watch out!" Bobby shouted as the mattress began sliding off the wagon.

"Hold it, Bobby!" I yelled. "Hold it!"

"It's too heavy!"

I ran over to his side to help, but the momentum of the runaway wagon, making us feel as if we were about to become airborne, pushed us farther into the road. With its radio blaring and its muffler roaring, a midnight-blue El Camino swerved around the corner at full throttle before the driver slammed his brakes. Our mattress flew into the street, taking the box spring with it. Bobby and I jumped back, watching the dresser crash to the pavement, landing hard on its back. Tires squealing, the driver sped off, leaving us all in a cloud of fumes.

We dodged zigzagging cars, trying to rescue our belongings from the busy intersection. Horns from swerving vehicles blasted as angry drivers hurled invectives at us.

Honk! "Get out of the road!"

Honk, Honk!! "What the heck are you doing?"

Honk, honk, honk!!! "You boys are gonna get killed out here!"

The clamor became so intense and traumatizing that Bobby and I froze in the middle of the second lane. That's when Ricardo dodged oncoming traffic, grabbed us each by the hand, and pulled us to the sidewalk.

"You okay?" His voice trembled as he wiped sweat from his forehead and looked us over. "You're okay," he assured us.

Bobby and I stood speechless, quivering with fright as we each clung tightly to Ricardo's legs. He stooped down, wrapped his arms around us, and heaved a sigh of relief.

Seeing our meager family belongings scattered all over the street was a devastating blow. It was bad enough getting kicked out of our apartment, but it was even more heartbreaking to see Mama's favorite records run over by the wheels of passing cars. We stood together, clasping hands by the curb, watching it all getting mangled. When I looked up at Ricardo, his eyes pooled with emotion. That's when, under the safe protection of our big brother, Bobby and I both burst into tears.

"Nah," Ricardo said, standing strong. "You're safe now. I won't let anything happen to you. You know that, don't you?"

I nodded. Bobby did too. Following Ricardo's lead, we balled up our fists, wiped our eyes, and ran our forearms under our runny noses. When the coast was clear, we ran back into the intersection to gather what remained of our belongings.

In a mad dash, I scooped up as many of Mama's records as my skinny arms could carry. "Look, they're still okay!" I cried out to my brothers, holding up some vinyl recordings of Frank Sinatra and Nat King Cole.

Bobby, whose hair was now plastered against his sweaty forehead, smiled as he and Ricardo grabbed the dresser. Thankfully, a small crowd of pedestrians helped us reload our damaged furnishings back onto our wagon.

By the time we reached the new rental, we had all agreed not to tell Mama about our near-death experience. She had enough to worry about already.

That night, she gathered us all together around our new living room with a resilient smile. Then she put Frank Sinatra on the record player, having no idea the album had barely survived the harrowing disaster. Bobby, Ricardo, and I shared knowing glances, and I was certain they were thinking what I was thinking—that Mama looked beautiful as she danced with our three sisters to "You Make Me Feel So Young" and that we were the heroes who had saved her favorite songs.

As she pulled each of us boys to our feet, spinning us over the shabby carpet, she made us feel at home again. Even then, I sensed that moment would remain unforgettable, all of us there together, singing, laughing, dancing, and celebrating the journey, no matter how scary and chaotic it could sometimes be.

I don't know how Mama did it. None of us knew how. But we all knew why: because she loved us.

CHAPTER 3

Loves Me Like a Rock

As the fifth of Maria Islas-Bravo's children, I made my grand entrance into the world at 8:04 a.m. on June 13, 1962, at Harbor General Hospital in Torrance, a small coastal city in the South Bay region of Los Angeles. I was the first of Mama's kids to be born in the United States and, therefore, her first US citizen. My older siblings Armando and Mary were from Mama's first marriage in Mexico. Ricardo and Patricia were from her second relationship in Mexico. By the time I came along, she had been happily married to my Irish American father, Daniel Christopher Donnelly. John F. Kennedy was president, and the American dream was well within her reach.

But while the Four Seasons scored hits on American radio with "Sherry" and "Big Girls Don't Cry," and Johnny Carson was taking over as host of *The Tonight Show*, something happened that would forever alter the course of our lives. My father deserted us, fleeing back to his hometown, Chicago, where he told his friends that Mama and I had died during my birth.

I can only imagine the sympathy he must have garnered after sharing his horrific phony fate over a beer at one of the local Irish pubs. Truth was, we *were* alive, but barely. There were seven of us by that time, including Mama and our maternal grandmother, Conchita, all struggling to survive with no father figure left to help us. When he'd left and considered us *dead to him*, a postage stamp cost four cents; gas, twenty-eight cents a gallon; a dozen eggs, thirty-two cents; and the average rent set a family back $110 per month—all more than Mama could afford, no matter how many extra hours she worked at the shipyard and the diner.

To make matters worse, not long after my father made a run for it, immigration refused to renew my grandmother's visa. Heartbroken, Conchita had no choice but to return to Mexico even though she'd been our primary caregiver during Mama's long, double shifts. Naturally, Mama was tempted to go with her, but she knew the opportunities for us would be limited in their native country. So she made the tough decision to go it alone in the United States, hoping to give her children a brighter future by sticking it out in the "land of opportunity."

Conchita had always served as Mama's backbone, and her absence left a gaping hole in our day-to-day life. The separation proved devastating not only for the close-knit mother and daughter but also for my older siblings, who loved their grandmother dearly. At the time, I remained protected by the blissful state of infancy, but I would soon experience the increasing difficulties my single-parent family now faced.

After my father rolled out of our lives, a second man courted my mother and then deserted her when he learned she was pregnant with his child. Another broken promise, another broken heart. As sad as it was for her, though, for me it proved a blessing, because that's how I got my baby brother, Bobby, my best friend and partner in crime.

Another slick man, another abandonment, and, well, that's how I got my baby sister, Lisa. Being the last of the magnificent seven, Lisa was another welcome addition to the family.

For a devout Catholic like Mama, birth control was strictly forbidden. She followed that rule, yet she was eager to land a husband the only way she knew how. Her physical beauty enraptured many a man who'd whispered promises—all of which were eventually broken. Temptation proved to be Mama's Achilles' heel, and before she knew it, seven children were depending on her, and only her. For everything.

Between us, we had five different fathers—one was Mexican, and four were Americans—all of whom were now absent from our lives. And because of immigration issues, we were growing up without the support of grandparents. Without uncles. Without aunts. Without cousins. Without the presence of a single relative living anywhere near us. With all of Mama's extended family residing across the border in Mexico, our mother was all we had in the world.

Despite her struggles, we never lacked for love or attention. Not only was she present, she was lavishly present, from early morning until late at night. Even when she was working, we were in her every thought, every prayer, every dream. This we knew for sure.

In addition to my mother's selfless and devoted parenting, I grew to love and depend on my siblings for everything. My oldest brother Armando was the proud Mexican with slicked-back hair like his idol, Elvis. He called Bobby and me "Prangacio and Bonifacio" after two Mexican puppets he remembered as a child and was a father figure to us all. His vigilance kept us safe too many times to count. Mary, my oldest sister, had fair skin and long straight hair. A nurturer from the start, she provided maternal care when Mama was at work. Next in command was my brother Ricardo, the great adventurer, and the one with whom I would share many future exploits. His strong sense of leadership guided us all, and I'd come to rely on him in more ways than one.

Four years older than me was Patricia, a gregarious girl with striking features and bright eyes, who would do anything for us. Like Mama, she carried a sparkling magnetism that seemed to glow, and her startling beauty was admired by all who crossed her path. Along with the two youngest, Bobby and Lisa, this was my family—the people I belonged to. My tribe. The ones I would do life with. And, boy, would life give us all we could handle!

I don't remember what day I realized I didn't have a father, though this fact was repeatedly brought to my attention by a few of my classmates at Augusta A. Mayo Elementary School in Compton, where I was attending second grade. One day my teacher, Mrs. Williams, made an announcement about the upcoming father-and-son breakfast. Details were written on the blackboard, but, seeing as I didn't have a dad, I just gazed at the laminated world map, wondering what all the other continents were like. Any place in a distant land intrigued me, and I imagined myself traveling far away, doing something heroic to win the affections of the most beautiful princess in the land.

On the playground during lunchtime, Billy Davis, a rosy-cheeked boy with a rotund belly, yelled out, "Hey, I hope you're not thinking about coming to that father-and-son breakfast, because *guess what?* You don't have a dad." I stood silently in shock as he continued. "You don't have a dad because your mom's a loser, and you are too."

"My mom is not a loser."

"Oh, yeah? That's not what my mother says. How come she has so many kids and no husband, huh? She's nothin' but a Mexican tramp."

With emotion swelling in my throat, I yelled, "You're just jealous because my mother is pretty and yours looks like the Goodyear blimp."

The first sound was my lunch box being thrown across the playground. The second was my body hitting the ground. I lay in pain on the asphalt. Trying to save face, I got up as quickly as I could, but Billy and his minions pushed me back down, pouncing on me even harder. I prayed they would stop, but they just kept punching and kicking me with my face smooshed against the blacktop. At that moment, I wished I had never been born. Wished I had the power to be invisible. Wished I had a dad.

When they finally ran off in laughter, I slowly pushed myself back up. With my head spinning, I brushed off the dirt and plucked small pieces of asphalt from my cheeks.

Under the monkey bars, Billy ate my ham and cheese sandwich while his friends feasted on my Twinkies and chocolate pudding. When they finished devouring my lunch, the beast wiped his mouth with his pudgy hands and then jumped on my space-themed lunch box until all the astronauts were smashed to smithereens.

Too embarrassed to go back to class, I sat alone on one of the swings, wondering why they had done this to me. I was angry that I didn't have a father, knowing that if I did have one, none of this would have happened. Holding back my tears, I walked to the edge of the school property and plopped down against the chain-link fence. Then, when I was certain no one could see, I cried my heart out.

Later that afternoon, I was lying on our couch at our apartment, nursing my wounds with an ice pack that Mary had prepared for me. When Mama walked through the door after work, she took one look at my fat lip and screamed, "What happened to you?"

I wanted to tell her what they'd called her, but I decided to keep that part to myself. "Some kids were making fun of me for not having a dad."

Mama's merciful brown eyes penetrated mine as she sat on the couch next to me. "Come closer, Danny."

I flipped myself around and lay my head on Mama's tangerine skirt. She twirled her fingers through my hair and went into a beguiling story as she caressed my face. "Do you know that before you were born, I went every day to the Basilica of Our Lady of Guadalupe and got on my knees at the steps of the church to pray? I prayed to Saint Anthony for you to be born on June thirteenth. Saint Anthony was the patron saint of lost things, and he died on June thirteenth."

"Why'd you want me to be born on the day somebody died?"

"I wanted *you* to come into this world on that day so you could pick up where he left off, and you know what?"

"I know. I know," I said with a sigh. "I was born on June thirteenth."

"That's right. Isn't that incredible? Out of 365 days you could have been born, you arrived on the very day I prayed you would. It was a sign from God that he had heard my prayers, proof that Saint Anthony petitioned the Lord himself for us. Then something miraculous happened in the hospital right after I gave birth to you," she whispered. "I saw a halo around you, confirmation from God that you were set apart for great and noble things, just like the blessed Saint Anthony."

I turned my head upward and eyed her suspiciously. "You're just telling me that to make me feel good. I'm not an angel."

"No, *mijo.* I never said you were an angel—just that God has a

special light on you. I would never lie about something like that. I'm a
Catholic woman, and, as God is my witness, I'm telling you the truth."

Mama's claims sounded unbelievable to me, even at that young age,
but she was adamant and believed these miracles had really happened.
Just telling the story seemed to bring her pleasure.

I always wanted Mama to be happy. But her story about my birth had
piqued my curiosity about something I *knew* was real—my not having a
father. Bobby and Lisa had the television on full blast, watching *Captain
Kangaroo*, and my older siblings were listening to their radios in their
bedrooms. With our home as loud as usual, the timing seemed right to
broach a subject that hadn't yet been addressed. "Mama, if God has a
special light on me, then how come I don't have a daddy? Is he dead?"

Mama took me by the hand and walked me outside, away from the
noise, so she could answer me.

"Your father's not dead, Danny." She paused. "He left us, just like
all your brothers' and sisters' fathers."

"But why? Did he join the army? Go to jail?"

"No, no. Nothing like that." She took a deep breath. "When you
were about six months old, your father told me he was going to get some
groceries. Then he drove off in our only car . . . and he never came back."

"We had a car?"

Mama nodded.

"I wish we had that car now. Then we wouldn't have to take the
bus everywhere."

"Me too, Danny. Me too."

"But why did he leave? Was it because of me?"

"No, of course not, my love. The truth is, he'd only married me to
avoid getting drafted into the Vietnam War. But look, *mijo*," she pulled
on both my cheeks, "if he hadn't married me, then I wouldn't have you,
my precious son, and we wouldn't be here in the United States. So, I
choose to see all the good that came out of this marriage, and believe me,
there was a lot of good. Your father and I rarely fought, and I thought
we would stay together forever. I think maybe taking care of all of us was
just too much for him. It's a lot. Especially for a young man, I guess."

"Did he leave us any pictures? A letter? Money?"

"Well, no. But he did forget to take his bongos."

I stared into my mother's eyes, wishing for more words, words that never came, and I wondered, what in the world was I supposed to do with a lousy set of bongos?

CHAPTER 4

How Can You Mend a Broken Heart

I was getting ready to send my G.I. Joe down a slalom run in his blinding white ski outfit when the doorbell rang. It was our first time renting a house instead of an apartment, and we'd all been making the most of the privacy. Mama always told me never to open the door unless I knew who it was, so I peered from behind the living room curtain of our humble home on East Palmer Avenue. There on the concrete porch stood an elderly lady with white hair and pearl-colored sunglasses. I didn't recognize her, but since she appeared harmless, I went against my mother's instructions and opened the door.

"Hi there, young man. Is your mommy home?"

I nodded.

"Please tell her Marion Donnelly is here."

As I walked to Mama's bedroom, I wondered who Marion Donnelly was and why we shared the same last name. I was also curious why there was a younger man and woman standing on the steps behind her. With white skin and rich-people clothes, they didn't look like most folks from our neighborhood.

I found Mama folding laundry. "Mama, Marion Donnelly wants you to come to the door."

Mama looked as if she'd seen a ghost. "What?"

"A lady named—"

"Yes, I heard you the first time, Danny."

"Then why'd you say *what*?"

Mama rushed to the mirror to comb her hair, then sprayed a squirt of perfume on both sides of her neck before hurrying to the front door, where the three strangers were waiting.

"Oh, my goodness, Marion," she said, "this is quite a surprise. Come in, please."

The house was chaotic as usual, and Mama yelled out for Ricardo to take everyone out back to play. Everyone except me. Mama insisted I stay with her.

The mysterious woman sat on the couch next to Mama and me. The young couple sat across from us on the gold velvet loveseat.

"*Mijo*," Mama said to me, "I want you to meet your grandmother, Marion. Your father's mother."

"My grandmother?" I glared at the woman suspiciously. "Then how come I never met you before?"

The two on the loveseat exchanged a silent scowl. Marion cleared her throat and said, "Well, honey, I live far away. In Chicago. Near your dad."

My dad?! "You live by my dad? What's he like, my dad?"

"Well, let's see." She smiled but gripped her hands tightly in her lap. "He likes to play his drums. And he's a successful businessman, very well respected in his field. More importantly, he's a terrific son."

My brows pinched tighter. "Then how come I never met him before?"

Another uncomfortable silence filled the room, and the couple sent a coded message to each other through their eyes. Finally, my grand-mother broke the quiet. "I want you to meet your aunt Marybeth," she said, gesturing toward the loveseat, "and her husband, Jean-Claude. We're on our way to Baja, Mexico, for a fishing trip, and we decided to stop over to meet you."

"A fishing trip?" I jumped up. "Can I go?"

"No, honey, I'm sorry. Not this time." She sat stiffly and shook her head. Then, perhaps out of guilt, she added, "But we're going on a trip to Europe in the summer. Maybe you can come with us then."

"Really? Yeah, I wanna go to Europe with you. Where is it?"

"In Europe, honey," she said, amused. "We have to fly on a plane for several hours across the United States, then all the way across the Atlantic Ocean."

"Mama, can I go on the airplane?" I asked, the pitch of my voice high and eager. "With my daddy?"

"Of course, Danny, but let's not get carried away. That's a long time from now."

Later that night, I stretched across our braided rug, studying the European map from our half set of encyclopedias. I circled all the places I wanted to visit. Then, with Mama's help, I wrote my first letter to my father:

Dear Daddy,

I've been dreaming about meeting you all of my life and I can't believe we're finally going to be together. I can't wait to go to Europe with you. I've already written down all the countries I want to visit, and by the time we go this summer, I will know everything about them because I have an Encyclopedia, and I'm going to study and memorize it.

With love and super-duper excitement,
Your son, Danny

From that day on, I began sending more letters, report cards, and pictures to my father, care of my grandmother's address because she wouldn't give us direct access to him. Anytime the phone rang, I ran to answer it, hoping it was Dad making his first call to me. Every day after school, I ran to the mailbox to see if a letter from him had arrived. But day after day—nothing. Days turned into weeks, weeks turned into months, and this all turned into a great and terrible sadness. After a year with no response, I felt worthless.

One evening after an early dinner, when the rest of my siblings went out to play, I stayed behind to have a heart-to-heart with Mama. "How come my daddy never answers my letters? How come he never calls or visits? Didn't my grandmother like me?"

"Of course she did. Marybeth and Jean-Claude thought you were adorable too. When you accidentally wrote the D in Danny backward, they thought it was the cutest thing they'd ever seen. They even took that piece of paper with them."

"So why doesn't he want to know me?"

"Well, I can't figure that out for the life of me, Danny. But it's his loss. He has no idea what a wonderful little boy you are."

"Maybe he didn't like my pictures I sent him. Maybe I'm just not good enough for him."

"No, *mijo.* Don't ever say anything like that again," she said, shaking her finger at me.

I threw my arms around her and started to sob. She held me for a moment, then pulled away. "Wait right there," she said, walking to the record player. She grabbed a Nat King Cole album from the gold metal rack. A bewitching sparkle came across her face after she threw on the song "Smile." She took hold of my arms, but I was being difficult and made them go limp.

"Come on, dance with me," she pleaded.

I resisted.

As the melancholy strings and the twinkling of the xylophone played, she leaned down and sang with Nat about smiling through heartbreak.

With the sound of jazz brushes sweeping across the snare drum, Mama tilted my head back and wiped my tears with her soft brown hands. Then she held me close to her chest, where I could hear her heartbeat as we danced.

I tried to stay sad faced while she ran her fingers through my hair, but her enthusiasm was irresistible.

As she sang, I finally cracked a slight smile.

"Aha," she said, poking her finger into my dimple. "There's my Danny boy, with that sweet smile I love. I knew you were in there somewhere."

With six siblings, our house was almost never quiet, but on this rare occasion it felt as if God had cleared the room so we could have this special moment together—just Mama, the music, and me. As the scarlet and gold sun shone through the living room window, a sense of serenity surrounded us.

While the needle drifted across the record, Mama said, "Promise me something, *mijo*. Promise me you won't ever let anyone change your beautiful heart. This world can be cruel sometimes, but if you stay the sweet boy you are, you'll see that everything will work out."

A couple of months passed, and Christmas was just around the corner. One December evening, the thought of Santa paying me a visit was the only thing on my mind. Mama came through the door with her shoulders hunched, lunch pail in hand, exhausted after a full shift at the Long Beach Naval Shipyard. But somehow, she managed to muster up enough energy to make us dinner and clean up the kitchen. Afterward, while we played in the living room, she sprawled out on the couch and fell asleep.

Patricia, Bobby, and I stretched out in awkward positions all over the Twister mat. Lisa was forming something indistinguishable with Play-Doh in the hallway, while the architect of the family, Ricardo, was creating a masterpiece on his Etch A Sketch. Armando and Mary were in their adjoining bedrooms, cranking the volume knobs on their record players, trying to drown out each other's music: the Four Tops versus the Doors.

Aside from the circus-like atmosphere, it was a fairly peaceful night—by our standards, anyway. Until the phone rang. It was a call that would forever change my mother's life. After several rings, Mama lifted herself off the couch and puttered over to the phone. "*Hola*," she said, half-asleep. She perked up when she realized it was her sister calling from Mexico. With her head leaning to one side and her ear pressed to the phone, she suddenly sunk into herself. She listened more intently, hanging on every word. "What? What?" she kept repeating.

After a few seconds of silence, she screamed, "No, no, no!!!" This was no ordinary scream. Not the kind that summoned us to do our chores, nor the one that insisted we stop fighting with one another. No. This was not like any scream I had heard before. She wailed at the top of her lungs, bringing the entire household to a sudden and silent stop.

Armando and Mary ran to the kitchen with fearful eyes. When Mama told them her mother had died, they held each other and bawled. They had been so close to our grandmother when they were young, and they had maintained that relationship through letters and the occasional long-distance call.

I sat at Mama's feet, listening carefully as she apologized to her sister, explaining that the cost had prevented her from flying home to Mexico City when her mother was sick at the Juarez Hospital. "And now I don't have enough money to attend the funeral," Mama said between tears.

Even at my young age, I sensed this would remain among Mama's greatest regrets, something that would cause her tremendous guilt from that moment on. Despite many hurts, this seemed the worst day of our mother's life, and she cried like nothing I had ever seen before. I cried along with her, because if Mama was sad, that was enough reason for me to be sad. It hurt to see her in such pain, and anything that hurt her hurt me.

After Mama hung up the phone, we all gathered around her in a huddle, trying our best to console her. But she was inconsolable.

Once she finally caught her breath, she began telling stories, sharing memories of her mother and the life they'd lived in Mexico, a life that seemed as distant as a dream to me.

"I want you all to know your grandmother. She loved you very, very much, and she always wanted to get back here to live with us. Conchita loved this country, but she was also a proud Mexican woman who was born in Guadalajara, which is about as Mexican as you can get. At least that's what she would have told you."

Mama smiled, and I felt a burst of hope that she might eventually stop crying. Small boned with a shiny black mane, Mama was beautiful. Her eyes were hypnotic, even when they weren't glassy with tears, but now she held us all captivated as she doled out pieces of her story.

"I was born July twelfth, 1930, and your grandma named me Maria Concepción Beatriz Flavia Livia Evangelina Islas-Bravo Jaime."

Lisa giggled at the long name as Mama spoke it in her thick Mexican accent.

"It is kind of funny to say, isn't it?" Mama said, rubbing Lisa's sandy blond hair and smiling at us. "But part of my name came from Conchita, whose birth name was Maria Concepción Jaime. Oh, she was a woman of fierce pride and strong spiritual conviction. During the Mexican Revolution, when she was a young woman, one of the brutal generals in Porfirio Díaz's army wanted to take her horse. 'No,' she refused. 'Give it to me,' he insisted. 'If you don't, I'll shoot you.' 'Go ahead,' she said. He pulled out his pistol and shot right next to her foot. She didn't flinch. Then he mounted his horse and rode off. She was a brave woman who lived a very adventurous life. Before she married your grandfather, she worked as an actress in the Mexican theater. She even had some parts in the silent movies. She was quite talented, and she loved to tell stories. Do you remember her telling you stories?" she asked my oldest brother and sister.

Armando and Mary nodded.

Mama turned to Ricardo and Patricia. "She read to you too, but you were so little you probably don't remember?"

I felt robbed. Because Conchita had to leave the States when I was just an infant, I'd never gotten the chance to know her. But I had always looked forward to spending time with her someday. Especially because I wanted to listen to her tell her wonderful stories, for which she was legendary.

"Conchita was the first to encourage me to come here to the United States," Mama continued. "She loved this country and had brought us all here to visit many times throughout my childhood. One thing she made sure of was that I was fluent in both English and Spanish, and she insisted I attend the American high school in Mexico City. I guess she knew I would need that knowledge someday."

More tears flowed, and then Mama squeezed my hand and said, "Oh, Danny. I wish you could remember her too. She loved to sing to you and rock you. She's the one who chose your middle name when you were born."

"Christopher?" I asked, surprised to learn this new fact.

Mama nodded. "That's right. She named you after Christopher Columbus in hopes you, too, would one day embark upon a great adventure."

Knowing this, my heart grieved the grandmother I would never get to know. And it touched me that somehow Conchita must have known what was in the stars, not only for Mama, but also for me.

CHAPTER 5

Soul Man

It was the night before my second-grade portrait, and I had just finished laying out my clothes for the big day. I was going with my corduroy jeans, a short-sleeved button-down, and a hand-me-down pair of Chuck Taylors. I wasn't crazy about my selection, though. It lacked pizzazz. I went looking for Mama and found her sitting at our yellow Formica kitchen table with a worried look on her face.

"Why are you putting the mail in two separate piles?" I asked.

"These are the bills I have to pay immediately," she said, pointing to one of the stacks. "These can wait a bit longer."

"Why so many?"

"Because it costs a lot to live." She forced a smile.

I had no insight to offer except to tell her how lovely she looked with her scarf draped around her neck. Mama never carried herself like a person who lacked self-esteem, no matter how little she earned, and I was proud of her sense of style. "You always look so pretty in your scarves, Mama. Like a movie star."

"*Ay, qué precioso, mijo.*" This was a phrase she often used whenever she thought we said something endearing. "I wish I were a movie star. Then we wouldn't struggle to pay these bills."

"Don't worry. One day when I'm rich, I'll buy you a big house and take care of you. Then you won't have to pay another bill ever again."

"I believe you would, Danny."

"Tomorrow is school picture day. I want to wear one of your scarves and look fancy, like you."

She raised her left eyebrow in a magnificent arch and giggled. "You're so sweet, my special boy. But I can't let you do that. The kids will make fun of you."

"They make fun of me anyway, for being skinny and for not having a dad. So, will you please let me wear it?"

"Boys don't wear scarves here in the States. If you do, the kids will call you a sissy and try to beat you up again."

"Tom Jones wears scarves on his TV show. So does Elvis. And they're not sissies. They're famous singers." She ruminated on the idea as I kept chipping away at her. "Please, Mama. Please? I don't care what those numbskulls say."

The next morning before heading off to school, she knelt down to tie her orange silk scarf around my neck. Then she slowly raised her eyes and whispered in my ear, "One day, my precious son, you will do something *fantazmical* with your life. I just know it."

That afternoon I stood in line to get my picture taken. Just as predicted, the students heckled me mercilessly. But I was determined to be like Tom Jones and Elvis, and I was willing to pay the price for it. When the beatnik photographer with the black beret signaled it was my turn, I proudly stepped in front of his camera and gave him my best smile. Then—*click!* It was over in a flash.

A few weeks later, I brought the pictures home. Aside from my missing two front teeth and dirty fingernails, it came out perfectly. The scarf stole the show. When Mama gazed at my eight-by-ten glossy, her face lit up. She stooped to give me a big hug, then kissed me on my forehead and said, "This is the most adorable picture I've ever seen."

I may have been the only boy in the history of elementary school photos to wear his mother's scarf, but in doing so, I had achieved my goal of setting myself apart. That mindset would stay with me for the rest of my life. I didn't know it then, but when Mama tied her orange silk scarf around my neck, she was passing hope from one generation to the next and giving me the guts to be myself—no matter the risk.

While I was still in search of a dream to call my own, Armando was already working a few jobs to pay for college. He rode his bicycle to each one. Early one evening, a platinum-blond woman with a bouffant hairstyle pulled out of nowhere and accidentally backed her car into him. Evidently, my brother went flying onto the pavement. The driver slammed on her brakes and ran out to check on Armando. "Oh my god!" she screamed, kneeling next to him. Then she poked his body to see if he was still breathing.

"I'm all right, ma'am," Armando assured her as he slowly got up and dusted himself off.

Frantic, the lady persisted. "I'm so sorry. I didn't see you. Can I drive you home?"

Armando pulled his bike from the ground. "No, thanks. I've got to get to work."

"I don't think you should go anywhere after what just happened. Where do you live?"

He started pushing the damaged bike. "Just down the street. But I'm fine, ma'am. Really."

"If you don't mind throwing your bike in my trunk, I should drive you home so I can apologize to your parents."

Bertha was a refined woman who wore chartreuse-colored cat-eye glasses and who would not take no for an answer. In bringing Armando home, she would soon learn that Mama had her hands full raising seven children alone. Through that chance meeting, my mother and Bertha became friends. Once in a while, Bertha would take Mama to the Holland House for lunch. Mama always appreciated a nice meal she didn't have to cook, and sharing her struggles with a sympathetic ear became a blessing to her. Bertha was compassionate and kind, noticing our family's needs, including my penchant for soulful rhythms. One evening she invited us to see two of my favorite Motown groups in concert—the Supremes and the Temptations.

A little before dusk, she pulled up in her mint-green Cadillac DeVille convertible, a magnificent machine with rocket-like tail fins and gleaming chrome bumpers. Like an angel, Bertha stepped out of the car wearing white from head to toe, including long gloves, a pillbox hat, and choker pearls with matching earrings. I could tell by the way Mama looked at her that she wished she had clothes like Bertha's. And I wished I could buy them for her.

After Bertha and Mama exchanged hugs, Ricardo, Patricia, Bobby, and I piled into her back seat and then waved goodbye to Mama, who held little Lisa on her hip. Armando was working, and Mary (who was a regular concertgoer) had joined her friends at the Forum in Inglewood to see the Doors. This would be my first concert, and I couldn't have been more excited.

With the wind blowing on my face, riding in Bertha's car at high speeds felt as if we were in a rocket ship headed to the moon. I recognized many of the streets in Compton I'd only seen on foot or from the seat of a crowded bus. We drove past our redbrick church with stained-glass images, then past miles of chain-link fences and windows barred with steel rods.

Bertha made small talk during the drive to the Long Beach Memorial Auditorium, a venue surrounded on three sides by a lagoon. Before the concert, we walked around the half-circular Rainbow Pier, taking in the beauty of the Pacific Ocean at sunset and breathing in the salty air.

While the scene was splendid, it was nothing compared to the thrill of listening to so many of my favorite Motown songs come to life on that stage. Hearing the Temptations sing "My Girl," "Beauty is Only Skin Deep," "Ain't Too Proud to Beg," and "The Way You Do the Things You Do" was nothing short of ecstasy. Not to mention when the Supremes harmonized on "Baby Love," "Where Did Our Love Go," "Come See About Me," and "Stop! In the Name of Love." When the Temps and Supremes came out together at the end and sang their duet, "I'm Gonna Make You Love Me," I was on cloud nine.

Bertha had purchased seats on the mezzanine level, giving me a bird's-eye view of the drummer. Throughout the show, I was bewitched by the beat of his drums, and the spell lasted all the way home as I continued to pound out rhythms on the seat.

"Will you stop that, please?" Ricardo snarled, thinking Bertha might be getting agitated.

"I'm sorry, I can't help myself."

Bertha turned around and smiled. "That's quite all right, honey. I'm just glad you liked the concert so much."

"Are you kidding? I didn't like it. I loved it!"

What I didn't have the words to say was that something transformative happened to me during that show, and I couldn't get those rhythms out of my head.

That night I dreamed the Supremes and Temptations took me on the road with them, and I had my very own drum set that sparkled when the lights hit it. When I awoke the next morning, I was still charged from the energy of the live performance. I scrounged through some trashcans in the alleyway, looking for anything I could use to make some drums. After finding some empty Folgers Coffee and Almond Roca cans, I climbed on a chair and raided Mama's kitchen cupboards.

"What are you looking for up there?" she asked, steadying the chair so I wouldn't fall.

"It's gonna be a surprise."

"Ooh, you know I love surprises," she said, smiling.

I grabbed some Tupperware canisters and a set of old wooden salad spoons and put on a show for Mama right there in the kitchen. Her enthusiastic cheers fed the fire in my belly, so I threw the makeshift drums into my red Radio Flyer wagon and hit the streets to make my big debut. Wanting to be seen by as many people as possible, I set up at the busy intersection of Long Beach Boulevard and Palmer Avenue, right next door to the Dodge dealership. Directly across the street stood the Taj Mahal (well, not the real one). It was the Angeles Abbey Memorial Park—a Byzantine-style mausoleum with vibrant colored tiles that ran across the top of its spires and turrets to form a mystical landmark.

As I set up my drums, I imagined Arabian knights rushing through the majestic building, racing outside to hear my performance.

I flipped my transistor radio to my favorite station, KRLA, 1150 on the AM dial. Wolfman Jack came on with his gravelly voice. "Check out this soulful rendition of 'Grazing in the Grass,' by Friends of Distinction," he howled, and—*bam*—in came the blaring horns with the percussionist pounding away on his bongos. By the time it got to the funky drum solo, I was pounding out my best riffs with Mama's spoons.

Right away, a crowd began gathering, as was a common occurrence in our part of the city. Before I knew it, the street was filled with glistening Afros and funky hats, one with a feather sticking out of it. An older man peered down at me with a smile through his red, heart-shaped sunglasses. Straightening his black leather double-breasted maxi coat, he grinned at his friends and said, "Da boy's got 'im some serious rhythm."

"Ah right, little brother man. You gots it," muttered a woman with pink curlers and threadbare leopard slippers. "James Brown's gonna hear about this funky little brother one day."

I clung to every affirming word and the heartfelt ways they were offered by these encouraging strangers. At one point, a couple started toe-tapping in their scuffed-up platforms. Like a Black Fred Astaire and Ginger Rogers, they drew an even larger crowd, and soon others were dancing in the street alongside them. It turned into a block party, and I loved their jubilant expressions as they were gettin' down to the radio, my coffee-can beats keeping time with every soulful track. Then someone threw a quarter in my wagon, which started a domino effect. The more passionately I played, the more money came flying in, so I dug in harder and put on the charm.

I was so inspired that my imagination took flight—yet again. Suddenly, a beam of light flashed out of the sky. Under it, the Supremes appeared, smiling over me with admiration. Then, descending out of the shadows, came the Temptations, dressed in emerald suits, pink tuxedo shirts, and white boots. Eddie Kendricks took out his pocket square and dabbed the sweat off my forehead. "You've been given a great gift, little man," he said in his angelic falsetto.

David Ruffin slid his thick-framed glasses off his nose, hunched over my left side, and with his raspy voice encouraged me. "Keep after it, boy. Your groove will take you places you can't begin to imagine."

I felt the ground shudder when Melvin Franklin's deep voice seconded the thought: "Daaaaaaaaarn right."

The other two Temps, Otis and Paul Williams, high-fived each other, then looked at me with a gleam of approval, as if to say, "Go 'head now." Then the Motor City musicians ascended into a cloud, their footprints slowly dissolving in the sky.

After that enchanted moment, I became fixated on fulfilling their prophecy. Maybe they really could see the future. After all, I'd just discovered I had an uncanny ability to make people dance, to make them smile, to make them happy in a world that wasn't always happy.

A sense of destiny began welling up inside me.

Drumming was proving to be a powerful tool, but I was realizing it could offer even more than that. Remembering how I had learned that African tribes used drums to send messages across the distance, I began to believe that if I played loud enough, I could send a signal all the way to my father in Chicago.

Perhaps he would pick up the signal somehow.

Perhaps he would respond to the call someday.

Someday . . . somehow . . . perhaps.

CHAPTER 6

Beyond the Sea

Like most kids in the '60s, we spent summers outside, running free and exploring everything. The Southern California climate gave us ample opportunity for fun, but that sun could get brutally hot, reflecting off all that concrete and asphalt. All a kid really wanted on days like that was to go swimming. But no one in our neighborhood had a pool.

When Mama wasn't waiting tables, welding at the shipyard, or ironing someone else's clothes, she might take us to a public swimming pool in the adjacent community of Lynwood. On more special occasions, though, she would take us on an adventurous outing to the beach. Of course, getting there and back without a vehicle was a challenge. Mama didn't have the greatest navigational skills, but fortunately, Ricardo had an innate sense of direction. He could read a map, and he understood the public transportation system, enabling all of us to escape the inner-city inferno of our neighborhood, if only for a day.

The smell of diesel and the sight of smoke always foreshadowed the quest, as both spewed out of the city bus pulling in front of our stop. The door would open, and Mama would lead the way up the steps and down the aisle, all of us following her in a row like ducklings. Because the bus typically ran at full occupancy, she would usually end up clutching one of the hand straps while the rest of us clung to any piece of her clothing we could grab.

Being a kid had its disadvantages, like being so short you had to stand under the armpits of strangers. After what felt like an eternity, we would get off at the corner of Ocean and Long Beach Boulevard.

By now, if Armando and Mary were with us, they would have already bolted, heading off to meet their friends at the beach. But for the rest of us, the first order of business usually involved a brisk walk to the Long Beach Barber College with its swirling, striped red, white, and blue pole. Mama couldn't afford the seventy-five cents for the professionals who worked in the front, so she would march us straight to the back, where students cut hair for a quarter.

One particular day, Ricardo, Bobby, and I took turns plopping our bums on the swiveling leather chair. A potpourri of hair tonics filled the room, while the barber in training wrapped us each in a snug white cape and warned us to "hold still."

After the student barber's showdown with my stubborn cowlick, Ricardo's unmanageable wave, and Bobby's dense mane, Mama had three new sons. Patricia and Lisa waited for us in the lobby while Mama fished quarters from her wicker beach bag.

One at a time, we self-consciously shuffled to the front, our heads held low as if we were young Samsons who had just been stripped of their strength. Mama smiled and ran her hands through what remained of our hair, "Oh, my goodness, look at you boys. You're all so handsome."

I don't know if we were, but Mama sure thought so. From there we took a short walk past the elegant Villa Riviera Hotel on Ocean Boulevard. From a distance, I gazed at the tall palm trees that swayed like slender giants around the Tudor Gothic structure.

As we walked closer to "the castle," as I called it, I had to tilt my head all the way back to see the gargoyles that perched along the highest ridges. I stared upward in amazement and said to Mama, "Wouldn't it be fun to live way up there on the top floor? Then we could see the ocean every day."

She smiled and patted me on the head as if she knew I would always be a dreamer.

I loved walking those sidewalks. Not only were they safer than the ones in our neighborhood, they also seemed twice as big and far fancier, with silvery flecks embedded in the cement that made the path sparkle in the sun. I pretended we were walking on diamonds as we watched aircraft carriers and battleships furrowing the waters at the shipyard. From time to time, boatloads of sailors would disembark, spilling onto the streets in their crisp white uniforms. As they walked past us, they rubbernecked Mama, making me jealous because I wanted her all to myself.

Staying near her side, we puttered along the boardwalk at the Pike, a turn-of-the-century amusement park that featured hundreds of attractions and arcades. On another day, we would explore that bewitching land, complete with a petting zoo and the Cyclone Racer, a colossal wooden roller coaster built on pilings that jutted over the water. But on this particular day, Mama had other plans. Her smile grew with each step closer to the luxurious Crest Theatre on Atlantic Boulevard. Gazing up at the sacred structure, she seemed to have stars in her eyes. Lisa was reading out each of the vertical letters on the central spire, c-r-e-s-t, when Mama took my hand and said, "Are you ready to experience some real Hollywood glamour?"

We followed her to the ritzy entrance, where she minced out the cost of admission to the frizzy-haired woman who granted us the keys to this wondrous kingdom. As we crossed the threshold into the foyer, our steps slowed, then stopped. Craning our necks at the overarching grandeur, I became entranced by the elegant Art Deco design, the shiny brass fixtures, and the coordinating floral carpets that spilled from the balcony all the way down the stairs.

It seemed we had stepped back in time to another era. Indeed, we had.

Smells of hot buttered popcorn and freshly roasted peanuts lured us to the concession stand. We kids stood salivating at the glass display that held assorted boxes of colorful candy, behind which a soda fountain offered a tantalizing array of drinks.

I glanced at Mama, who was counting money again. We weren't expecting her to buy us a snack, because we knew that money was tight. Money was always tight. But she was intent on making a memory of this day, a memory we would take with us long after the movie was over. And so she sprang for a tub of popcorn, which had just overflowed from the popper.

"Butter?" the attendant asked.

Mama smiled and said, "Why not?"

By this time, we were all licking our lips as we followed her to the cavernous auditorium. The lighting was subdued, the temperature cool, and the mood bustling with anticipation as dolled-up ticket holders searched for perfect seats. The ceiling seemed to vault to the heavens, its expanse made more glorious by a constellation of elaborate chandeliers. The woodwork was exquisite too, with carefully crafted seats upholstered in plush velvet. When I sank into mine, it seemed to swallow me, and I never wanted to leave.

We were like strangers who had stumbled into Wonderland. All except Mama. She was the only one among us who didn't seem like a stranger here. I studied her carefully, taking in every gesture, every word. Until that moment, I had only seen her in impoverished settings—rat-infested tenements with threadbare carpets, windows without curtains, and unreliable plumbing. But now, I was watching her change right before my eyes. Here, my mother was elegant, almost queenlike. Here, she became her truest self. Here, she belonged.

As we passed the popcorn, the house lights dimmed. The red velvet curtains, ruched at the top and cascading to the floor, slowly opened. The backlight washed over the majestic pleats as the projector sent sudden images shimmering onto the massive screen. When the music swelled, I fell under the spell of Max Steiner's stirring score. The chimes rang in rhythmic succession, giving way to triumphant horns. Then the title swept over the screen in bold lettering: *Gone with the Wind*.

Mama's face was lit with excitement, making me wonder who she had been as a girl, before she was our mother. Before the seven of us, one by one, changed the course of her life. Suddenly, the woman I thought I knew so well seemed a mystery, and I wanted to learn all I could about her past.

But that would have to wait, because never in my life had I seen such vibrant colors and images as were now projected onto the screen. The grandiosity was enlivening. What stood out most, though, was the rapturous expression I saw on Mama's face when Clark Gable first appeared. Her eyelashes fluttered. Her mouth grinned broadly. "Oh my lord, he's a dreamboat," she whispered. No matter how many men had burned her, she remained a romantic through and through. Still, it seemed there was something about Mama that remained hidden behind a veil, something deep in her heart that she had not brought into the light. Her passion for the cinema bordered on a divine obsession, which proved as intriguing to me as the film itself.

The movie was so long it had an intermission. As the audience made its way to the restrooms, I stayed behind. Then, when no one was looking, I combed the aisles, searching for unattended bags of popcorn. With quick hands, I poured the contents into our empty bucket, cramming as much into my mouth as possible before my family returned to their seats. Although it did fill my stomach, the popcorn was a temporary fix. But the names Rhett Butler and Scarlett O'Hara, along with the brow-raising line, "Frankly, my dear, I don't give a damn," would stay with me forever.

At dusk we walked out of the theater, now lit up in neon with massive searchlights sweeping the skyline as if we'd attended a real Hollywood premiere. We marveled at the spectacle of it all as we made our way to a little inlet in Belmont Shores known as Naples Beach. Along the way, I raved about the film, asking when we could come back to that theater. Mama smiled and said, "Did you know I was in a few films in Mexico? I was an actress on the big screen. Just like that one."

My eyes widened in disbelief as I imagined my mother a Mexican Scarlett O'Hara.

"It's true," Mama said, laughing. "I was sure I'd be a movie star someday, and I was on my way too. Thanks to my godmother, María Félix. She was one of the most important movie stars of the Mexican cinema. She helped me go on casting calls and coached me until I started to land bit parts in films."

"No way," Bobby said. "You never told us that."

Mama shrugged. "There's a lot you don't know about me."

Just as I'd suspected, Mama was a mystery waiting to unfold.

"Tell us," I said. The others echoed my request.

Then she slowly opened the curtains that had draped her past. "Well, I was working on a black-and-white movie called *Salón México*. That's when I met my first husband, Cesar, Armando and Mary's father."

Bobby smiled. "And . . ."

"And . . . it was 1949, and I was just eighteen years old when that tall, dark, handsome actor caught my eye. I was a goner. But . . . I should've listened to my father."

"Why?" I asked. "What did he say?"

"We know this part already," Ricardo said.

"Yeah," Patricia added.

"You two do," Mama said patiently, "but Danny, Bobby, and Lisa don't know any of this, so it's time they learn my story too."

"Tell us, Mama," I begged.

"Well, as I was saying, my father, you know, he could see right through that smooth-talking playboy. Called him a 'cad who would never provide anything, not even a broom to sweep the floor.' He warned me that he was a schemer. But I was in love." Then, after another laugh, she added, "Papa actually wanted me to marry the son of the president of Mexico. So I just figured no one would have been good enough in my father's eyes."

"What happened?" I asked, dazzled by the fact that my mother had been in the movies.

"I was stubborn and married the actor anyway. And then, ten days after the wedding, my father died of a heart attack. He was only sixty-two, but I had broken his heart."

We walked the rest of the way without speaking another word. Mama's mood seemed to grow heavier with each step. By the time we reached the sea, though, she looked out at the waves and pulled her summer dress over her head to reveal the purple bikini that perfectly matched her scarf. "My father would have loved all of you," she said. "He was a great man. And if he were here today, he'd tell you all to go swim!"

Then she laughed and chased us into the water, each of us leaving a trail of shoes and clothes in the sand as we stripped down to our swimsuits.

With no riptides, this pristine beach community proved safe for us to swim. And swim we did, long after the moon had claimed the sky. I took a keen interest in the rhythm of the crashing waves, timing each in my head. The more I listened, the more I became engrossed by the sounds of nature. I tuned in to the cawing of the seagulls, the fits of the wind, the foghorn call of sea vessels—so much rhythmic beauty in them all.

Mama knew how much I loved to feel the sea breeze on my face, but she also knew how much I loved rhythm. That night, while Bobby and I were putting the final touches on our sandcastle, she knelt beside me and placed a giant seashell to my ear. "Listen to that sound," she said. "God is everywhere, Danny. And his rhythms are in everything he has created. Isn't his creation wonderful?"

Somehow, Mama always knew just what to say to let me know that she believed I was one of God's wonderful creations too.

Later that night, Mama walked us to Tiny Naylor's restaurant. From a distance, it looked like a spaceship ready to take flight with its slanted canopy roof and recessed lighting. Up close, a medley of shiny cars was parked snugly underneath as waitresses in roller skates bobbed back and forth carrying trays of food. Inside, Mama bought one hot chocolate for us to split so we could use the bathroom and change out of our wet clothes before embarking on the long trip home. Mama had done her best to show us a good time, but once again her accounting came up short. Without enough money to take the bus home, she had to improvise. She had long been an advocate for carpooling, as long as it was someone else's car we were pooling in.

"You guys stay put while I look for a ride," she said. Then, like witnessing the great Houdini do the impossible, we watched as she worked her magic in a supermarket parking lot. Ever so slowly she walked up to a friendly-looking female shopper loading groceries into her car. With an impossible-to-refuse smile accompanied by her impassioned plea, Mama spoke politely. "Excuse me, but my children and I seem to have lost our bus tokens. Would it be possible for you to give us a ride up the street?"

As soon as she got the go-ahead from our newly vetted chauffeur, she waved us over, calling out in Spanish, "*¡Vámonos!*" Darting toward the car, we piled into the back as inconspicuously as possible, and away we went!

That night, we got lucky, and the woman drove us all the way home. But that was rare. Usually, these unsuspecting do-gooders would only drive us as far in our direction as they were headed, then drop us off on the side of the road, where Mama would perform the same routine all over again, putting her acting skills to work. She would do this again and again, even if it took two, three, or four drivers to get us all the way back to Compton.

It was dangerous to hop in a car with complete strangers, but if anyone ever tried anything, there were more of us than them. At least, that's what Mama always said. Plus, she had developed a sixth sense for discerning who was trustworthy. Almost exclusively she chose women since they were less likely to be sexual predators or a threat to our safety. Through it all, Mama had a way of making it seem like a fun adventure without ever letting on how dangerous or embarrassing it really was.

That tactic worked well when I was too young to know any better. In time, though, my innocence would eventually come to an end. Soon enough, I would realize the severity of our situation and the danger we were often in. As my awareness of our desperation grew, so did my shame. But that time had not yet arrived. Mama's optimism and enthusiasm had shielded me from that. And yet the contrast between our meager rental and that majestic theater could not have been starker. Although I didn't have the words then to express the tragic juxtaposition, I somehow knew that the glory of my Mama's past was a way of life that, for her, was now gone with the wind.

CHAPTER 7

High Hopes

Bobby and I jumped at the chance to join Mama and Lisa on a grocery trip one Friday after school. We followed her down each aisle as she picked out what she needed for dinner. After marking off every item on her list, we headed for the checkout line.

Lisa was sitting in the front of the cart, playing with a Pez dispenser. Bobby and I were standing by Mama's side, pestering her for some last-minute treats while we thumbed through the latest issue of *TV Guide*. "Stop it, boys," she snapped. "Quit asking me for everything you see. We might not even have enough to pay for the food we need." She looked dazed as the cashier with a bushy mustache rang up the groceries.

"Your total comes to six ninety-seven," he said.

Mama's eyes were fixed on something in the distance—her heart was clearly in another time and place, another world altogether.

Bushy Mustache scowled and said again, "Six ninety-seven."

Mama still offered no response.

Bushy Mustache became perturbed. "Ma'am, your total comes to six dollars and ninety-seven cents. Pay it or leave."

She was now staring right into his eyes as he challenged her, and there was no way she couldn't hear him. I tugged her shirt, "Mama? Are you okay?"

Suddenly snapping out of her trance, Mama seemed flustered as she said, "Oh, I'm so sorry, sir. It must be my medication. Please forgive me." She rummaged through her purse for the money, but a mortified look flashed across her face as she muttered something about being a couple of dollars short. She dug deeper.

Bushy Mustache began tapping his thick fingers on the register.

"I'm sorry. Please, just give me a minute."

His eyes twitched, and he mumbled something under his breath while she continued searching her bag, finally pulling out two more crumpled dollar bills. With that, the man bagged up our groceries, and we were on our way.

Back at our house, we helped unload the food. In the kitchen, with Dean Martin's "That's Amore" playing in the background, I took my chance. "Mama, what happened at the market? You scared us."

"I'll tell you later," she said, setting cans on the shelves. "Right now, I have to get dinner ready. It's family night." She smiled.

There was a huge age gap between Mama's oldest, Armando, and her youngest, Lisa—sixteen years, to be exact. This meant there was a short window of time when all eight of us were able to have dinner together at the same time. Naturally, Armando and Mary, being the oldest, would rather hang out with their friends than attend a family dinner with their annoying little brothers and sisters. And since Armando had moved into his own place with his new bride Diane, our family dinners had become even more of a special occurrence. But Mama insisted we have dinner together once in a while as a family. These family nights could be chaotic or end up in a squabble, but this evening there wouldn't be any family feuds.

Mama tried to get our attention a few times, but we were too busy telling jokes or teasing one another. Finally, she clinked her knife against her glass. "Listen up. I want to tell you a story."

Whenever Mama wanted to tell us a story, we knew she had something important to say, and we always stopped to listen.

"I want to share some more things about me that you younger ones don't know. Things you can all be proud of. My father, your grandfather, was the honorable Antonio Islas-Bravo, one of Mexico's most revered supreme court judges."

"Judge?" I asked, picturing a scary man in a long black robe.

"You didn't know?" Armando asked me.

I shook my head and turned back to Mama.

She shrugged. "It's hard to talk about my past. It's just so different from the life we live today. But I want you to know you come from a strong, proud Mexican family. A good family. A well-respected family."

"¡Viva México!" Armando shouted as Diane rolled her eyes. He remained passionately loyal to his home country, despite his young wife's indifference.

Mama smiled, then continued her story. "My father served on the supreme court from 1941 to 1947. But he wasn't born into power. He was a self-made man who'd worked very hard to reach that position. He'd served in the Mexican Army and fought alongside Emiliano Zapata and Pancho Villa during the Mexican Revolution, defending the peasant communities that were being driven off their land. After the war, your grandfather went on to become a deputy sheriff, an attorney, and an ambassador to Denmark. He also became a well-known writer, making his mark with an impassioned work called *La Sucesión Presidencial de 1928*."

My ears perked up. "A writer?"

Mama smiled and nodded. "He was a hero to the common man, but he also had the respect of the elite. In fact, the supreme court closed for a week to mourn your grandfather's passing. His picture still hangs in the Hall of Justice in Mexico City. When he died, the president of the supreme court said, 'We have lost a great man, a great leader, and a great friend.'"

"A great man like me," Bobby said, flaring his chest with pride.

I punched his arm teasingly. Patricia laughed, but Mary gave me a stern tilt of her head.

"What else?" I asked, eager for every last detail about this family hero.

"Well, your grandfather . . . the great man," said Mama, smiling at Bobby, "he had the funeral of a diplomat. The president of Mexico, dignitaries, celebrities—they all came to pay their respects. But others attended the funeral too. The hardworking citizens of Mexico came to honor him because he'd fought all his life to improve their rights. And that's what I want you to learn from your grandfather's story. Everybody matters. Everybody deserves to be treated with respect. Including your-selves. Don't ever let anyone treat you as if you don't matter."

Then she went on to explain how her father had demanded impec-cable manners and expected his children to excel in school. "To give us an appreciation for culture, he often took us to the opera and the theater. And to give us an incentive to learn, he would pay us for every book we read."

"Will you pay *us* to read books?" I asked. This I could do!

Mama laughed. "I wish I could pay you all to read—I really do—but you should read for your own good, to enrich your life, especially if you want to become successful like your grandfather."

"I don't understand. If your father was so important, how come we're not rich?" Bobby asked.

Mama didn't answer. Instead, she slipped back into a melancholic state and said she would tell us more tomorrow.

The next morning, Mama woke us up early by blasting Fred Astaire's "Something's Gotta Give."

"Get ready, children. We're going to do something special today!"

Patricia registered complaints from her bedroom. "We want to sleep in." It was, after all, a Saturday.

"Yeah, let us sleep," Ricardo moaned.

"Not today," Mama said, rushing her five youngest out the door.

After spending much of the day transferring from one bus to another, we finally arrived at the corner of Sunset Boulevard and Doheny Drive. From Sunset, we explored neighborhoods where rows of charmingly ornate streetlights were interspersed along both sides of the boulevard. In contrast to Compton, Beverly Hills was vibrant with color—red tulips, white geraniums, lavender roses, burgundy hollyhocks, and orange dahlias dangled from planter boxes and garden beds—not to mention the bougainvillea that spilled over trellises in cascades of hot pinks and deep violets. I felt like Dorothy when she was swept from the sepia tones of her home in Kansas and plopped into the technicolor land of Oz.

We walked down the tree-lined streets, our heads turning from one side to the other, mesmerized by this upscale world. To add to the fantasy, colossal bushes had been trimmed into the shapes of animals. I tried peering through them to get a glimpse of what life lay behind them, but the shrubbery was too tall and dense. The meticulously manicured lawns and ingenious landscapes made me giddy. I wanted to stay in this celestial kingdom, to play in those yards, and to live in one of these mansions. To be a part of that world.

The visual splendor was so beguiling it spun me into a terrific trance. I daydreamed my father was a master of one of those estates—a learned man with a depth of character to match. As I built more stories to heal the hole in my heart, I imagined I had been kidnapped, and now, years later, having escaped my captors, I was wandering the streets of Beverly Hills, trying to find my way back to him. I would discover him on his morning stroll dressed in his scarlet robe and black velvet slippers. He would wrap me in his arms and spin me 'round and 'round until I was dizzy. "At last!" he would exclaim as tears streamed down his face. "I *knew* I would find you! I just knew!" Then he would take me home to our columned mansion with its dignified doors and luminous chandeliers, where he would say, "One day this will all be yours, son." How wonderful it would have been if this wishful reverie weren't merely the delusion of a boy who ached to have a home in his father's heart.

While we strolled through these stately streets as a tribe of tall, thin Mexican Americans who couldn't have looked more out of place if we'd tried, Mama told us more about her past. She pointed to one Spanish-style home with terracotta shingles and creeping ivy. "I grew up in a house much like that one. And you, my children, you can have a home like that too, if you work hard enough."

It was difficult to believe my mother had ever lived in such a grandiose place, but I knew she was telling the truth by the tears in her eyes.

"We lived in the best district in Mexico City. Just like the families who live here in Beverly Hills. We were a diplomatic family with a lavish home at the top of a hill. Maids, cooks, tutors, butlers, drivers, and even a governess were a normal part of our everyday life. My parents had both come from families of lawyers, and they had great expectations for me, their firstborn. My father, especially, hoped I would follow in his diplomatic footsteps. He sent me to the most prestigious private Catholic schools and exposed me to all the fineries of life, encouraging me to take part in the state dinners and to entertain when important dignitaries came to visit. I would play piano, sing, and impress them with my English. But the only ones I really cared about impressing were the ones from the United States. We had traveled here many times when I was young, and I fell in love with this country."

While Mary and Armando had long known of Mama's past and still maintained deep ties to Mexico, the rest of us were just beginning to understand how different her childhood had been in comparison to ours. From the sound of it, her upbringing had been stable and esteemed, while ours was shaky and shameful. It was hard to relate to her life of privilege when all we had ever known was poverty and struggle. But knowing she had come from a world far better than mine proved inspiring and became a much-needed catalyst for my aspirations.

"You come from a long line of high achievers," she continued. "And your grandfather's greatness runs in your veins. So just remember what the Bible says: 'All things are possible to those who believe.'"

"Believe what?" I asked.

"Believe in something you can see with your heart, even if it's impossible to see with your eyes. It means you have faith."

I looked my mother in the eye. "Do you have faith, Mama?"

"I wish you knew just how strong my faith has been, Danny. Faith is what got me through all the tough times of my life. It's the only way I'm able to remain hopeful when there's nothing to be optimistic about."

Before starting home, we looked west on Sunset, where immense shafts of gold filled the skyline and the sun dissolved into the horizon. It had been an exhausting day traveling back and forth on all those buses, but I would never forget those glorious images, nor the words my mother spoke to us. Whatever faith was, I knew she had it. And I wanted it for myself.

Later that night, when I was lying next to Mama as she tucked me in for bed, she said to me, "Do you want to know what happened to me at the cash register?"

I nodded my head.

"For a minute, I felt I was actually back in Mexico. I got lost in time."

"Like in the *Time Machine* movie?"

"Exactly like that. There I was, dressed in a flowing pink and white embroidered gown, seated next to President Truman, amusing him with my girlish charm during one of our state dinners."

As Mama continued her enchanting tales, I was spirited away to the land of make-believe. Her seemingly mythical past filled me with a once-upon-a-time hope that someday I might serendipitously fall into a fairy tale of my own. Especially since her childhood story wasn't a fairy tale at all; it was true! This made me believe that maybe, just maybe, my handsome prince of a father would come for me, take my hand, and walk me to a happily-ever-after ending.

All I had to do was believe.

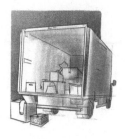

CHAPTER 8

I Feel the Earth Move

On February 9, 1971, shortly before 6:00 a.m., I was sound asleep in my family's single-story bungalow when I felt a rumbling. As the noise grew louder, I thought I was dreaming about thunder until I was jolted from the top bunk onto the floor. When I hit the ground, I knew it was no dream. I tried running to Mama's room, but the floor beneath me swayed like an ocean swell. Then the ceiling above me cracked, and a hunk of plaster fell on my head.

"Earthquake!!!" Mama screamed. "Run to the living room!"

I grabbed Bobby's hand from the bottom bunk and yanked him out of bed. We climbed over our dresser that had just crashed to the floor and stumbled down the dark hallway. I flipped the light switch. Nothing. My siblings yelled frantically from different places in the house. Windows cracked. Pictures flew off the walls. Light fixtures rocked. Dishes shattered. Shards of glass littered the floor.

Our bookcase toppled to the floor with a crash. Bobby squeezed my hand, and we looked at each other, our faces both panic-stricken. We clung to each other as our house groaned and Lisa cried.

"Under the table!" Mama yelled, pulling us all together to the safest place she could find. As we huddled in the small space, she prayed in

Spanish, her rosary in one hand, her crucifix in the other. The only thing we kids could think to do was to pray with her.

Then, everything stilled. The nightmare was over. We exhaled a collective sigh.

Mama made the sign of the cross and thanked the heavens. But they must not have heard her, because suddenly the house started shaking even harder. Our eyes filled with terror once again as we wrapped our arms around each other, pulling together. No one spoke. Then, with one final jolt, it was over. For good this time.

We would soon learn that the 6.7 quake took 64 lives and injured 2,543 others. In the days that followed the Sylmar / San Fernando earthquake, the aftershocks unsettled the landscape of Mama's soul. "That's it," she said. "We've got to get out of this place!"

Mama had been talking this way ever since the night Armando had rescued Lisa when she disappeared during our hide-and-seek game one day. After we scoured the neighborhood desperately looking for Lisa, Mama broke down. "There're just too many of you for me to keep track of by myself!" While we tried to console her, Armando showed up with a disheveled Lisa in his arms. Where had he found her? "A seedy place," he said angrily. "Full of drunks. I walked to the end of the bar and found her sitting on the lap of a gringo who was giving her a drink."

In the months that followed, Mama came to believe our rental house, which was next door to a liquor store, was cursed. It was there that I'd almost died by choking on a grape, and once, while Patricia was taking a bath, the tub had plunged through the rotting floor, crashing all the way to the ground. A piece of glass had fallen from a window, gashing Ricardo's hand. Also in that house, I had almost been electrocuted. We'd even gotten robbed, which was terribly frightening and had left us all feeling unsafe, even in our own home. Enough strange things had happened there for all of us to be convinced that something evil possessed the house.

It was time to get out, and we all knew it.

A couple of months later, Armando and his wife Diane took a trip north to Grants Pass, Oregon, to visit her parents, the Diffins.

They invited Ricardo and Patricia to ride with them for Easter break in Diane's red Pontiac convertible.

After returning, Ricardo and Patricia lobbied Mama to move our family there.

"It's beautiful!" Patricia exclaimed. "We could go hiking through the forests instead of walking on cement all day."

"And they don't have any smog. The sky is clear blue," Ricardo added. "There's lots of trees and mountains, rivers and lakes. We can live off the land, hunting, fishing, and growing our own food."

Along with Mama's fear of earthquakes, her fear of the streets of Los Angeles was an ever-present one. Times were changing, especially in our neighborhood, where crime, drugs, gangs, and the cost of living were all on the rise.

One night soon after, Mama made a startling announcement. "I think Ricardo and Patricia are right. We should move to Oregon. The earthquake was horrible. We were lucky none of us died. But things are getting worse. If we don't get out of here soon, I'm afraid you guys might join a gang, end up in jail, or . . . worse."

We all agreed.

And so on Friday, April 2, 1971, Mama prepared a traditional meal of tamales, tacos, enchiladas, and her favorite dessert, flan. "This is our last dinner here," she said as we all gathered around the dining room table. "Tomorrow we cross over into a new season of our lives. I believe it will be our best yet. Now, let's make a toast. To Oregon."

"To Oregon," we answered as we clinked our mismatched water glasses together.

Bobby and I were so excited that we talked through the night about all the great adventures that awaited us in Oregon and about how much we wanted to get a dog.

In hopes of a better life, we packed whichever of our belongings would fit into the smallest U-Haul available and headed north on the I-5 Freeway for the 719-mile journey to our future. I was about to turn nine, and we were leaving the only world I had ever known.

Because Mama hadn't learned to drive yet, Armando drove the truck with her, Bobby, Lisa, and me all crammed together on the front seat. Mary, who had just turned nineteen, drove Ricardo and Patricia in the used '62 Chevy Nova she had just purchased from her friend's dad.

At some point, after chugging up Interstate 5 through the Tehachapi Mountains and then descending down into Grapevine Canyon, we became separated from Mary. We pulled over at a rest stop to try to re-connect, but the other half of our family was nowhere to be found. Mama was worried sick. Oblivious to her anxiety, we three kids played I Spy and Slug Bug and sang songs like "She'll Be Coming 'Round the Mountain."

As we drove past the "Leaving California" sign, I wondered if we would ever return. And when we passed the rustic Welcome to Oregon sign, carved out of wood, I sensed it was the end of the life I had known. Mama's eyes peered behind us, then ahead like an eagle. "Where the heck are they?" she shouted. "I should have had a mechanic check that car. It was making strange noises."

A few miles into Oregon, the landscape shifted from barren high desert to dense evergreen forest. All around us stretched a sprawling mountain canvas, stippled with Douglas firs and conifers, their thin tips spired toward the skies, a complete contrast to the scrappy junipers and palms we had tried to climb back in Compton. As Bobby, Lisa, and I gazed out the window, the expression on their faces was the same as mine—one of sheer wonder.

But not on my mother's face. "I hope they're all right," she said, still searching for the rest of our crew.

"Don't worry. I'm sure they're okay," I said, but I had no idea what I was talking about. None of us knew whether our siblings were really okay or not.

We continued north on I-5, passing quaint towns like Ashland and Medford before taking the exit for Grants Pass. On the sharp turn toward the city center, a gust of wind blew through our open windows, filling our lungs with the sweet scent of pine. Bobby and I couldn't stop smiling.

We crossed over the striking arches of the Caveman Bridge and peered out at the sparkling waters of the rugged Rogue River. At the outskirts of the city, Armando steered onto Williams Highway and headed south toward Murphy. Along the way stood a lumber mill that bellowed smoke, and an endless array of ferns was strewn across the woodlands. After a bend in the road, Armando said, "Welcome to the Diffins' house!" as he turned into a long gravel driveway.

The rest of us cheered, "We're here! We're here!"

Straddling the wire fence, prickly patches of overgrown blackberry bushes crowded both sides of the drive. Woven among them, I'd soon learn, were strands of poison oak. Once we had piled out of the truck, we were greeted by Geronimo, a friendly Australian shepherd with freaky-looking blue eyes. He seemed as excited to meet us as we were to meet him, and he wagged his tail so hard it almost gave me a welt. Mama looked relieved to get out of the truck, but she couldn't bring herself to smile, not with the other half of our family still missing.

Excited by our new surroundings, Bobby and I, with Lisa in tow, crunched over gravel, branches, and pine needles toward a goat that was bleating in the pasture. He seemed more tentative the closer we got, as uncertain of us as we were of him. Bravely, we reached out to touch him, the first time we had ever petted a goat.

Like something we had only seen on TV, the Diffins' property offered us green, hilly meadows near a creek. There, I was drawn in by the murky wonders of the underwater world, where we spotted a school of tadpoles and a few frogs. A tapping sound drew my attention to a wooden bridge, where I looked up at my first woodpecker, chipping away at a ponderosa pine. When we came to the family's red barn, we discovered huge stacks of freshly cut firewood that gave off a delightfully homey fragrance. This new world felt vibrant, the opposite of everything we had ever known in LA.

"Boys, come here right away!"

"What's wrong?" Bobby asked as we ran toward the back of the house, where Mama was motioning for us to join her.

"Mary just called from a pay phone. They're okay! They'll be here in a little bit," she said, clearly relieved.

As soon as they drove up, we hugged one another and had our first happy moment together as a family in this new land.

I was straight outta Compton, a place where I had been surrounded by concrete, graffiti, and hoodlums, and I was eager to do some exploring, eager for unique experiences. Little did I know how *unique* those experiences would prove to be.

CHAPTER 9

Food, Glorious Food

Josephine County was teeming with hopyards, gladiola fields, and grassy meadows, each of which gave off a distinct fragrance. When the northerly winds blew across the vivid landscape, the scent of sugar pine, sequoia, and Pacific madrone trees breezed through the air. These were the smells of southern Oregon. Whenever a fresh aroma wafted our way, Mama would inhale and say to us, "Breathe it all in and savor this moment. It will only feel new once."

It was exciting to be someplace different, but I was experiencing a serious case of culture shock. I was a city boy who had suddenly found himself in Grants Pass. Population 523 cows, 242 pigs, 87 horses, 63 goats, 57 ducks, 47 chickens, and 12,971 people. Well, not exactly. There were tons more animals, but the population within the city limits was official.

We had left Los Angeles because street-smart predators lurked everywhere, all waiting for an easy mark. When we arrived in southern Oregon, a different but equally dangerous demographic roamed: country bumpkins, bearded gnomes, and loners dressed in army surplus clothing. White folks, mostly. Lots of them. I had never seen so many in one place. I looked everywhere, but I couldn't find even one Black person.

Adding texture to this throwback culture was the ever-present caveman theme. From Caveman Plaza to the Caveman Bowling Alley and everywhere in between, there was no escaping the town's prehistoric mascot.

With its lack of ethnic diversity, Grants Pass proved more culturally challenging than we had anticipated. It was there, in the midst of that agrarian community, that we first witnessed something that shook us to our core: square dancing. At a local Grange hall, we stood in shock watching boys in western shirts and blue jeans promenading at their hootenanny with girls in skirts and petticoats as they do-si-doed with the stiffness of an ironing board. Given the fact we had grown up watching *Soul Train* every Saturday morning—a Black show that featured the best dancers, wearing the hippest fashions of the day, dancing to the latest R&B hits—we should have known that we wouldn't fit into this community.

Our first rental property was a cold, damp green bungalow on Redwood Avenue, just outside of town. It sat kitty-corner from the Old Red Barn Country Store, directly behind Redwood Elementary School, where Bobby and I would attend for the remaining two months of the school year and the beginning of the fall semester.

The "new school" routine had become all too familiar. In the years leading up to this, I had learned to recognize what an eviction notice looked like and to understand the reasons we were being kicked to the curb yet again. When we weren't getting thrown out for being late on the rent, merciless landlords would hand us our walking papers once they had realized how many of us were sharing the rental. If we weren't being booted out, Mama would sometimes jump ship to protect us from unsavory characters who lurked around our apartment complexes—drug dealers, lowlifes, pimps, predators. There was always someone looking to prey on an overwhelmed single mother with a throng of seven vulnerable children. The perilous streets had been consistently unpredictable, and Mama was always on the hunt for a safe place for us.

By the time we reached Grants Pass, we had moved more than thirty times. The instability had become numbing. Through the years, we had drifted, rudderless, from one place to another without a compass to guide us or a plan to protect us. Along the way, we landed in

Long Beach, Lynnwood, Paramount, and North Long Beach. We were innocent outliers in search of a place to call home, but while we lived in abject poverty, our spirits were kept afloat by the buoyant resilience of our mother—a brave and indomitable woman who always kept her heart soft and her head held high.

While I had grown accustomed to new starts, here in Oregon, I was facing many firsts. My first chore at the green rental house was to mow the grass, but that was only because I kept bugging Mama to let me use the mower we had borrowed from Diane's parents. It had rained a lot that spring, which made the grass as tall as it was thick. In spite of that, I couldn't wait to get my hands on that powerful piece of machinery and have a go at it.

Shortly after I began mowing, dense clumps of moist green gunk shot out the side of the mower. I made good progress as I zigzagged back and forth, making straight lines, until a long, black snake slithered right in front of me. I froze. Another first! Terrified I might get bitten, I reacted instinctively, pushing the mower over the snake as fast as I could and sending bits of him flying into the irrigation canal. Just as I had hoped, every day in this foreign land offered some wild, new adventure, and I was learning lessons from each one.

Around the time George Harrison of the Beatles was preparing for his New York City concert to help feed the starving kids of Bangladesh, the kids in my house were in desperate need of food as well. Happily married, Armando and Diane had rented a small white cottage on Booth Street, and he'd found work at Rogue Community College as a science and Spanish tutor—a job that suited him well since he was modeling his life after his favorite uncle in Mexico City, a man known for being an impassioned teacher and activist who, like our grandfather, fought for social justice. Armando carried that torch too, and he had long been the one to fight for all of us. But now that he and Diane had a one-year-old daughter, Anna, they had financial responsibilities of their own and could no longer afford to contribute to our family as much as he had done in the past.

The week after she helped us move to Grants Pass, Mary had gone back to Los Angeles, where she enrolled as a freshman at Compton Junior College and worked in the admissions office as part of a work-study program. Both Mary and Armando were driven to create a better future for themselves and continued to go to college while working full-time. With them gone, that left the five remaining children and my mother to fend for ourselves. As we quickly neared the end of our savings, we had to think of new ways to earn an income.

Frustrated by her unsuccessful job search, Mama went door to door, offering ironing, housecleaning, and babysitting services, but people were skeptical and turned her away. Determined to help, Bobby, Lisa, and I hit both sides of Redwood Highway, trying to sell the shiny rocks we had collected from the stream. But no one seemed as fascinated with them as we were, and so we slunk away in dismay.

When things were tight in Los Angeles, we remained hopeful because as long as you were a hard worker, you could always find a way to make a buck in the city. In Grants Pass, things were different. We wanted to work. We tried to work. We had always worked. But this new town wasn't exactly quick in offering us the opportunity to earn a living.

Running out of money meant coming to the end of our food supply. Mama scoured the cupboards for whatever was left. One by one, she opened them, only to be disappointed. We had already gone through the last cans of Spam, SpaghettiOs, and corned beef hash. The only thing left was a can of chicken noodle soup and a loaf of Wonder Bread. Mama lit up the stove, opened the can of soup, and poured it into a saucepan. After she rationed out a small portion to each of us, she said, "I think we might have made a mistake moving to Oregon. It feels like no one wants us here. They won't even give us a chance. I wish we could afford to move back to California, but we have no choice now but to stick it out."

The soup didn't last long, and the slices of white bread were so thin and squishy it was a *"wonder"* they called it bread at all. We doctored it up as best we could by smearing each slice with margarine and sprinkling sugar on top. Most mornings we went without breakfast. But we did get a free lunch at school, which we had always looked forward to. The big challenge was dinner.

My mother had no way of knowing how long it would be until she could put some real food on the table, so she insisted we cut the bread into slivers, one for each of us. To boost our spirits, Ricardo told us stories of tribes he had read about in *National Geographic*, indigenous people who had survived long periods of time on small portions of food, which they could do as long as they had water. Like hungry wolves, we stared at each other in desperation, trying to come up with a survival plan. With little sustenance, I tried to fill my stomach by drinking glasses of water, but our normally rambunctious family was running out of steam. Our energy waned in the evenings as we would spread our sleeping bags over the damp and drafty floor. Most of our furniture had been left behind in Los Angeles, unable to fit into the only moving truck we could afford to rent.

Mama had always been a miracle worker when it came to stretching a dollar, but in order to put her superpowers to work, she had to have at least a few dollars to start with. After all, even Jesus needed five loaves and two fish to multiply them for the crowd. We had long been poor, but we had never gone hungry.

One night my mother adapted a few lines from *Gone with the Wind*. "As God is my witness, Grants Pass is not going to lick me!" Strong. Resolute. Defiant. She said it with the fervency of the actress she had always wanted to be. "We're going to live through this, my children, and when it's all over, we'll never be hungry again. As God is my witness, we'll never be hungry again." Mama could be dramatic at times, but in this case, her histrionics were warranted. We all needed to believe she could lead us out of our despair, and her resolve convinced us she could.

With determination, she continued scouring the classified section of the *Daily Courier*, looking for work. That's when she stumbled onto an announcement for Boatnik, the Memorial Day weekend carnival at Riverside Park. Speedboats would race up and down the Rogue River, while a smorgasbord of family-friendly games and competitions took place at the park.

Mama tapped the paper and smiled. "Looks like God is making a way for us to eat."

"How?" we all cried out.

"According to the paper, they're going to have a variety of food-eating contests throughout the weekend. And there's no cost to enter."

"We're gonna win!" I shouted, driven not only by hunger but also by my competitive drive to be the best at anything I set out to achieve.

"I have no doubt, son. But even if we don't win, we'll get to eat, and that's all I care about for my family."

We lived on bread and water for the next couple of days. All we could talk about was the food that awaited us. The mere thought of stuffing our faces kept our spirits alive.

The weather was marvelous on that opening day, but it was no comparison to the variety of enticing smells floating throughout the park. Once we descended upon the acres of lush grounds, the aroma of fresh corn dog batter and fried chicken was almost too much to bear. Like a poised bird dog, I was ready to capture my prey once the command was given.

Throughout the park, colorful, hand-painted signs listed the games you could participate in. As we strolled around the carnival to see what caught our interest, the sound of giggling children filled the air. Patricia and I were the two most aggressive of the family, so we decided to enter the fastest-runner contest. We ran with all our hearts, because we would get a prize if we won. We didn't care what it was. We knew whatever it was, we could use it.

The sound of boat engines roaring nearby spurred us on to the finish line. For taking home the gold in each of our categories, we were both presented with a brand-new T-shirt with the words "Honorary Jr. Jaycee" on the front, along with a humorous drawing of the city's caveman mascot. We walked around in our new T-shirts, feeling the pride of Olympic champions.

Ricardo and Bobby entered a potato sack race. Mama and the rest of us screamed at the top of our lungs from the sidelines. "Go, Ricardo! Go, Bobby!" Determined not to let us be the only winners, they hopped across the lawn, edging themselves into first place. They, too, were awarded the same caramel-colored T-shirts. Suddenly we looked like one happy family in our matching attire, which was very uncharacteristic of us. We were not the matchy-matchy kind of family, but we *were* happy—happy to be wearing something new, something clean. And happy to know we would soon be able to eat.

After the races, we scurried to a wooded corner of the park, where the watermelon-eating contest was about to take place. As the sun peeked through the branches of the tall trees, oodles of kids sat at the picnic tables, each with half a watermelon in front of them. The tables were jam-packed.

Once we heard the word "Go," Ricardo, Patricia, and I plunged our faces into those melons. When the whistle blew, the only thing that remained, besides the drippings on our faces, was a thin white layer of rind in front of each of us. From there, we found the fried chicken–eating contest near the river. Along the bank, people sat in lawn chairs, watching the speedboats race by as mallard ducks waddled over the grass. As quickly as the bell rang, we sunk our teeth into the crisp chicken. By the end of the competition, the only thing left on our plates was a pile of bones. Each day we continued to gorge ourselves with the same determination at the pizza, corn dog, and flapjack-eating contests, knowing this could be the last food we would have for a while.

Between contests, we watched the Grants Pass High School pep band march in the parade down Sixth Street. Sitting on the edge of the bridge with a full belly for the first time in weeks, I found myself drawn to the pulsing cadence of the drum line. "I want to play the drums, Mama," I said, wishing I could march in the band like those musicians. "Am I too little?"

"You're never too little to dream big things," she assured me.

CHAPTER 10

The Little Drummer Boy

On the first of October, we left the drafty place on Redwood Avenue and moved into a small rental house in downtown Grants Pass on B Street, right around the corner from Armando and Diane's place. Early one crisp evening, I heard the cackling of women and the rustling of paper on our front stoop. A gentle knock followed.

I opened the door to a big surprise. On the steps stood three nuns—Sisters Nancy, Vivian, and Vicki. They were wrapped in habits so intimidating I suspected I had been found out. But I couldn't figure which mischievous act had done me in since there were so many to choose from in the short time we had been attending St. Anne's Church. Like the time Mama gave me a dollar for the offering basket, and after dropping it in, I pulled out five quarters when she wasn't looking. Or when I snuck into the back of the church and took a box of communion wafers, spread peanut butter over them, and gave them out at school as sandwiches. Or when I took a few hymnals and tried to sell them on the street. With all that tomfoolery on my résumé, I knew I could never be the altar boy Mama wanted me to be. Still, I figured it best to let them make the first move on the off chance they might call me out on one of my lesser offenses.

"Hi there, Danny. Is your mother home?" pale Sister Nancy asked. I said nothing, because I was afraid she was about to tell how I kept my comics hidden in my book of Bible stories. Then Mama popped up behind me with a slightly worried look on her face, placing a reassuring hand on my shoulder as she greeted the sisters.

"How are you, Maria?" Sister Nancy said, launching into a friendly exchange with Mama. Meanwhile, each of the nuns stood there, holding two grocery bags, some of which were on the verge of splitting open, prompting Sister Vivian to politely speak up. "Can we put these down on your kitchen table?"

"Of course," Mama said, welcoming them out of the blustery cold.

After plopping her bags down, Sister Nancy made an announcement. "Maria, we wanted to do something special to let your family know you are loved and welcomed here in Grants Pass."

Mama's eyes welled with sudden emotion as the sisters began to unpack the bags.

A Butterball turkey wrapped in yellow plastic netting. A couple of boxes of Mrs. Cubbison's stuffing. A bag of potatoes. Bread rolls, chicken stock, gravy mix, and butter. *Real* butter! When Sister Vicki pulled out a can of Libby's pumpkin pie mix and a graham cracker piecrust, I couldn't contain myself. I cheered aloud, "Woo-hoo!"

Bobby looked in one of the sacks, spotting a bag of marshmallows and a couple of bottles of Martinelli's Gold Medal sparkling cider, the fanciest drink we had ever seen. He and I looked at each other in amazement. Ricardo and Patricia grinned from ear to ear as they gathered around the table. Lisa was jumping up and down, gleaming with excitement.

The church called this gift a "Thanksgiving basket." After the nuns presented us with their offering of love, we thanked them and gave each of them a big bear hug. Their eyes filled with tears too. Before the sisters left, they said a prayer over our family. Afterward, Mama looked at us sternly, then glanced back at our guests. "You can expect to see all of my children at Mass this Sunday," she said.

That Thanksgiving, Mama spent all day singing while she cooked.

By evening, the entire family gathered around the table. We all ate like kings. It was the first time since the Memorial Day Boatnik festival that we had felt full.

A couple of weeks later, six inches of snow fell on Grants Pass. School was canceled, leaving us free to play in the magical snow globe of that December morning, a flurry of snowflakes wisping around us. With no snow gear, Mama held Lisa, who was five now, and both of them tried to catch the flakes in their mouths while the rest of us built our first snowman, using rocks for the eyes and branches for the arms. We topped him off by placing Mama's wool beret on his head, then we spent the next few hours sliding down hills on a wooden sleigh with the neighbor kids.

That night, as I relived the perfect day, all seemed right with the world. Christmas was just around the corner, and one of our favorite activities was to flip through the *Sears Wish Book*. Just as we would do every evening, Bobby and I sat together on the couch and pretended we were getting everything on our side of the page.

"I'm getting the Sno-Cone machine," I insisted.

"I'm getting all the Johnny West action figures," he replied.

Then we switched sides and started all over again. That's how we would entertain ourselves in our land of make-believe, where wishes were horses ridden by beggars like us.

But the reality of our circumstances became clear to me late one night when I saw Mama go into her closet. Just a few days before Christmas, her demeanor made me suspicious. I snuck closer for a peek. I couldn't get a good look without her seeing me, so I put my ear to the door. She was counting, "Six seventy-five, seven, seven twenty-five, seven fifty, seven seventy-five, eight." When she got to ten, she stopped. After I heard her putting her coin jar away, I walked out of her bedroom as quickly and quietly as I could.

Now pregnant, Mary had moved back from Los Angeles to be with the family for a couple of months, and we were all so happy to be reunited with her. On December 23, she gave birth to her daughter, Lydia, at the Josephine Memorial Hospital, making our first Christmas in Oregon extra special. The next night, we attended midnight Mass, a must for any Catholic family. Even with Mary in the hospital with a new baby, Mama wouldn't dare let us skip the Christmas Eve ceremony, especially after the church had been so kind to us. After the service, we each looked forward to opening one small present—our family tradition. With Perry Como's "'Twas the Night before Christmas" playing on the record player, Mama handed each of us a red mesh Christmas stocking. In it were walnuts, an orange, a candy cane, a miniature set of checkers, and a couple of cheesy toys that broke in a matter of seconds.

We would have to wait until Christmas morning to open our real presents, some of which were made possible by the Salvation Army and the Marine Corps Toys for Tots Program. As soon as the sun came up, we gathered around the tree in our pajamas, eager for the fun to begin. When I spotted a large gift with my name on it, I tore off the wrapping paper. As soon as I got a glimpse of the box, I jumped to my feet in a frenzy of delight. It was the groovy *Disney Rocktet* drum set from the *Sears Wish Book*—the very drums I had wanted for months. Pictured on the front of the bass drum were Goofy strumming the banjo, Minnie and Mickey rocking out on guitars in bell bottoms and beads, and Donald Duck quacking away on drums.

"Thank you, thank you, thank you, Mama!" I hugged her tightly. "You knew how much I wanted those drums, and you got them for me. I love you so much."

Standing next to the wood-burning stove in her pink quilted robe, she smiled at me and said, "I love you even more, *mijo*. I'm so happy you like it."

For the rest of the day, I pounded the drums with all my heart. By Christmas evening, though, I had already ripped the thin skins on the tom-toms and put a hole through the bass drumhead that was not much thicker than construction paper.

Mama was infuriated, but not at me. "Whoever made those drums should be ashamed of themselves for making such cheap junk!" she yelled. "You get a kid all wound up, and then you drop him from the sky." She paced the floor with a look of disdain, rambling off impassioned sentences in Spanish.

"Mama, it's just a toy," Patricia explained. "He needs a real set of drums. I saw one in the *Sears Wish Book* for a hundred dollars."

My mother's veins protruded from her forehead. "We don't have a hundred dollars! I had to scrape up every loose quarter I had to get these. It's not fair, I tell you. It's just not fair."

It broke my heart to see her so disappointed. In fact, I was more upset about how she felt than I was for myself. Though that drum set lasted only a day, it connected me to rhythms that would last a lifetime. From that moment on, I felt as if some ghost of Christmas future was beckoning me to my destiny, the sounding of a beat that was yet to come.

Our B Street house was the last place Mary lived with us. After the holidays, she moved with her new baby, Lydia, forty-five minutes south to attend Southern Oregon College, where she resided on campus in Ashland and relied on Mama for babysitting when needed. Before moving, she gave Mama her '62 Chevy Nova so we could have a car. In the wake of her departure, we would have to make another adjustment to our continually changing family. This would prove to be a difficult one because Mary had always served as an anchor of dependability, especially for my mother.

When school resumed in January, I inquired about playing the drums in the school band, only to learn that they didn't offer percussion. Their orchestra featured strings and woodwinds exclusively. The only opening was for a violinist, something I had no desire to be. Mama encouraged me to give it a try, but I had my heart set on the drums, so I resisted.

She came up with a clever idea to change my mind. On a cold wintry day after school, she walked me down the street to the library, one of our favorite haunts. That day she checked out *The Lives of the Great Composers, Volume 1*. When we got home, she gathered Bobby, Lisa, and me around her and read the stories of Johann Sebastian Bach, Ludwig van Beethoven, Wolfgang Amadeus Mozart, and Frederic Chopin.

As she read, her voice took on an inspired tone that set my heart to longing. "Did you know I play piano?" Mama asked. The three of us shook our heads. I certainly knew Mama loved music. She was always singing and dancing around the house, pleading with us to join her, but I'd never imagined her playing the piano. Once again, she was full of surprises.

"I loved making music, and my parents used to take us to the opera, the theater, and concerts. They encouraged us to develop our talents. So I studied piano from a very young age and eventually added acting, voice, and dance classes in high school, then continued all the way through the prep school at the University of Mexico, where I studied Latin, Greek, philosophy, cooking, and sewing. But it was music and drama that I loved most. I practiced every day. And eventually I even joined a band."

"You were in a band?" Bobby asked.

"What kind of band?" I added.

"Yeah," echoed Lisa. "What kind?"

Mama smiled. "We were well known in our area because we sang all the popular American songs in English. We performed at high school dances, college parties, weddings, and *quinceañeras*, which are celebrations for girls when they turn fifteen. Conchita usually came with me to auditions, acting classes, and band rehearsals and performances. She loved being a part of the fun. She really was my best friend, not just my mother."

"You're my best friend," I said.

Mama hugged me tighter, and I knew she could tell I was telling the truth.

I was so enthralled by Mama's adventures, not to mention the lives of all those musical geniuses we had read about in the book, that I asked if we could go back to the library for more. It seemed to please her that I showed such interest, and the next evening, she read us the stories from volume 2 in the series, this time detailing the lives of Franz Schubert, Johannes Brahms, and Franz Liszt.

Mama sensed I was hungry for more and used her winsome

personality to convince the Rogue Theatre to bring in some films about the lives of the great composers. Her gifts of persuasion worked. Before long the marquee boasted such titles as *The Great Waltz* and *A Song to Remember*—both films she had suggested they run. At the theater, I would pan the audience and think to myself, *You're all having a good time because of my mother.* I was proud of her vision to enrich the area with culture. She may not have been able to give us what her parents had offered her as a child, but she always found a way to expand our world beyond the small sphere of influence we were limited to otherwise.

As usual, Mama's plan worked. Not long after my exposure to the books and movies about classical musicians, I decided to give the violin a try. I practiced every day after school, thinking I might be the next Paganini, Beethoven, or Bach. At the end of the semester, we put on a concert. Mama sat in the front row with the rest of my family as we performed a children's version of *The Nutcracker Suite* by Tchaikovsky. The power of performing with an ensemble in front of a live audience was invigorating.

From that moment on, there was no turning back from the music.

CHAPTER 11

We Are Family

As I learned more about the lives of classical composers, I continued to practice the violin. While I didn't exactly love it, I was beginning to learn basic music notation and how an ensemble played in tempo together. Suddenly the wide world of rhythms opened up to me. I studied the four-count rhythm of fly fishers casting for salmon on the Rogue River. As the sun broke through the clouds, bald eagles soared overhead, catching the movement of thermal updrafts. My mind tuned into the swift sound of water, gurgling around boulders, and the swirling eddies, which collided resoundingly, then settled harmoniously downriver. Those ancient rhythms rose and fell in that riverbed, and something of their music rose and fell within me, soothing my soul and somehow resolving the discord that lived there.

A year had passed, and we were slowly adjusting to life within the city limits of Grants Pass. Mama had cobbled together a mishmash of part-time jobs, and she was able to stretch them far enough to make ends meet. Before we knew it, though, we were in for another transition. Our mother had grown tired of renting. She had always wanted to purchase a small piece of property and build a house on it. It seemed ridiculous when money was so scarce. But Mama was often ridiculous. Her hope was to establish stability for us by having some land of our own, a noble goal for a family that had always been on the move.

Gathered around our usual meeting place—the kitchen table—she shared her vision with us. It would require tremendous sacrifice and hard work, neither of which was unfamiliar to us. We all bought into it. Ricardo, who was now fourteen, took a job with Josephine County Parks and Recreation. At age thirteen, Patricia found work at the Riverside Motel. I was about to turn ten, and Bobby was seven. Together, with five-year-old Lisa helping out however she could, we did every odd job we could get our hands on. From shoveling horse manure and mowing lawns to washing cars and feeding animals, we did it. And happily. Because this was *our* dream now, our *family's* dream, and not just Mama's.

As our mother cleaned houses and ironed clothes, we all scrimped and saved and sacrificed. Traveling light had become a way of life for us, but to facilitate our next move, we would have to lighten our load even more. We sold practically everything we owned in a yard sale. Everything, that is, except my *Sears Wish Book* and Mama's orange silk scarf. And our record albums. We couldn't get rid of *those*. The catalog remained my window to the outside world—a window from which I could see my dreams, however far-fetched they might be. In the midst of so many uncertainties, those dreams—and the words Mama spoke over me when she tied that scarf around my neck—were the two things that gave me hope. And the music, well, the music was oxygen to us all. It kept our hopes alive. And it kept us dancing toward our dream, however slow or halting our steps.

Mama looked for property on the outskirts of town, where land was cheaper. Soon she found an acre-and-a-half lot for five thousand dollars in the Jerome Prairie area, just below Bolt Mountain. But after working our fingers to the bone, we didn't even have enough for the down payment. And it seemed we never would. We were all discouraged, especially Mama. Still studying in Ashland, Mary learned about our situation and came to our rescue again by giving us a portion of her financial aid for college. It was just enough for the down payment. And just enough to keep our hopes alive. Mama accepted the help on one condition—that Mary would continue her schooling and not give up *her* dreams.

Since Mary had also given us her car, and Sister Nancy had taught Mama how to drive, Mama drove us out to take a look at our future home. Our hopes were buoyed on the corner of Jerome Prairie Road and Sleepy Hollow Loop, where a sensational brown house claimed the space, surrounded by a ranch-style white fence. Within the pristine grounds grazed a herd of Hereford cows and a few haughty horses. But as we continued up the street, our eyes met a shanty town of tin-roofed shacks, their yards littered with jacked-up cars and a hodgepodge of rusted machinery. There was a long abandoned mobile home with trees growing straight through it, along with a few atrocious A-frames. The only thing unifying this patchwork of rural living seemed to be the dense blackberry vines and decomposed granite that flanked both sides of the street.

As Mama pulled up to our designated lot, I felt a rush of anxiety. With the exception of a few scraggly oak trees and some thick brush in the back of the property, the land was nearly barren.

With a twinkle in her eye, Mama said, "I know it doesn't look like much, but with a little hard work and faith, we can make something of this place. The best part is that one day it will be ours, and we won't ever have to move again." Then she sang the classic line about fairy tales coming true from "Young at Heart" by Frank Sinatra, one of her favorite songs.

Mama was unrelenting in her optimism, and we rallied behind her with gusto, believing that together we could do anything. What I didn't know then was that Mama was going to move us out to that deserted terrain on Sleepy Hollow Loop *before* any shelter was in place for us. Having spent all our savings on the down payment and sold nearly everything we owned for that lump-sum deposit, she piled all six of us into our old white two-door Chevy Nova and parked it on the rural lot. This small used car would now serve as our family's home. As this realization hit me, I felt a desolation so great I could hardly breathe. It was hard to understand how we had arrived at that situation after working so hard.

The days in the car were long. The nights, longer. Mama slept in the driver's seat, cramped behind the steering wheel. Ricardo sacked out in the bucket seat next to her, while Patricia, Bobby, and I all squeezed into the back with Lisa stretched across our laps like a mummy.

The benefit of this being summer was that it was not freezing—yet. Instead, we sweated our way through each restless night until about 4:00 a.m., when the temperature would finally drop. Then we would make good use of our blue U-Haul moving blankets. With all the squirming going on, it was fitful sleep at best. But despite our confined quarters, I always woke up in a good mood and could be counted on to find humor in every situation. Early one morning, I nicknamed our car "the White House." My family cracked up, which made everything seem okay.

While President Richard Nixon was in the midst of the Watergate scandal at the real White House, and the country remained at war in Vietnam, we were knee-deep in our own challenges, struggling just to survive. The undeveloped lot gave us no access to irrigation or running water, no gas, no electricity, and not even a bathroom. All we had were the clothes on our back, a few possessions in the trunk, the cheapest nonperishable food we could buy, and a piece of the American dream, *if* we could keep up the monthly payments for that acre and a half of southern Oregon.

During the day, my mother would take us to Schroeder Park along the banks of the Rogue River to use the restrooms and outdoor shower facilities. While locals peered at us with disgust, I felt such shame as I cleaned myself under the cold stream of water. I ached for a normal life. Or at least to be invisible. I wanted so badly not to have people look down on us, and I wished that the fairy tale really could come true for people like us. But no amount of wishing seemed to make it so. No amount of working either. Each day, before leaving the park, we would fill plastic jugs with drinking water and carry them back to "the White House" to prepare for yet another day without a real home.

We may not have had a house, but we did finally have an address. The first thing that went up on our lot was a mailbox. Mama helped us glue the numbers 3-5-5 to the post with a proud look on her face. It didn't seem like much, but for the first time in our lives, we had something to call our own.

One balmy night, Mary took a break from her college studies to visit us. We sat under the stars as she told us about a group of young "Jesus freaks" in town called the Shilohs. They were reportedly following the command to "love your neighbor as yourself." After one too many scrub downs under the cold showerhead and cement floors of the park, we begged Mama to take us to the Shilohs to see if they might let us take hot showers. Reluctantly, she swung by their place on the corner of D Street to see if they were for real. Just as Mary had reported, they had claimed a lilac-colored two-story house with ivory-white trim and a big wagon wheel out front. To the right grew heaps of sumptuous sunflowers so high they leaned over to form an enchanting canopy. On the left, a thriving garden bloomed behind a wire fence. The entire place looked loved.

Mama knocked on the door while we sat in the car, shivering in our wet clothes. A hippie with a beard answered, and we eavesdropped curiously, overhearing bits and pieces of their conversation. "My children and I . . . no running water . . . hot showers . . ."

"Welcome you . . . house of God . . . what's ours is yours."

Mama looked back and smiled at us, motioning us to come to the door. As we entered through clouds of burning incense, we were greeted by long-haired young men with bandannas wrapped around their heads and earthy young women who looked like they could bust out in sweet harmonies on cue.

On my way to the bathroom, I ran my hands through the colorful glass-bead curtains that reflected the light from each doorway, giving the home an iridescent glimmer as if I were looking through a kaleidoscope. And then, the spell continued as I stood under the warmth of the pulsating showerhead.

I never wanted to leave.

CHAPTER 12

Livin' on a Prayer

One by one, we took turns being washed in the goodness of this group of flower children from the Jesus Revolution. As the filth ran off our bodies, our spirits were being reinvigorated too. But not everyone in the region shared the Shilohs' desire to "love thy neighbor as thyself," and nothing could have prepared us for the hardships we were about to face. Each of us would be tested, and the only way to survive was to do what we did best—lean on each other.

Like many of her college friends, Mary wanted to go on weekend camping trips with her classmates. Scrimping and saving her hard-earned money, she was finally able to buy a used, eleven-foot camper. Two aqua racing stripes ran along the outside, one on the top and one in the middle.

Inside was a kitchenette, including a dining table with seats that converted into a bunk bed. It was charming, and she couldn't wait for her new adventures to begin. But as much as she wanted to take to the road with her friends, she couldn't bear the thought of leaving her family behind, wedged into a Chevy Nova.

That is who she was, who we *all* were. And we were that way because of Mama. How many adventures had *she* given up because she couldn't bear the thought of leaving *us* behind? We were not people going in different directions, thinking only of ourselves. Not seven kids and a single mom complaining about what we didn't have. Not a bitter mother shaking her fist at God—or at us—for all she had left behind. We had no idea what all she had sacrificed. All we knew was that it wasn't us. It was never us. Not once.

That is how we survived, leaning on each other, one uncertain day at a time, sharing what we had, however small the space, however meager the meal. And that is what compelled Mary to give us her camper.

We were overjoyed about the increased living space and thankful for her never-ending generosity. Because there wasn't enough room in it for all of us, Mama, Bobby, Lisa, and I slept in the camper, while Ricardo and Patricia continued sleeping in the car. At night they flipped a coin to see who would get the coveted back seat.

It had been more than three months since we had moved to the lot. Mama was desperate to get Ricardo and Patricia out of the car and knew we all needed a place to change our clothes before the school year started, so she took us on a search for some additional shelter. Her first stop—an army surplus store. Her first purchase—a tattered brown tent. We stuffed the tent in the trunk and ventured onward. She was a woman on a mission.

"What are we looking for now?" I asked.

"Army cots," she said with resolve. "So Ricardo and Patricia can get a good night's rest in that tent when school starts."

"We'll keep our eyes peeled," Ricardo said, saluting her as if she were a general. As we drove down Rogue River Highway, we scoured the storefronts for cots and military blankets.

At the north end of town, Bobby spotted the Mr. X Swap Shop, and Mama pulled over. We all tumbled out of the car to have a look. Her eyes lit up when she saw a cot, but when she noticed the five-dollar price tag, they dimmed.

The clerk, an old codger with gray tufts sprigging out his ears, tried to rekindle her interest by saying, "That's a mighty fine cot there, ma'am. Army issued."

"I'm sure it is, but unfortunately, it's way over our budget." Mama moved in closer, her brown eyes fixed and determined. "All I can afford is a dollar. Will you sell it to me for that?"

Despite having reared seven kids and endured decades of hardship, Mama remained a beauty, turning heads everywhere we went. The old man didn't stand a chance. After a little resistance, he surrendered. The dollar changed hands, and so did the cot. As we walked away, though, Patricia spotted another one just like it through an open door to the back room. She tugged on Mama's hand and nodded in that direction.

Mama marched out to the car to grab another dollar out of the glove box, then marched back in with the reinforcement of precedence. The salesman's arms were folded across his chest, braced against the on-slaught of her logic. "Since you sold me the first cot for a dollar, here's another dollar for the second one." Arms folded tighter. Dollar pushed closer. Tighter, closer. Her brown eyes giving him no room to retreat.

He took the dollar. "All right, lady. Go ahead, take it."

That was Mama, as tenderhearted a woman as you'd ever meet, and equally as tough, especially when it came to caring for her children.

The day's search had proven fruitful, but there was more that needed to be done. Mama pulled into the parking lot of a laundromat, where Ricardo and Patricia helped wash our clothes. Bobby and I, meanwhile, carted Lisa around as fast as we could in a large rolling laundry basket. When all the clothes were dried and folded—and all the fun depleted—we drove back to the vacant lot we called home.

There we turned on the stove in the camper and cooked some Spam. The saltiness made us thirsty, but we didn't have enough drinking water, so we took turns taking swigs out of the plastic jug until we had emptied it.

By the soft light of the moon, we set up camp like a circle of tee-pees—one car, one tent, one eleven-foot camper. With doors open, windows down, and tent flaps pulled back, we entertained one an-other, spinning tales of wild imaginings, until suddenly the headlights of a late-night driver blinded us with a flash I feared more than the darkness. We were all together, but also alone, with not so much as a baseball bat for protection. Every time I heard a car approaching, I was afraid it might stop and that men who *did* have baseball bats, or worse, would get out and hurt us. Despite all the dangers of LA, I had never felt as unsafe as here.

In the morning, we had a family powwow to plan our next steps. First and foremost, we needed water. For that, new friends from church helped us dig a well, proving yet again that this challenging community held many people with good hearts. Next, an outhouse needed to be built. My only worry about that was the possibility of being carted off by Bigfoot in the middle of the night. Rumors of his existence were legendary in the Northwest.

Ricardo was gifted with an architect's intellect, which made it possible for us to construct both a protective structure around the well and our very own outhouse. Borrowing tools from friends, Bobby and I worked hard alongside Ricardo, following his instructions until the three of us got the job done with scrap materials. Meanwhile, the girls rustled up food to keep us going.

Our property sat near the road with no trees to give us shade. In an attempt to keep the summer temperature down, we covered the windows with aluminum foil. But it was still hot. Roasting. Broiling. Baking hot. Our only relief from the oppressive heat was an outing to one of the rivers or lakes in the region. When we had enough gas, we would make the drive out to Jumpoff Joe Creek or Indian Mary Park. But when the needle was near E, our only option was the Applegate River.

One sweltering afternoon, we piled into the car and headed out to that nearby watering hole. After Mama parked, Patricia bolted into the river as fast as she could, then shimmied up a gargantuan tree and swung from a long rope before plunging into the water with a huge splash. Ricardo plopped himself in the center of an inner tube and floated in the lazy currents. Bobby and I raced each other across the narrow section of the river, while Lisa played at the edge of the bank.

All the while, I could hear the wind whispering through the trees. It brought such peace to my soul, that wind. I had always loved the sound, but *that* wind, *that* day, was—well, some things can't be expressed, only savored.

While we were basking in the simple pleasures of that sun-drenched day, Mama fired up the charcoal briquettes in the Hibachi grill. Soon the smell of sizzling hot dogs filled the air. All was perfect and peaceful.

The mood shifted when a caravan of bikers pulled up, riding the loudest motorcycles I had ever heard. They were a motley crew, sporting bandannas, sunglasses, and unkempt mustaches. They dismounted their hogs and stood like a horde of invading Huns, wearing long chaps, Nazi-like helmets, and black leather vests embroidered with the words "*Gypsy Jokers.*"

One with demonic eyes and a scar from ear to chin stared menacingly at Mama, his face pitted and grim. Apparently their leader, he shot a glance at a few of his henchmen, then murmured something indistinguishable. They made their way toward us, their footsteps as heavy and foreboding as storm troopers. My heart pounded. My mouth went dry and my eyes darted, searching for something I could use as a weapon to protect my mother. The closer they walked, the stiffer I became. I cut my eyes back to Mama's terror-stricken face. She cupped her hands, yelling across the river, "*¡Vámonos! ¡Vámonos!*"

She grabbed the grill, its coals still burning, and hurled it into the trunk. The rest of us ran as fast as we could, throwing ourselves into the car as she screeched out of the parking lot in a spray of gravel, praying our gas wouldn't run out and that the biker gang wouldn't catch up with us.

Clutching the steering wheel, Mama never looked back. As the car shuddered across the truss bridge on Fish Hatchery Road, her face seemed possessed with a fear that shook me to my core. Only when we reached the other side did she pause to look in the rearview mirror. "They're gone," she said with a sigh of relief. "Thank you, Jesus. Thank you, Jesus," she repeated more times than I could count. When she finally flipped on the radio to ease our nerves, the Bill Withers song "Lean on Me" came on.

And that's exactly what we did.

Assured the gang hadn't followed us home, we lurched into our dirt driveway. With the coals still burning, Mama pulled the grill from the trunk, set it up, and continued barbecuing in the middle of our lot as if nothing had happened. But she remained eerily quiet, her brows furrowed, her face forlorn.

After the run-in with the bikers, Mama feared for our safety. With no father to protect us, and Armando no longer living with us either, she decided it was time to get a guard dog. One day she returned from the library with a massive book entitled *The Encyclopedia of Dogs*. We flipped through every colorful page to see what kind of dog we should get. I wanted an Old English sheepdog, like rich people had. But Ricardo suggested a German shepherd since they were known for their protective instincts. And they were cheaper.

Mama agreed. "We need a dog that will bark at intruders," she insisted, "especially at night."

After walking out of Byrd's supermarket one late summer day, we came upon some kids with a cardboard sign: *Free German Shepherd Puppies*. Squirming around in a tall box were some of the cutest puppies you ever saw. We couldn't believe our luck!

Mama, however, had her suspicions. "Are you sure these puppies are free?"

"Yes, ma'am. One hundred percent free."

"Okay," she said to us warily. "Go ahead and choose one."

We took our time and picked out the prettiest one in the litter. She had distinct markings and a noble face. On our way home, I asked if we could stop by the pet store. With the little money I had saved, I bought a thin black book: *How to Raise and Train a German Shepherd*.

I made believe our puppy was of pure and noble blood, like the regal-looking dogs in the book, so she deserved a royal name. We settled on Duchess. Maybe it was the way she wagged her tan and black tail. Or the way she gazed at me with those longing eyes and rolled back her ears when I said her name. From the moment we brought her home, she became a member of our family. We loved Duchess dearly. And she loved us.

Not everyone loved her, though, especially our neighbors.

Hidden away in the dark woods behind us lived the Huxleys, a group of roughnecks who liked guns, liquor, and not much else, as far as I could tell. Bobby and I were afraid to go near their place because of the violent screams we often heard coming through the trees. They had made it clear they despised us from the moment we arrived. Every time they drove past us, they would rev the engine, yell some racial slurs, and throw something into our yard—usually a beer can or an empty bottle of Jack Daniels.

One day I asked Armando why they kept calling Mama a "taco bender." He explained they were saying "taco vendor," a derogatory label that insinuated she had no education or desire to improve, which of course was an outright lie. I wanted to sock them in the face for making fun of my sweet mother. Grants Pass was the first place I witnessed hatred toward my mother simply because she was Mexican. I couldn't understand how people could hate someone who had never done anything to them. She just wanted to make a better life for us. Was that so wrong?

I complained to Mama, asking her why they were so mean to us. "We never gave them a reason to hate us," I argued.

"You're right, Danny. We've done nothing wrong. But some people hate for no good reason, and it seems the Huxleys are those kinds of people."

Boone Huxley was a lanky, pimply-faced high school delinquent. But that's just what he looked like outwardly. Inside, he was a degenerate, mean and cruel. The only thing that seemed to bring him gratification was inflicting pain on others—especially us.

Whenever he walked past me with his snarled lip and beady eyes, shivers ran down my spine. It was terrifying to know someone that sinister lived so close to us. Little did I know, it would only be a matter of time before his evil manifested itself.

CHAPTER 13

Kung Fu Fighting

Our summer vacation was fast coming to an end, and I would be entering fifth grade at yet another new school—Jerome Prairie Elementary. I had changed schools so many times I'd lost count. A couple of days before classes started, Bobby and I decided to scrounge through one of the dumpsters downtown to see what interesting things we might find.

If you were willing to get past the smell, the fear of getting caught, and the shame of being seen, you might get lucky and stumble upon something worthwhile. The key was to have a childlike faith that while sifting through other people's trash, you might find buried treasure. It was just before sunset when I spotted something at the bottom of that dumpster that gave rise to a flurry of excitement—an instructional book titled *Boys' Judo*.

From experience, I had learned that how you carried yourself as a new student determined how you would be treated for the rest of the year. Going from one school to the next, I was always "the new kid," always the one who got shoved in the halls or bullied on the playground. This time around I wanted to be feared and revered. To do that, I knew I would have to set a precedent, so I decided I would be—wait for it—a black-belt kung fu master! *Ta da!*

The only problem was I knew nothing about martial arts. That is, until this large paperback book fortuitously fell into my hands. On the first day of school, I told everyone I was a kung fu champion from LA. "I've studied with the masters," I announced on the playground. "If you mess with me, I'll take you down."

The kids *oohed* and *aahed* as I punctuated that claim with a high kick, ending in a kung fu pose. Then with an Asian accent, I shouted the word *kiai*, like they did in the movies. I mesmerized my audience with tales of bigger boys I had taken down and tournaments I had won. They bought it. All except the biggest kid, a bruiser named Willoughby. "Okay, tough guy, prove it," he said.

With Zen-like composure I responded, "My *sensei*, Harold E. Sharp, taught me never to use judo to show off, but only in true self-defense." Willoughby couldn't possibly know Harold E. Sharp was one of the authors of my dumpster-dive book, *Boys' Judo*.

"All right then," Willoughby countered, glaring at me. "How's about you just break this pole-vault stick in half? That way, you're not hurting nobody."

"That's school property. My masters taught me to respect the property of others," I said, bowing in respect. To the gaping admiration of everyone, the flummoxed Willoughby stood down. I had established myself as a force to be reckoned with. *Victory!*

At home that night, I perused the book, noting its clearly sketched illustrations and simple-to-follow instructions. While trying out the moves on Bobby, I got the idea that I could teach this stuff. And charge for it!

The following day I announced my offer. "If anyone wants to learn the ancient art of judo, I will share the secrets of my masters . . . for twenty-five cents a day." I convinced the spellbound crowd I was giving them a really good deal for the wealth of knowledge I possessed. Based on the number of eager takers, they agreed.

With dollar signs in his eyes, Bobby later counted the chapters, multiplied them by the number of students, then by twenty-five cents per student. Our con was simple. He'd manage the money. I'd handle the instruction. Soon, we'd be rich!

On day one, I enlisted the help of my pupils in taking down the gray tumbling mats in the gym to get set up for the lunchtime lessons. I taught them the key judo stretches first. This took the entire lesson. *Cha-ching!*

That night, I studied the book intensely, carefully going over each step with Bobby in preparation for the following day's lesson. I didn't know the first thing about judo, but as long as I could just stay one step ahead of the class, I was golden. And that's all that mattered to me. By the middle of the week, I had kids sparring with each other while I oversaw their progress and helped them perfect their technique. Soon, everybody was kung fu fighting. Bobby collected quarters daily from each pupil and put them in our pencil box. Barely a week into it, and we were making money hand over fist.

Until Friday.

On Friday, the principal, Mr. Belt, was walking past the gymnasium when the noise inside suddenly caught his attention. He pressed his face to the window of the double doors and peered in. Then he pushed his way through, hastening to the middle of the gymnasium. "What in the world is going on in here?"

The room fell silent.

Cracking under the pressure, a dingbat named Freddy Farnsworth pointed to me. "He's giving us judo lessons, and it's only costing us each a quarter."

Mr. Belt walked toward me, jaws clenched, eyes blazing. "What kind of racket are you running here, buster?"

"N-nothing," I stammered.

He leaned down to glower at me. "It looks like a lot more than nothing to me."

"Everyone wanted to learn judo, and I thought twenty-five cents was fair. Don't you think?" I squeezed out my best smile.

An austere man, Mr. Belt was not amused. "Well, that's the end of your hustle here, pal." He dismissed everyone except Bobby and me. "Follow me, boys!"

We slogged behind him in a walk of shame, our shoes squeaking over the linoleum tiles all the way down the long corridor, all the way to the next building, all the way to his office, where he commanded, "Sit."

We sat.

"Wait here."

We waited.

The delay was excruciating, made even more so by the wooden paddles hanging on the wall behind his desk. My body twitched as I looked at Bobby. He was panting so rapidly I feared he was on the verge of hyperventilating.

When Mr. Belt returned, he reached for the paddle. "Get up."

We got up.

"Bend over and grab your ankles."

We bent over and grabbed our ankles.

Bobby's face was flushed red with anger. "I knew that book would get us into trouble," he fumed.

Then, in an unexpected moment of mercy, Bobby reached for one of my hands to stop it from trembling. Just when Mr. Belt was about to take his first whack, his secretary interrupted with something that required his immediate attention.

More waiting. More trembling. When he finally returned, the look on his face had changed. Instead of whacking us, he lectured us on the virtues of honest, hard work. He agreed not to notify Mama in exchange for us cleaning the cafeteria for a week. We sealed the deal with a handshake, nodding our compliance and thanking him profusely for his leniency.

But then he asked for the day's profit. Confiscating our hard-earned cash was a far worse fate than a spanking or being assigned to the janitorial crew. Reluctantly, and somewhat resentfully, I handed him the pencil box.

Bobby and I left disappointed at being out a day's pay, but we had still pocketed the profits from the previous four. By the time Mr. Belt shut down our clandestine operation, we had already earned sixteen dollars.

At home that evening, Mama sat bundled in frayed towels, the smell of Vicks VapoRub steaming from the humidifier. With the weather turning colder, her lifelong bout with arthritis was causing her pain. She had told us several times that we didn't have enough insulation for the coming winter, but now it seemed she really was worried we might freeze. I glanced over at Bobby, then took him aside. "I know we wanted to spend that money on something for us, but how happy would Mama be if she could buy the insulation instead? We could all be warm in the addition we're going to build onto the trailer."

It was never hard talking Bobby into doing something sacrificial. He could easily part with anything if he felt someone else needed it more. When the two of us presented Mama with our cash, her eyes narrowed in suspicion. "Where did all that money come from?"

"We've been doing some odd jobs and wanted to surprise you with it. We want you to use it to buy the insulation."

She pulled us both into one big family hug. "One day the Lord is going to really bless you, my sweet boys. You have such good hearts."

After purchasing the insulation, Mama handed us back the leftover change. It was just enough for us to buy a few packs of Topps football cards at the store across the street from school.

Speaking of school, I loved the admiration I had received during the week I was a kung fu master. When it ended, though, I was back to being a nobody. Filling that void were musings of what I might do that would give me the same feeling of distinction, something that was legitimate, an identity that was not built on deception but on a truth that I could claim as mine.

One day after school, Ricardo drove Bobby and me to Ashland. We cruised down Siskiyou Boulevard, the main drag in town, where many professors from Southern Oregon College resided. Both sides of the street were lined with tall pine trees and lovely Victorian homes decorated with bird baths and flower gardens. The high-end neighborhood might not have held the matchless opulence of Beverly Hills, but compared to the arid landscape of Sleepy Hollow Loop, this university district seemed to me a suburban Shangri-la.

We were going to a thrift store to purchase some cheap items. But Ricardo came up with a better idea after he spotted a lady in a nice car unloading bags at a Salvation Army drop box next to Safeway. He pulled into the parking lot, and we waited for her to leave.

When no one was looking, Ricardo and Bobby clasped their hands together and hefted me up through the chute. I dug through the heap, trying to get to the bottom. When I was about to hand things up to my brothers, Ricardo whispered, "Hide! Someone's coming!" As they drove off, I pulled a blanket over me, lying still, holding my breath.

There was the sound of footsteps approaching.

Then the sounds of someone breathing and metal creaking as the chute was pushed open.

A wedge of light revealed my exposed feet.

A hand pulled back the blanket. Above me, the scruffy face of a cadaverous hippie looked down at me, his long hair falling over his eyes.

I trembled.

"Whoa, little man. What are youuuuu doing down there?"

"I, eh, I . . . I'm looking for my marbles. My dad accidentally dropped them off here earlier this afternoon. They're my favorites."

He leaned in closer, so close I could smell a wretched stench on him. "How would you like to go on the road with me, kid?"

I gulped. I wanted to climb out and run off, but he was blocking my way.

"We could have a lot of fun traveling together," he said.

Now fully terrified, I feigned an excuse. "I can't because I, um . . . my dad, he's coming to get me any minute. He's in there," I said, pointing toward the Safeway. "He's picking up something for my mom."

An awkward pause loitered between us.

"Whatever, my man. If you say so." Then, after a pause, he shifted gears. "Hey, while you're down there, can you see if there's a pair of size-ten sandals?"

My heart raced as I rummaged through the pile of junk, hoping to find what he wanted so he would leave. I handed him a pair of tennis shoes, and wished I could have found a bar of soap for him as well.

After a quick examination, he said, "Far out. Right size too. Thanks, little man. Hope you find your marbles." Then he tramped off.

You too, I thought.

When the drifter was gone, Ricardo pulled the car in front of the drop box. I tossed him and Bobby everything I could grab without even slowing down to see what I was grabbing. And they didn't look either. They just crammed it all into the trunk. Then we tumbled back into the car and sped off.

Once we got home, we unloaded the trunk and sifted through the thrown-away parts of other people's lives.

An electric blanket—perfect to ease the pain of Mama's arthritis, which seemed to be worsening by the day.

Some dishes—to fill in some of the missing ones in our small mix-and-match collection.

Assorted clothing—what didn't fit could be used for cleaning rags or to stuff into drafty spaces to keep out the cold.

A bowling ball in its bag—we'd think of something.

A few albums—who doesn't need a little more music in their life? And one of those albums, Sandy Nelson's "Let There Be Drums," would become a breadcrumb along the path to my destiny.

It was a good day.

CHAPTER 14

Rock 'n' Roll Fantasy

One afternoon I heard our school was hosting its annual talent show. My teacher, Mrs. Middleton, posted the sign-up sheet in the hallway. I was tempted to write my name on it, but I had no idea what to put down as my talent. Each day I grew more anxious. A few of my class-mates pestered me to karate chop a brick in half since, after all, I *was* a kung fu master.

Well, I knew *that* was never going to happen. Still, I wanted to do something spectacular. So I asked around to see if anyone was putting a band together that needed a drummer. A friend told me about Doyle Foster, a freckle-faced boy with wispy red hair who played the guitar and sang. After class, I approached him in the hallway.

"Hey, Doyle, I hear you're a really good musician." He grinned at me through hair that swooped past his eyes. "You should put a band together and enter the talent show."

He liked the idea, saying he had a couple of musician friends who might be interested. "One plays bass, and the other keyboards."

"And *I* could be your drummer."

"You play drums?"

"Yeah. I'm pretty good, actually."

"You got a drum set?"

"Of course," I lied. I didn't own one piece of drumming equipment, not even a pair of drumsticks. In fact, I had never touched a *real* set of drums in my life. But I was determined to make my debut at the talent show in spite of that minor limitation.

Turns out, Doyle and I were both big Elvis fans and thought it would be fun to play the King's version of "Never Been to Spain." We scheduled our first rehearsal after school in the gymnasium, the same place where Mr. Belt had shut down my judo operation.

The lively Ernie Adams was setting up his bass equipment when he asked, "Hey, where's your drum set?"

"At the shop getting fixed. But don't worry, they promised it would be ready for the show. For now, I'll just tap on the back of a chair with my hands to give you guys a steady beat."

"Okay," he said disappointingly.

At the start of our next rehearsal, Doyle saw me on stage pounding on the back of the chair again.

"Where are your drums?" he asked, now concerned.

"Sorry, Doyle. They had to order a special part."

"All right, man, but we really need those drums by showtime."

"Don't worry. They'll be fixed by then."

After school, I shared my predicament with Ricardo and explained how I had been playing on the back of chairs with my hands. He thought for a moment, then said, "Get in the car. We're going to look for something we can turn into a drum set."

During our hunt for anything percussive, we drove behind a variety of stores and through numerous alleyways, but no luck. While passing by the Music Shop on Sixth Street, I spotted a shimmering, blue-sparkle drum set in the front window. "I wish we had the money to get those," I said.

"Me too. But we don't, so we'll have to get more creative," Ricardo said. "Okay, you've been playing with your hands on the back of a chair, right?"

"Yep."

"I have an idea, but let's hope they have what we need." Ricardo pulled the car behind the General Electric appliance store by Byrd's Market. "There it is," he said. "That's *exactly* what we need."

"*What's* exactly what we need?" I asked, confused.

"That. You're staring at it."

"You mean that big, empty box?"

"Yeah, it's perfect."

"How is that a drum set?"

"With a little ingenuity we'll turn it into one. But first, we have to get it home."

We folded the cumbersome appliance box down flat and stuck it in the trunk as far as we could, but half of it was still hanging out over the road. Ricardo tied the trunk closed with twine, adding his red T-shirt as a flag so the cops wouldn't give us a ticket. Driving slowly, we soon arrived at home with the box fully intact.

"What now?" I asked.

"You still have that *Sears Wish Book*?"

"I'd never get rid of *that*. They have the drums I want in there."

"Great. Because when I get back, I'll need you to open it to those pages."

"Where are you headed now?"

"Just sit tight. I'm running to grab some supplies from the hobby store. Everything's gonna work out. You'll see. You just have to trust me on this."

Nearly an hour later he returned with a bag full of paints, brushes, glue, and glitter. "Now, let's take a good look at those drum sets."

I handed him the catalog with my dog-eared pages. He studied the images for a while, then began to draw freehand on the front of the box. Once he had his outline of the drum and cymbals to scale, he enlisted Patricia and Bobby to help. Lisa handed us the supplies as needed, making it a family affair. We followed his detailed instructions and painted carefully through the night until we were all exhausted.

Ricardo stayed up longer to put on the finishing touches. To give the cymbals some shimmer, he glued on gold glitter. Then he sketched our band name, the Rhinestones, on the bass drumhead before adding silver glitter to make it look like rhinestones. I couldn't believe I now had a dazzling drum set painted on the front of the box.

On the evening of the concert, while my bandmates were setting up, Ricardo, Patricia, and Bobby helped me haul my contraption up the back stairs of the gymnasium and onto the stage. While I waited for the other acts to finish, I confided in Mama about my apprehension. "I'm afraid everyone will make fun of me when they see my box."

She knelt down and looked me in the eyes. "Don't worry about what anybody else thinks or says. Just go up there and show them your stuff, *mijo*. God gave you the gift of rhythm, and nothing can stop it from shining." Then she pulled out some Dippity-Do from her purse, patted down my cowlick with hair gel, and adjusted my cape, which I wore in honor of Elvis. "You're going to be fantastic."

Moments later, when they caught sight of the box, my fellow band-mates voiced their frustration. After hustling through a few more excuses about the repair part not coming in and forgetting my drumsticks on the dresser, I finally said, "Look, guys, we can still make this work. Let's go out there and give it all we've got."

Doyle looked down disappointingly, and with zero enthusiasm in his voice, he said, "I guess so."

Seconds later, the announcer came on. "Ladies and gentlemen, please welcome . . . the Rhinestones!"

I jumped behind my box and counted off the song. In the midst of hammering out my best rhythms by hand, I noticed people pointing at me and whispering to one another. A few even chuckled, but I refused to let them bring me down.

I kept my eyes fixed on Mama's loving gaze and on a few of the pretty girls from my class. The small audience seemed to have a nega-tive effect on my bandmates' performance. I, on the other hand, was lost in the fantasy of a million screaming fans.

When our song ended, my family jumped to their feet as if we had given a command performance at Madison Square Garden. Sadly, no one else shared their enthusiasm. Deep down, though, I wanted my drummer father to see me play. I wanted him to surprise me with a real drum set so I wouldn't have to lie. *But how could he do either*, I thought, *when he wasn't even in my life?*

Doyle cut me some slack. "I can't believe a box could sound so good," he said to me after the show. "Can't wait to jam with you when you get your real drums back."

Later, I would break out in a cold sweat, trying to figure out how I would get those drums. But for now, I just savored the moment—my first live performance as the drummer of a real band, even if it was just with glitter, glue, and cardboard.

I would never be the same after feeling the sensation of those rhythms vibrating from that appliance box. That night a twinkle in my eye emerged—a twinkle that turned into a sparkle, which gave birth to a dream.

The next day, I was so eager to hit some real drums that I went to talk to the band director. "Mr. Loveless," I said with great conviction. "I'd like to play the snare drum."

"How long have you been playing?"

"Actually, sir, I haven't played yet, but I'd like to learn."

He rolled his eyes. "It's a little late for that now, son. Our drummers have been playing for a couple of years already, and you should have started at the top of the school year. If you joined us now, you'd be too far behind."

"What if I come back at the start of next year?"

"I just couldn't sanction that, because then you'd be in way over your head. Besides, we already have too many drummers as it is." He walked away, murmuring, "Everybody wants to be a drummer."

It felt as if the door to my future had been slammed shut, and my shoulders slumped in despair.

With no place for me in the band program, I had to consider a new pursuit. Camping was something I had wanted to do ever since we moved to Oregon, something most boys my age longed to do with their dads. I thought camping would be the perfect way for him to teach me the survival skills I was dying to learn, and for us to finally bond as father and son. The Rogue Valley held majestic mountains, raging waters, and all manner of wildlife hidden in the overgrown sprawl of the forest. It was only natural for an eleven-year-old boy to want to explore it. But since Mama couldn't afford to send me to camp, and my dad wasn't interested in my survival, I turned to books to learn the skills I'd need to stay alive in the wild.

I checked out every library book on the subject, leafing through the pages, jotting down notes. But it seemed each one I read lacked something—not enough pictures, not enough descriptions, not enough adventures. A light in my head turned on. I would compile the most exhaustive, definitive, authoritative book on the subject.

I never left home without my little red briefcase that Mama called a *mochila*. In it was my *magnum opus*, or at least the beginnings of it. When I wasn't banging out rhythms, I was writing. I scribbled in the back of the car, on the school bus, in the supermarket, in the barbershop, even in the waiting room of my doctor's office. Mama said to me, "Remember, your grandfather was a writer in Mexico. You can do it too, Danny."

Everywhere I went, I wrote. Mind you, I didn't know when I split an infinitive or dangled a participle. And I couldn't tell you the difference between a colon and a semicolon or when to use a comma and why. But my lack of grammar skills didn't bother me in the slightest. With the innocence of ignorance, I threw myself into every page, every sentence, every word.

Why?

Because Mama said I could.

CHAPTER 15

Get Up, Stand Up

Monday mornings were my least favorite. One, because the school week started again. Two, because I was usually sleep deprived from listening to the radio and writing into the wee hours of the morning. One such morning at the crack of dawn, Bobby and I waited alongside the road for our school bus while Duchess signaled it was time to play. A year had passed, and she was almost full grown now but still on the smaller side for a shepherd.

"Fetch, Duchess," I said, hurling her favorite bone as far as I could into the woods.

She barreled into the dark forest, crunching leaves and jumping over twigs before racing back to drop the bone at my feet. As she wagged her tail and begged for another round, I waved the bone in front of her nose, leading her in circles until she rolled on her back with her paws wrestling the air.

When she yelped with excitement and sprang to her feet, I gave in, stuffing the bone into her mouth. She clamped her teeth and gave Bobby a good round of tug of war. Playing with Duchess was always the best part of our morning.

"Good girl," I said, giving her a hug as the bus approached. She stared back at me with those gentle and loyal eyes, the ones that were there to greet me when I got home every day. "We'll be back soon, girl. Watch after Mama."

Sitting behind the steering wheel was Mrs. Trenton, a peculiar woman with crinkly skin the color of ash. As usual, Bobby and I jockeyed for position to board first. This time he elbowed me, plowing his way up the stairs. Unfortunately, Boone Huxley's stop was just before ours. This meant he could see where we sat, and we hated that, especially since he and his high school flunkies loved to taunt us. Among other things, one of the misfortunes about living in a rural area was having to ride the bus with kids of all ages—elementary schoolers, junior high kids, *and* high schoolers.

On this particular day we didn't see them. But they saw us.

"Ouch!" I yelled, reaching for the back of my head. "What the heck was that?" Then something hit me again, this time on the edge of my ear. "Stop it!" I demanded, looking back.

Suddenly, an onslaught of spit wads came flying at us full speed. It was a surprise attack from Boone and his blowhards, who'd clearly been waiting for just the right moment to declare war. Using his high-powered slingshot, Boone had excellent aim, no doubt something he had perfected by killing small animals in the woods.

"I love hunting me some daaawg," he threatened. "Next time one comes sniffing around our property, I'll make me a fur coat out of it. Watch me."

"You better not be talking about our German shepherd," Bobby said.

"You call that a German shepherd? That runt looks more like a Chihuahua." He turned to one of his cohorts. "Hey, aren't Chihuahuas from Mexico?"

His sidekick barked at us. "Yep. Just like those two little beaners."

Bobby clenched his hands into fists, and my cheeks flushed with rage.

Oblivious to the battle at hand, Mrs. Trenton pulled off Woodland Park Drive into the school parking lot. The elementary kids leaped out of their seats, sprinting to class because the bus had arrived late to campus. Boone and his thuggish posse kept pushing us as we worked our way to the front, flicking the back of our ears and jabbing us with their elbows.

When one of them grabbed a book and smacked me on the head with it, Bobby yelled for Mrs. Trenton to intervene. "She ain't gonna rescue you now," the big one with flaming orange hair said. "She already left for her bathroom break."

They pushed us off the bus onto the blacktop. We got up and tried to run, but they spilled out and circled around us.

Boone glared hard at me and said, "Get out of our country, you wetbacks."

I was skinny as a rail, and the only weapon I had were my words. I shot them with all the force I had. "Shut up, you ugly white honky!"

"Rednecks!" Bobby added.

One of them punched Bobby in the chest so hard I could hear the wind leave him. Calling us names was one thing. Hitting my brother was another. I took a swing but missed. The next thing I knew, Boone was squeezing the bejesus out of me while the others threw punches.

With blood gushing down our shirts, Bobby and I fought back with all we had. But our efforts proved futile as the crew of ruffians struck us repeatedly with fists and kicks. They bellowed with laughter over each and every blow, pounding us relentlessly until they stood with a gleam of satisfaction in their hardened eyes.

As Bobby and I staggered off the school grounds, Boone followed us. "You spics need to swim right back across the Rio Grande and stay in Mexico, where you came from!"

Ironically, neither Bobby nor I spoke Spanish. Nor had we ever been to Mexico. In fact, we both probably spoke better English than Boone's clan of illiterates. At that moment, I wanted to move back to California more than anything in the world.

"One last thing," Boone said brusquely. "Just in case you're thinkin' 'bout reportin' us to the po-leece, my uncle is one of the sheriff's deputies. So if you don't want no problem from the law, you'd best keep your traps shut!"

Bloodied and bruised, Bobby and I shuffled down the rural back roads, sulking in the shame of it all. We crossed a shallow gully and came to a nearby creek to wash off the blood. After splashing water on my face, I could see how badly my little brother had been beaten. The flesh around his eyes was swollen and already starting to darken. His eyes were reduced to slits. I was certain I looked the same, but I was too afraid to look at my reflection in the water. I put my arms around Bobby instead. "Sorry I couldn't protect you from those thugs," I said. "I'm your big brother, and I should have been able to stop them."

"I'm sorry I took so long to get off the bus," Bobby said. "Maybe if I'd moved faster, we wouldn't have gotten beat up."

"It's not your fault. They were out to get us one way or another. They've had it in for us ever since we moved here."

With several hours to kill before school let out, we were in desperate need of a hiding place. Bobby came up with a brilliant plan—the Jerome Prairie Bible Church. Careful to sneak in from the back, we found sanctuary within those walls. But the place felt different from St. Anne's. Less reverential. No stained-glass windows, no candles to light, no holy water. No crucifix of Jesus nailed to the cross behind the pulpit either. Walking through it felt more like we were at a recreational hall. We would hardly have known we were in a church if not for the blue and white banner that read, "He is love," plus the stash of hymnals in every pew.

We hid inside one of the classrooms until we were certain no one was there, then we stealthily made our way to the banquet hall to search the refrigerator. All we found in the fridge was a pale green Tupperware container. I opened the lid and was greeted by a smell so pungent I thought I would throw up.

Undeterred, Bobby popped open the freezer, hoping to find Popsicles or ice cream, but the only thing there was a metal ice tray. I popped out a few cubes and placed them on our faces, trying to reduce the swelling.

By midday our stomachs were growling. We snuck out and went blackberry picking on the backside of Redwood Highway. With swollen lips, we carefully ate just one berry at a time, slowly chewing through the pain.

As we ate, Bobby turned to me. "It feels like my jaw is broken."

"Mine too," I admitted. What neither of us said aloud was that our hearts were broken even more.

With the day nearing its end, we trudged homeward after the school buses had finished their routes. As we turned up our driveway, Duchess was wagging her tail, eager for her afternoon round of fetch. But we were in no mood to play. We felt bad about it and bent down to pet her. She sensed something was wrong and immediately began licking our wounds. We crept into the trailer, knowing it would break Mama's heart to see us like this. With her back facing us, I mumbled a greeting.

"Hi, Mama."

"Oh, hi, boys" she said, slowly turning around. "*¡Ay, Dios mío!*" she screamed. "*¡Ay, Dios mío!*" Utterly hysterical, she rattled off more in Spanish. We stood before her in silence, filled with so much disgrace we could barely look her in the eye. "Tell me right now. Who did this to you?"

"We didn't do anything wrong," Bobby said.

"Yeah. We were just walking off the school bus when these high school creeps ganged up on us for no reason," I explained. "They called us dirty Mexicans, wetbacks, beaners. Told us to go back to Mexico. Said we were illegal aliens."

Mama snapped. "I don't know who these people think they are or where they think *they* came from. The truth is we're all immigrants in this country. We just arrived at different times. Furthermore, I entered legally with my four children, and *you two* were born here. So was Lisa. Plus, your fathers are from this country. *You are* American citizens."

It didn't matter to our haters that we *were* citizens. Didn't matter that we all had jobs. Didn't matter how hard we worked or how resourceful we were. It didn't matter how good of a mother we had. Didn't matter how happy a family we were, how we all pitched in, helped each other, loved each other, looked out for each other. None of that mattered to people like Boone.

Beside herself with anger, Mama called Armando to tell him what had happened. He got off work from Rogue Community College and rushed right over. Never one to back down from a fight for justice, Armando was always there for us. Whether it was rescuing Lisa from the pedophile in Compton or the numerous times he had defended

Mama from lecherous landlords. Day after day, incident after incident, my oldest brother laid his life down for us. Without his protection we would have suffered even more than we did, and we all felt safer when Armando arrived.

"Where are those *pendejos*?" he asked as he knelt down, putting his arms around us. As we told him the story, he slammed his fist into his palm and went on a rampage, his sentences bristling with Spanish curse words. "If those *cabrones* think they can beat up my little brothers and not pay the consequences, they've got another thing coming. I'm gonna show 'em how it feels to be punched by someone bigger than them!"

After we told him how they verbally assaulted us, the proud Mexican in him became even more enraged. "Wait 'til I get my hands on those gringos! They're going to wish they'd never laid hands on you!" The atmosphere grew even tenser. He vented as he paced. "Tomorrow I'm going to ride the bus with you so you can point them out to me."

As much as we wanted him to pulverize our assailants, we didn't want Armando to get into trouble with the law. We told Mama what Boone said about his uncle being a sheriff's deputy, and she tried to calm Armando down. Bobby and I hugged him, pleading with him to let it go.

With Boone's connections to local law enforcement, we had no choice but to suck it up and deal with the shame. The only good thing was that no one had seen us getting the crud beaten out of us, since our peers were all in class when it happened. I would have never lived that down, especially after proclaiming myself a kung fu master.

The next morning, when I awoke, Bobby was still sound asleep, snoring away with his blanket pulled up to his neck. I leaned down and examined his fully swollen face, which was now almost unrecognizable. I felt so bad for him and so terrible for not being able to protect him. I had let him down and was torn up over it. After seeing his injuries, I was afraid of what mine looked like, especially given the amount of pain I was in.

Squinting through my swollen eyelids, I finally caught sight of myself in Mama's compact mirror. I was horrified. My face was bloated, purple as an eggplant. I felt like a total loser. Worthless. I didn't want anyone to see me like this.

Thankfully, Mama let us stay home from school so the kids couldn't mock us. I was hoping we'd never have to go back.

Later that evening, after she kissed us goodnight, I got up to get a drink of water. I could see Mama on her knees, weeping quietly into her pillow. I wanted to ask her what was wrong, but I figured it must be because of the way we looked. Even though my face hurt, I felt worse for Mama than for Bobby and me. Our faces would heal, but I wasn't sure she would ever be the same. How much more heartache could our mother endure?

Under my covers I prayed. I prayed God would punish those tyrants for hurting us. I prayed he would take us away from this place that was bringing us all so much pain. But in the morning, I could see that he hadn't answered my prayers.

We were still there. And nothing had changed.

I couldn't understand. Didn't he see? Didn't he care? If God was real, couldn't he have done something, *anything*?

CHAPTER 16

With a Little Help from My Friends

Mama's dream of having a house built on the property seemed an impossible one. But we made one step in the right direction, courtesy of Mr. Stars, Ricardo's junior high Spanish teacher. In exchange for our eleven-foot trailer and a few extra dollars, we upgraded to his twenty-foot trailer, which gave us nine additional feet.

Around this time, my mother developed chronic anemia. In addition to her lifelong struggles with arthritis, this disease had devastating effects on her health and resulted in oral surgery to remove all her teeth. Not only was the surgery painful, it proved a tough blow for an attractive woman in her early forties to have to wear dentures. This further diminished her pride, but it didn't sink her.

After her surgery, she went to recover at the home of Francis and Ferrell Buckley, a kind, elderly couple we had met at St. Anne's. With long, wavy hair and a soft smile, Francis was the sweet old lady you wished was your grandma. Ferrell was a bona fide ham radio operator who tuned in to the Mexican radio stations so Mama could listen to them while recovering.

At the time, Ricardo was fifteen, still too young to care for Bobby, Lisa, and me on his own, so Mama arranged for us to stay with the Stars up the road, while Patricia went to stay with Mary in Ashland, a choice she made every chance she got since she was having a particularly rough time with the local yokels.

Experts in living off the land, Mr. and Mrs. Stars embodied the words *earthy* and *resourceful*. The muscular Mr. Stars was not only a good Spanish teacher, he was a modern-day frontiersman who had built his modest log cabin and everything in it from the trees on his property. Mrs. Stars, a squatty Peruvian woman with long, thick hair, proudly served us her healthful concoctions in wooden bowls they had hand-carved themselves.

Too accustomed to free school lunches to appreciate Mrs. Stars's cooking, we sulked when we were served primordial stews made from foraged ingredients washed down with warm goat's milk—something I wouldn't have wished on my worst enemy. While Mrs. Stars had been generous and welcoming, we prayed extra hard for Mama's speedy recovery in hopes of getting back to eating Minute Rice with chicken-flavored bouillon cubes and Jell-O, staples I never thought I would miss so much.

Mr. Stars was a gracious man who let us cut trees from his property to build a fence around our trailer. With bare feet, Ricardo, Bobby, and I dragged one skinny log after another from the top of his steep incline, winding a mile back down the hot asphalt loop to our place.

Once in our yard, Ricardo asked Bobby and me to strip the bark from the trees while he did the backbreaking work of digging holes for the posts. We repeated this process all day, every day, until the Buckleys brought Mama home at the end of the week. Proud of our home improvement, we were eager to see her reaction. Her eyes brightened when she took notice of the fence. She did her best to smile, even though I could tell it hurt, and her appreciative expression made the effort worthwhile.

After Mama recovered and got used to wearing dentures, she bargained with a man who had broken down on the side of the highway while towing a twenty-four-foot silver trailer. Soon, we parked the aluminum heap of junk right next to Mr. Stars's twenty-footer.

We were always looking to upgrade our humble dwellings, so when we lucked upon some used sheets of corrugated tin at an abandoned construction site, Ricardo rigged up an awning between the two trailers. Once again, my brother's prodigious enterprise improved our living conditions, providing a bit of shade from the merciless sun.

Meanwhile, Mama also signed me, Bobby, and Lisa up with the Big Brothers Big Sisters of America program in order to bring more adult role models into our lives. Her hope was to find people who could take us on outings she couldn't afford and give herself a break from us kids, which she desperately needed from time to time. A caring couple named Beverly and Bill Large agreed to be our mentors and took us to our first football game, out for pizza and Chinese food, and even hosted overnight stays for us at their home in Colonial Valley, a choice community in Grants Pass.

On one such night—April 24, 1973, to be exact—they let us watch Elvis's concert "Aloha from Hawaii" on their big color TV console. It was the first satellite concert in world history, with an estimated 1.5 billion people watching from all around the globe. I was fortunate to be among them.

While the smell of Beverly's zucchini nut bread hung in the air, I sat transfixed by the King of Rock 'n' Roll in his bedazzled jumpsuit holding command over his audience. As the musical spectacle unfolded, I found myself drawn to the man directly behind Elvis, wailing away on a massive blue-sparkle drum set. It was Ronnie Tutt. With his long hair swaying, Ronnie seemed to be having more fun than anyone else on stage, heck, than anyone else in the world.

Beverly and Bill's son, Jeff, was a drummer in a rock band called Johnny Golden and the Family Jewels that toured around the state in a van with "America's No. 1 Rock & Roll Show Band!" painted on its side. Lucky for me, he too had a blue-sparkle set, which he let me bang on during one of the commercial breaks. And, boy, did I go to town, trying to do my best Ronnie Tutt impersonation. It was love at first sound hearing the *boom* of the bass drum, the *crash* of the cymbals, and the *crack* of the snare drum. It was the first time I had ever hit a *real* set of drums with *real* drumsticks. While my mother dreamed of homebuilding, I was contemplating how much fun it would be to travel from town to town like Ronnie Tutt and Jeff in a rock band.

With a spirit of resourcefulness, we continued making improvements as we could, even using leftover particleboard as skirting around the trailers. Then the Shilohs came to our aid once again. This time, the Jesus followers helped us dig a deep hole for a septic tank. It took us a couple of days to dig through the rocky ground, but they kept working until we were finally able to nix the outhouse for good. When they were done, they asked Mama if she needed help with anything else.

Mama shook her head humbly. "You've done so much for all of us. I don't know how to thank you."

"You just did," one of the hippies said. "You gave us a chance to love our neighbor, and that's what we're called to do."

Mama smiled and hugged the good Samaritans, thanking them again and again for their compassion. Then, the tallest of the trio said something we never expected to hear. "Every home needs a garden, don't you think?"

My ears perked up as I remembered the thriving plants growing at their place in town. Within minutes, they had unloaded a rototiller from the back of their truck and were hard at work tilling the land for our family.

As the Shilohs were leaving, they encouraged us to plant a fruit and vegetable garden as they had done on their property. We followed their advice and went to Albers Feed Supply to buy a variety of seed packets: radishes, corn, cucumbers, lettuce, carrots, pumpkins, strawberries, watermelon, potatoes, onions, and tomatoes.

Mama was all smiles as she put the seeds in the ground, while we came behind her and covered them with fertilizer and soil. Excited at the prospect of growing our own food, we watered the ground every night with a portable sprinkler attached to our well. To me, the sound of that water hitting the soil was the sound of empowerment. Water brought forth life, and I became absorbed by the daily progress of the plants.

Watching the early buds transform into something edible was really something. Thirty days later, we were pulling radishes out of the ground and dicing them into salads. Throughout that summer and fall, we harvested a bumper crop of fruits and vegetables. We now had a sustainable food source and were living off the land like we had wanted. Mama was happy she didn't have to go to the grocery store as often.

Always determined to make a safe and cheerful home for us, Mama splurged and ordered some rose bushes from the Jackson and Perkins Company in Medford. After receiving the shipment, she planted them with great expectation. When they finally blossomed, she beamed with excitement, taking in the fragrance of the petals as if they transported her to better days.

"Ah . . . this takes me right back by my mother's rose garden. How is it that a smell can be so deeply ingrained in your memory?" she asked us.

Bobby, Lisa, and I gathered around her, smelling the roses.

"Here, try this one," Mama said, pointing to a delicate pink bloom and encouraging us to lean closer. "This one reminds me of the day we all came back together in the United States. Do you remember that day, Danny?"

I shook my head.

"Of course you don't," Mama continued. "Your father, whom you were named after, was an Irish American, a charming and funny man I'd met while he was studying at the University of Mexico. I'd already had my heart broken two times, but he convinced me to try again. So, on December 27, 1960, we married. Just two days after Christmas."

She moved to another rose bush, and we followed.

"Even though Dan was an American citizen, the immigration process was lengthy and costly. We eventually moved to Long Beach, where I worked as a waitress, helping to make ends meet. That was a long way down from the plans my father had for me, but I did my best. I even took a second job in that factory in Huntington Park, and later in Torrance, where I welded parts for ships."

When she paused, I nudged her to continue, telling her how much I loved her stories.

With a smile, she complied. "Your father was an outgoing, big-boned man with the gift of gab. Six foot three with strawberry-blond hair. And he worked as a door-to-door Fuller Brush salesman. A 'Fuller Brush man,' that's what they called them back then. He sold personal care and household cleaning products. They were a popular outfit at the time, and he was very good at it."

I clung to every word she offered, always hungry for any connection I could find to my mysterious "Fuller Brush man" father.

"We were happy and working hard, but there was one big problem. I couldn't bring my four older children across the border from Mexico. The immigration office made me wait for approval. You can't imagine how hard that was for me . . . to be apart from Armando, Mary, Patricia, and Ricardo. I couldn't have managed if not for my mother."

"Conchita?" I asked.

"Yes, Conchita. She kept the kids in Tijuana. Every Friday after work, I'd travel from LA to spend the weekend with them, always bringing food and gifts from the States. Each Sunday night, I'd tuck my babies into bed in Mexico and make the long trek back to earn more money the following week. It took me a year to save enough for the immigration fees and to get all the paperwork approved for the legal entry of my family. But I was willing to make that sacrifice, knowing we were building a better life here in the United States."

I looked around at our two tumbledown trailers and wondered how this could be better than the fabled life she had left behind in Mexico. Lisa had lost interest by now and started drifting through the garden with Bobby close behind. But I stayed with Mama, asking her to tell me more.

"Not long after giving birth to you, your older siblings were granted legal entrance into this country. You were just an infant when we all celebrated by going to Disneyland as a family. We were so happy to finally be reunited here in the States. All those labor-intensive work hours, the grueling double shifts, the frustrating legalities, and the painful absences from my children had been worth it. I remember it just as if it had happened yesterday."

Her eyes grew distant as she carried me back in time with her, word by word. "We entered those gates, and the magic was all around us. At

one point, we stopped to smell the bountiful roses that decorated the
theme park. I looked up at my husband and my five children, and I
thought, *Now . . . our new life begins.*"

Then she plucked one of the rose blooms and held it under my nose.
"Doesn't that smell divine, *mijo*? Now you'll have memories to share
with your children someday too."

Good news came in spurts, so a year later, when Mama informed us
that we'd be graduating to a seventy-foot mobile home, one that was
fourteen feet wide, we felt like we had won the lottery.

"Walker the Weeper sells 'em cheaper." That was the jingle that came
over the radio as we headed there to choose our new abode. While Mama
was finalizing the trade, we ran around the lot of the largest mobile home
dealer in the area. It seemed to take hours for her to sign her life away.

It was hard for Mama to get us as far as she did without the financial support of a husband, and we never took for granted a single inch
of the extra space she had found for us. Despite our deep love and devotion to one another, such tight quarters had long been a recipe for
conflict. At the end of one day, I described one of these typical skir-
mishes in my diary:

> *Then when Ricardo got home us three boys got in a big fight.*
> *Ricardo hit me, I hit him, he hit Bobby, Bobby hit him, and*
> *then he stopped for a second. Then he punched me as hard as he*
> *could again and again, but I didn't back down and I smacked*
> *him in the nose and gut. He gave me a bump over my left eye*
> *and a few bumps on the head. Afterwards we made up and went*
> *to Riverside Park then we watched* The Wizard of Oz.

Though we fought frequently, as boys do, we couldn't afford to hold
grudges. How could we? We needed each other to survive.

Despite the extra space, we quickly outgrew our new trailer too. And so Ricardo, our resident mastermind, drafted plans to build an addition onto the mobile home. Relying on his shop teacher for guidance, his clever design would give us two more bedrooms and a foyer.

We all spent the summer of '74 working wherever we could to raise money for the renovations. Any extra time was devoted to the first phase of construction. Our faithful Nova facilitated endless trips to the building supply store, and we hauled everything in that jalopy, from four-by-eight sheets of chipboard and drywall to cinder blocks, roofing paper, shingles, and everything in between.

Once the foundation, framing, and flooring were in place, we three boys spread our sleeping bags across the floor of the unfinished building, where the cool night air caressed our faces. There, in the midst of the moonlight, we gazed at distant constellations while talking about the dreams we had for our lives. With the mind of an engineer, Ricardo wanted to create solutions and design new things. Bobby wanted to be a cop and lock up bad guys like Boone. And me? Well, I wanted to make people happy. The best way I could think of doing that was by banging the drums. "I wanna play in a band," I said, remembering how it felt when I noodled behind Jeff's drum set only a short time ago.

Ricardo conceived the next phase of our building project and etched out a plan. "If I had that book on architecture I saw at the bookstore, I could put the roof on correctly, and a few other things I'm not exactly sure of."

"How much is it?" I asked.

"Twenty-five dollars."

"Twenty-five! Are you kidding me?"

"My shop teacher told me it's the standard manual for the kind of work we're doing."

"Where in the world are we going to get an extra twenty-five dollars?" Bobby asked.

No one had an answer.

With our construction temporarily on hold, we rustled up more work, scouring the classified ads in the papers and the bulletin boards

in town for any kind of employment. I even went door to door, asking
if anyone needed help with anything.

My diary revealed one such effort involving a friend's father:

*Then David's dad said he'll hire us to move a tree. I thought
it was a joke. I couldn't move a tree with a tractor, but for the
$15.00 he offered, I could do it blindfolded.*

Another day's entry recorded our progress:

*David and I went selling raspberries and looking for work. We
sold $2.25 worth of berries and left our names at a few people's
houses.*

We divided our time between school, work, and making progress on
the addition when we could afford the materials. Everybody pitched in.
Patricia, who had just landed a job at the Arctic Circle, a fast-food joint
similar to Dairy Queen, always gave all she had to the family's needs
and then some. Every day she made the dangerous, seven-mile jaunt on
her ten-speed. After her shift ended, she strapped a paper cylinder of ice
cream to her bike and navigated the dark country roads with only one
goal: to get home before it melted. Every time we heard the sound of her
tires treading over gravel, we ran to greet her. Patricia had always been
insistent on bringing a little more sweetness into our lives in whatever
way she could. This was just another one of her ways.

Mama may not have had the aid of a husband, but along with the
Shilohs and kind men like Mr. Stars and Mr. Buckley, she did get a little
help from the unsung hero of the family: our 1962 Chevy Nova. That
car gallantly fought for our survival, not only serving as "the White
House" when we landed on this empty lot with no other shelter to call
our own, but by faithfully transporting us and our dreams at every hour
of the day and night, through all kinds of weather.

If the engine was her heartbeat, then surely those headlights were
her eyes. At times I felt compassion coming straight from those low

beams—as if she knew our afflictions and made it her sole purpose to help us get through them. Among the list of her notable accomplishments, the old "White House" could be trusted with many family secrets. And we relied on her to perform whatever miracles we needed at the time—like stretching a dollar.

One of her inspired performances went something like this: Ricardo would pull up to the entrance of the Redwood Drive-In movie theater and pay the admission. After he found the perfect parking spot, we younger siblings would push the back seat forward from inside the trunk where we'd been hiding, and *presto*—it was family night at the movies! All for the price of one.

For a bunch of prepubescent pipsqueaks with no spare change, this ruse provided hair-raising thrills. The toughest part of it was holding back our laughter after Ricardo said, "One ticket, please." That was the ultimate test of our self-control.

One night we caught a double feature that I'm sure Mama wouldn't have approved of. It started with *Five Fingers of Death*, a future kung fu cult classic, followed by *Superfly*, a Black exploitation film featuring the innovative music of Curtis Mayfield—music that would continue to fuel my desire to become a disciple of soul. The sounds of bongos, shakers, cowbells, plus some spinning roto toms came through the static window speaker, and Mayfield's funky rhythms resonated in a way I couldn't shake.

That night I wrote in my diary about the day's adventure. But the last entry was the most telling:

I love God, Jesus, and family.
I stole an architecture book.

CHAPTER 17

Another Brick
in the Wall

Monday. Didn't go to school today.

Friday. Didn't go to school today.

So began my diary entries, week after week, month after month. School had become the epicenter of my anguish, and I skipped as much of it as possible. Home was my sanctuary, and I wanted to spend as much time there as I could. Most weeks I would come down with a case of Monday- and Friday-itis. I had perfected my sick routine so I wouldn't have to face some smart aleck or turn in an unfinished homework assignment. If I exhibited the slightest cough, Mama would say, "You don't sound good, Danny. You better stay home today."

But by late morning I'd be miraculously healed, ready to go outside and play with Duchess. As a lighthearted warning, Mama would sing a line to me from "Swingin' on a Star" by Bing Crosby, gently teasing me that I might turn into a mule if I didn't go to school.

Better than anyone, she knew my struggle to fit in. I believe she let me stay home to protect me from the cruelty of the world. And on some days, I suspect, she let me stay home to keep her company. Her health was becoming as unpredictable as our life had been. Despite her debilitating arthritis and anemia, she still had some good days, but the bad days were becoming more numerous. After years of working long, hard hours, ironing or waitressing or cleaning through the pain, the toll had finally become too much. With winter proving particularly difficult, those long, cold months were keeping Mama at home nearly as much as me. On days when she felt strong enough, she would take me into town to run errands with her, to pick up a new batch of laundry to be ironed, or to clean someone's home. And during these times, she never missed an opportunity to share her knowledge about history, life, literature, music, and art. In this way, she was informally homeschooling me.

Boy, how I loved those days with just Mama and me. I followed close on her heels and soaked up every bit of her attention I could get.

One frosty morning while I was eating a bowl of Captain Crunch and Mama was munching on Frosted Flakes, the phone rang. It was my elementary principal, Mr. Belt.

"Let me speak to your mother," he said.

"Uh . . ." I stammered, "she's very sick. I think she's sleeping right now."

"Why aren't you in school today, Danny?"

"Our Shetland pony got loose and I had to chase him, so I missed the bus."

He didn't buy my story, even though we actually *did* have a pony and that's really what had happened that particular day. So I gave him the harder truth. "My mother's arthritis is really bad today, and there's no one who can drive me to school."

"Well then, I'll be right over to pick you up."

I pulled off my jammies and threw on my clothes. As it was still cold, I wiped the condensation from the windows to keep an eye out. Ten minutes later, his sedan pulled into the driveway as ominously as an unmarked police car. I caught a look of disdain on his face as I climbed into the back seat like a common criminal. Neither of us spoke, making for the longest ten-minute drive of my life. When we finally arrived at school, I slithered out of his car, my head hung in shame.

Soon it would not just be Mr. Belt coming to put an end to my recidivism. Truant officers began dropping by unexpectedly to haul me back to school while attempting to frighten me with cautionary tales of other deserters. It wasn't that I disliked learning. I just disliked school . . . and math . . . and a few of the teachers . . . and all of the nitwits . . . and of course, the ever-vigilant Mr. Belt.

At home, I often immersed myself in the subjects that most interested me, spending hours poring over library books or our gap-toothed row of encyclopedias, a salvaged set that was missing a third of its volumes. But mainly, I loved staying home to help Mama. In those cold months, I would prepare her meals, usually a TV dinner and sometimes a prepackaged pound cake for dessert. Then I would massage her hands with Ben-Gay cream, trying to offer her some relief. As time passed, her hands began to gnarl. It pained me to see this, and I came to despise the smell of menthol. It was the smell of immobility, as Mama was too often confined to the couch or her bed while her body curled in on itself. It was also the smell of isolation, with Mama held captive indoors while the wrath of winter settled over us all. But the worst thing about the smell was that it reminded me how much Mama was hurting. And how helpless I was to make it better.

One day I wrote about how I was feeling in my diary:

Mama is not feeling well, she is always sick but I wish I could take the sickness from her. She sacrifices for us to please us. I don't know what I'd do without her. I'd probably die. She's all I got. I don't know why God allows this, but someday she'll be better. I pray for her all the time. She's always in pain, I cry for her but no one ever sees me, I'm crying while I write this, I always feel sorry for her, she's never well and does all she can for us when we're sick and she's still sick with arthritis herself.

As if the arthritis and anemia weren't bad enough, Mama also suffered from horrible dizzy spells and the fluctuating pain of an early menopause. In California, she had held down many jobs and worked hard like her father had taught her to do. She was proud of her Mexican culture, one known for its strong work ethic, and she had never com-plained about the hard labor. But with her health taking a turn for the worse, she was struggling to manage the physical demands of her many jobs.

Some days she sat in hot laundromats, folding mountains of clothes for strangers while I read a book. On other days, with steam mist-ing through the room, she would stand in front of the ironing board, hunched over while beads of sweat dripped from her forehead, working her fingers to the bone. Fingers that ached from the pain of her arthri-tis. Fingers that were aging prematurely. Fingers that now had to fill out forms for government assistance.

Going on welfare shamed Mama greatly. She had fought long and hard to avoid taking handouts, and the government support added one more layer of disgrace on the rest of us. I was painfully aware that we weren't like most people. I could tell by their condescending stares when Mama paid for our groceries with what I initially thought was "colored money" but eventually found out were food stamps. My face flushed when the cashier raised her eyebrows at some of the purchases, tacitly expressing her disapproval. Every time she cleared her throat when punching the keys of her cash register, I could feel her contempt.

My mother's declining health worried me, and I tried to make her happy in every way I could, hoping to lift her spirits somehow. Some-times it was watching the old black-and-white movies she loved, films like *Wuthering Heights*, *Laura*, *Rebecca*, *Great Expectations*, or *The Grapes of Wrath*. Other times it was listening to her favorite music or reading aloud to her. One day at Byrd's Market, she was flipping through the latest issue of *Sunset* magazine while waiting in the checkout line. She leaned over to show me the two-page spread of an A-frame home in New England. "Oh, my goodness, look at this house, Danny. Isn't it in-teresting? Look at the colors of those leaves." She always said she would like to live where the foliage changed with the seasons.

Mama handed me the magazine to put back on the rack. But I had a better idea. While the bagger was loading our groceries in the cart, I slipped the magazine into the sack when no one was looking.

Mama pulled it from the stash at home and said, "Danny, how did this get in the bag?"

I shrugged.

"Well, I know the magazine didn't just walk off the shelf and jump in the bag."

"I took it," I admitted shamefully.

"'Thou shalt not steal.' Wasn't that one of the commandments you just learned in catechism?"

Mama had no idea how much I struggled with that one because I had managed to keep my kleptomania from her until now. "Yes," I replied.

"Remember," she continued, "your grandfather was a supreme court justice and an upstanding man of the law. He would never tolerate dishonesty. I remember when a man came to our house and tried to bribe your grandfather to vote in an unethical way. Your grandfather got so mad that he dragged the man out of the house by his ears and told him never to return. This is who we are, and I don't want anything to taint your pure heart."

"I'm sorry, Mama," I said sheepishly. "I wanted you to have the magazine because I know how happy it makes you to look at all the pictures. I like looking at them with you too. It's not fair you couldn't afford it." I didn't have the heart to tell her that I wasn't as pure as she thought. There were things I desperately wanted, but without much money, I couldn't think of any other way to get them.

"Well, life's not always fair, but that's no excuse not to make good choices. But I forgive you, *mijo*. Now you have to ask God to forgive you. Even though what you did was wrong," she said, kissing me on my forehead, "I love how much you love me. I'm the luckiest mother in the world to have you as my son. One day you'll make lots of money to buy whatever you want. And the next time we return to the market, we will give them the fifty cents for the magazine."

Cozy under the electric blanket together, we flipped through the pages, imagining what it would be like to own our home rather than a mash-up of trailers and mobile homes. Thoughts of a gazebo, a trellis, a deck, flower gardens, and a swimming pool kept us talking excitedly. I told Mama I wanted to build a tree house and dig a moat around it. She thought that was a great idea. But our daydreams didn't end there. We fantasized about flying on an airplane to a tropical island or to Europe to visit all the places in the books she had read to me. We imagined ourselves having savory meals at chichi restaurants and hobnobbing with our favorite movie stars in Beverly Hills.

We flew to the future, making believe I had won an award—maybe an Oscar, a Grammy, a Pulitzer, or a gold medal at the Olympics—for doing something extraordinary. "Now let me hear your acceptance speech," she said. I went on and on while she smiled at me with eyes of love, finally concluding with, "And mostly, I would like to thank my mother, who believed in me and taught me everything I know."

She wrapped me in her arms and covered me in kisses.

"Have you ever given an acceptance speech, Mama?"

"No," she said with a smile. "I'm saving that experience for you, *mijo*."

"You know what I still don't understand?" I said. "If you were an actress and your family was so rich and famous in Mexico, why don't we have any money now?"

"Ahhh . . . I've never really explained that, have I?"

I shook my head and curled closer.

"Well, you should first know that my parents loved us all very much, and they took good care of me and my siblings. When I was young, just seven years old, I became very ill with rheumatoid arthritis. Just like today, I had good days and bad, but when I'd have trouble moving my arms, hands, and legs, your grandfather would send my mother and me to live in the warmer climates of Acapulco for the winter months. It helped to alleviate my pain."

"Let's move there," I said, "if it helps you feel better."

"Oh, my sweet son," she said, kissing me on the top of my head, and then continued, "the good thing about my parents is that they valued education. Even when I was out of school for my illness, my father would hire private tutors. Kind of like I tutor you today."

I smiled.

"As you know, your grandfather was a successful man. A respected man. A wealthy man. But when he died, the corrupt faction of the Mexican government, whom he had fought long and hard against while advocating for the rights of the people, came and seized our family's house, took all our assets, even emptied our bank accounts. My father didn't have a will, and so we went from riches to rags in one dreadful day."

"They stole all your money?" I sat up, incredulous.

"Something like that, yes," Mama said. "Of course, I'd just married my first husband, and his true colors started to show. He was thirteen years older than I was, and he'd had his eyes set on being a movie producer. Once he realized he'd no longer have access to my family's wealth or connections in the worlds of film and finance, he changed completely. Just like my father had predicted, he wasn't all he'd pretended to be. I went from being the darling princess at the ball to the despised house-keeper at his beck and call."

"Like Cinderella?"

"Yes, Danny. Like Cinderella. And just like the cruel stepmother in the fairy tale, he did terribly cruel things to me, locking me in my room for days at a time, yelling at me, cheating on me, humiliating me. I'd never been treated that way in all my life, and I was so young I didn't know how to handle it. Of course, I tried to save the marriage at first, trying hard to make him happy and keep him calm. But in time, I had no choice but to divorce him, another shame for my Catholic family."

"He was the one being mean. That's not your fault," I said.

"Thankfully, my mother didn't blame me either, and there were two incredible blessings that came from it all: Armando and Mary. No matter how painful the marriage may have been, I'll always be grateful for my children."

"What happened then?" I asked, hungry for more of her stories.

"After that, I was feeling scared. I was a young mother with two little kids, and without our family's wealth to help us financially, we had few options. As the oldest daughter, I felt responsible for helping my mother and my sisters too. We were all struggling to make ends meet when another man came along, offering rescue. I clung to him like a life buoy. Once again, the only good things that came out of that second relationship were Ricardo and Patricia."

"And then came me?"

Mama pulled me to her and smiled. "That's right, *mijo*. Then came you."

"Tell me again about my dad. Tell me everything you know."

"Oh, he was a nice man, Danny. Like you. He just wasn't as strong as you, that's all." With that, Mama drifted away again before returning with a smile to say, "Now, what shall we study today?"

I gave her a big hug, happy that she had considered me stronger than my father. Happy to know he had been a kind man, even if he hadn't been kind enough to stay.

Despite my antipathy for school, my education was in good hands with Mama. She was a natural-born teacher, a veritable repository of knowledge with an enthusiasm that was infectious. Unlike any other teacher I'd known, she made learning fun. Though her methods were unorthodox, I was given a first-rate education—one that would foster in me the heart of a lifelong learner.

She made good use of our public library and schooled me on everything from the French Revolution to the great operas, from Renaissance art to renowned scientists like Madame Curie. She borrowed volumes of classic literature by authors such as Mark Twain, Jules Verne, Jane Austen, Charles Dickens, Alexandre Dumas, Victor Hugo, Robert Louis Stevenson, and a host of others. We also studied the Bible, my two favorite stories being Daniel in the Lions' Den and David and Goliath.

Of course, Mama also loved the movies, so we devoured every volume of *The Illustrated History of the Movies*. It was a series featuring biographies of Hollywood luminaries such as Charlton Heston, Jack Lemmon, Henry Fonda, Cary Grant, Marilyn Monroe, and Rita Hayworth, along with a host of other stars.

Of all the books she read to me, though, one would stand out as my favorite: *Beautiful Joe: An Autobiography of a Dog* by Marshall Saunders.

We owned a tattered first edition from 1893 that we had found at a flea market for a quarter. That was Mama, always on the lookout for not simply a bargain but a steal. With great anticipation we turned the brittle pages ever so gently. Being a dog lover, I was engrossed in this heartfelt treasure, mainly because it was the only book I had known that was written from a dog's perspective.

My mother had a deep love for reading and made sure I read plenty of books. Each week in school, students received a copy of *My Weekly Reader: The Children's Newspaper*. On the back was *the Weekly Reader Book Club* order form, where kids could order the latest paperbacks from Scholastic. When the shipment arrived, the teacher would call out the names of students who had ordered books. Despite our financial constraints, I always walked away with the biggest stack, which I paid for from various odd jobs, and it was probably the *only* reason I bothered going to school at all.

I loved the smell of fresh books, and I knew those stories would transport me to places where dreams really did come true. I read about sports greats like Hank Aaron, Wilt Chamberlain, "Broadway" Joe Namath, and Muhammad Ali. Each story stimulated my own yearning to do something worthy of being highlighted in one of those paperbacks. Those days at school were the best of times.

They were also the worst of times.

One day I came home and told Mama about a nasty remark some twit had made about my lack of attendance and how stupid I was. Her response was, "He's just jealous because he knows you're smarter than he is." On another day, not long after that, Mr. Smith, my social studies teacher, called me up to the front of the class to answer a few of the test questions. Because of my frequent absences, the students burst into laughter as I walked to the front of the class.

"What is the capital of Switzerland?" he asked.

"Bern," I answered.

"Correct."

"Which mountain range contains the highest peak?"

"The Himalayan Mountains."

"Right again. Now, tell the class what continents surround the Mediterranean Sea?"

"I believe they are Africa, Asia, and Europe."

"Yes, that's right. Well done, Danny! Well done!"

The class looked stunned, but what they didn't know was that Mama's passion for international culture had rubbed off on me. At home we would go over the capitals of each state and review the various countries around the world. She had filled my head with the idea that I would one day travel the globe. In light of her affirming forecast, I wanted to know everything about this world that I would one day be exploring. I would memorize every detail in preparation for my future adventures.

After I sat down, Mr. Smith said to the class, "Don't be so quick to judge. Everything is not as it appears."

Maybe Grant Allen summed up my educational experience best when he said, "I have never let my schooling interfere with my education." I loved the quote so much that I pinned it on my bedroom wall, right next to the photos of legendary football stars from the NFL. Despite my horrible attendance and often poor grades, what could not be graded was my sense of wonder. Basking in the glow of Mama's presence, I was inspired to learn, to dream big, and to believe in myself. She convinced me that I could be anything I wanted to be while also assuring me that one day I would be a great husband and father because of my tender heart.

Though I had attended a countless number of schools along the way, Mama was my most influential teacher. I never became a Rhodes scholar, but because of her, I always felt like one.

CHAPTER 18

The Hustle

One afternoon in the fall of 1974, I was thumbing through a copy of *Boy's Life* magazine in the foyer of my dentist's office when I found an advertisement to sell greeting cards in exchange for prizes. A quick glance at the prize list, and I was hooked: a telescope, an archery set, a Kodak Instamatic camera, a microscope, a Daisy air rifle, walkie-talkies, and—drum roll, please—a sports bike.

In bold capital letters, the tagline read, SEND AWAY FOR XMAS PACKS AND PRIZE BOOK TODAY. Within a few weeks of mailing the postcard, I received my first shipment. The accompanying letter instructed me to sell each box of Christmas cards for $1.50, then send the full $21.00 in earnings back to the company. In turn, they would put points toward a prize of my choosing.

After doing the math, I realized I would have to sell a gazillion boxes to win the bicycle I had my heart set on. Even though I had never met him, I was hoping I had inherited my father's powers of persuasion as a "Fuller Brush man."

With sheer determination and salesmanship in my bloodline, I sold all fourteen boxes in no time. Now I had the $21.00 to send back to the company. However, being entrusted with that much cash was a test of my character, and every time I counted the dollar bills, I felt less sure I would pass that test.

Why should I send back all that money when I'm *the one doing all the work?* I asked myself. I got to thinking how I might con the corporate gangsters who were exploiting gullible kids like me, kids full of hopes and dreams, kids who would have to work until they were senior citizens to get the prizes they wanted. I figured the best way to get even was for one of those kids to seek revenge.

I nominated myself.

And so, with the same Robin Hood mindset that had inspired my early capers in LA, I decided to keep the $21.00 and buy my own bike. One Saturday afternoon I headed down to the local bicycle shop to scope out my options. After examining the merchandise, I handed the clerk all my cash and rode away with a used Schwinn. A steal of a deal for sure. I felt a sense of pride, riding tall on that metallic-blue banana seat, knowing I had pulled one over on "the Man."

But how could one bike make up for such a multitude of injustices against children across the land? It couldn't. There would have to be more recompense to make things right. And so I sent away for more greeting cards and then for seed packets from another company. I sold all of their merchandise too. I did the same thing with another company. And another. And another.

Things were going so well that anything seemed possible, including my dream of living next door to my favorite group, the Jackson 5. I even joined their fan club and ordered *The Soul of the Jackson 5* from *My Weekly Reader* for fifty cents. Inside were black-and-white pictures of their mansion in Encino, California.

As the twelve-year-old kingpin of my own greeting card and seed packet cartel, I felt this lofty goal was now within reach. I was building up a nice little nest egg at US Bank, and each deposit was recorded in my gold passbook.

Life was good—and full of hope and promise for a bright future. Until . . .

I began to receive a steady stream of letters from various law firms, asking for the return of their merchandise or their money. I didn't want Mama to know, so I hid them under my mattress.

The first letters kindly requested that I comply with their request, which I had no intention of doing. The tone of the next wave of letters was more hostile, which interrupted my otherwise childlike slumber. I grew anxious and my sleep became restless. I became so concerned that I scheduled an appointment to see an attorney downtown.

Mr. Salisbury's office was located in an ominous structure beside the train tracks. After climbing the stairs to the second floor of the crumbling redbrick building, I opened the door to his office. "Hello," I said to a beady-eyed woman with a face white as frost and just as cold. "I'm here to see Mr. Salisbury."

"Well, you need to make an appointment for that," she said sternly. "You can't just walk in . . ."

"I did, ma'am. This is the time of my appointment. I'm Danny Donnelly."

After a pause, she checked her calendar and said, "Oh, my. I had no idea you were a child."

"I like to think of myself as a young businessman," I said, straightening my back so she would take me seriously.

She chuckled. After shaking her head in disbelief, she buzzed the lawyer on her intercom. "Sir, your . . . um . . . your four thirty is here." She looked back at me. "A young businessman named Danny Donnelly."

I nodded in agreement and tightened my grip on my red briefcase.

Moments later, a plump, ruddy man waved me into his office. Stretching across his floor-to-ceiling bookshelves stood rows of law books. *Impressive*, I thought. *I obviously picked the right man for the job. I guess I really do have good business sense.*

"How can I help you, young man?" Mr. Salisbury scanned my face with intense curiosity. After I told him about my plight, I opened my satchel and handed him a sheaf of letters. He perused the corporate threats levied against me. "How old are you?"

"Twelve, sir."

"Do you know what a minor is?"

"Someone who digs for treasure?"

"No, not that kind. In the legal world, a minor is someone under eighteen years of age. *You* are a minor. This means those companies cannot prosecute you. But if I were you, I'd stop doing whatever generated these letters in the first place."

"Yes, sir. I certainly will—I mean, no sir, I won't do that anymore. Thanks so much for your help. How much do I owe you?"

"You don't owe me anything, son. Just try and stay out of trouble so I won't have to see you in the future for something more serious." He picked up a Bible, pointed at it, and said, "Go and sin no more."

I had heard those same words in catechism at St. Anne's, and though I wasn't sure where in the Bible they came from, I *was* sure what they meant. I slunk out the door and hurried down the stairs.

To celebrate this rare victory against the establishment, I walked to Blind George's newsstand on G Street and treated myself to some of their famous popcorn. Then I walked down the train tracks that ran through the middle of town before collecting my bike and racing home. When Mama asked me about the bike, I told her it belonged to a friend. "He's got two," I explained. "He said I could use this one as long as I want."

A lie to my mother. Another sin. I had one more to commit before I could "go and sin no more." I had to burn those threatening letters so Mama would never find out I had come so close to getting in trouble with the law. After burning them in our rusty trash barrel, though, I still felt guilty. Not even the ashes absolved me.

I felt the need to make things "right with the Lord." This led me to the eerie confessional booth at St. Anne's, which was fashioned out of the darkest wood on earth. I pulled open the creaking door, took a seat, and waited in the shadowy silence for Father Roberto. When I heard him enter his side of the dual chamber, I pressed my narrow chin against the screen. "Bless me, Father, for I have sinned."

"What is your sin, son?"

"I bamboozled some companies out of their money and bought a bicycle with it."

"Well, if you want to get right with God, you should sell the bike and give the money to the poor."

"Yes, Father. As you say."

"Then I absolve you from your sins in the name of the Father, the Son, and the Holy Spirit. Go and sin no more."

I left the church in a bit of a quandary. If I followed Father Roberto's command, wouldn't I just be giving the money to myself?

As I rode my bike home through the winding roads, a war was waging within my soul.

Should I sell it? Should I give it away? Should I tell Mama?

These were weighty concerns for a twelve-year-old whose soul was at stake, and I needed to sleep on the matter to get my head clear. After a good night's rest, I came to my senses the following morning.

I kept the bike.

CHAPTER 19

Hound Dog

Duchess didn't come home one evening, and I worried about her all night. In the morning, I was expecting to see her lying outside the trailer, waiting to gobble up her food. But when I called for her, she didn't come trotting out of the brush like usual. I knocked on every door on both sides of Sleepy Hollow Loop. "Have you seen our German shepherd?"

No one had. Bobby and I decided to look for her in the woods behind our house. "Duchess! Duchess?" we called out as we scoured the dense forest until we came to a slight ridge where Bobby spotted her lying on the bank of a little creek.

"Come here, girl!" I hollered. She appeared unable to move.

"Maybe she was attacked by a coyote," Bobby said as we ran toward her. We had heard their high-pitched yips on winter nights and long feared an encounter with the pack. I stooped low on the damp earth to take a closer look at Duchess. Just as we had feared, her fur was covered in dried blood. She turned her head toward me languidly as I petted her shoulder. When our eyes met, she whimpered, then put her head down.

"No animal did this to her!" I shouted, fury coursing through my veins. "It was that demon-possessed Boone. He shot her. Just like he said he would!"

Bobby picked up a branch and slammed it against a tree so hard it broke.

"Come on," I said. "We have to save her."

We gingerly picked her up. Then I cradled her against my chest. Each jolt through the hilly terrain caused her to whimper. It was a long and slow walk home. She was small, as far as shepherds go, but with each step she felt heavier. I thought about handing her off to Bobby, but I was afraid I might drop her, so I kept going, determined to save our cherished pet.

A few feet from our trailer, she made a dreadful groan and took her final breath in my arms. My cheeks were already wet with tears as I set her lifeless body on the dirt. Bobby knelt down to stroke her fur and say good-bye, and that's when he totally lost it. He sobbed his heart out. I did too.

If I had only used the money I had spent on the bicycle to finish the fence instead, Duchess might still be alive.

I was beside myself with grief and moped around for days. Mama, also distraught over her death, cried alongside us. Lisa grieved too.

My grief turned to anger, my anger to vengeance, my vengeance to vehemence. Before long I was plotting a way to take revenge on my cruel neighbors. But we had no proof, only our intuition. Even if we had been able to prove they had killed Duchess, we knew no one would do anything about it since we didn't matter to those in power in our community. To them, we would always be outsiders—poor and unwanted immigrants who didn't belong in Grants Pass.

Months later, Mama drove Bobby, Lisa, and me on Interstate 5, heading north. "What exit?" she asked.

"Seventy-six, Wolf Creek," I answered, reading her directions.

"*Sí, sí,*" Mama agreed, turning onto winding back roads.

"This place gives me the creeps," I admitted, as the rural paths pulled us far from civilization.

After a steep turn upward into the mountains, we followed a rough logging road before finally arriving at our destination. The second Mama got out of the car, she was greeted by the chaotic barks of dogs in the distance. She grimaced as she tiptoed her way up to the porch, ringing the doorbell of a single-story home where moss grew thick on the shingled roof. Told to wait in the car, the three of us couldn't figure out why on earth we had traveled to such a remote place.

A friendly woman with long golden hair came out to greet Mama on her veranda, putting us all at ease. With a smile, Mama signaled for us.

"Follow me around back," the woman said as she bounced ahead of us over red dirt that was as fine as powder. In the distance stood a dog kennel. The closer we got to it, the stronger the stench became—a toxic combination of wet dogs and dog doo.

"You've got quite the compound here," Mama said politely.

"Yes, we do. We've been at it for a long time."

"Those dogs look really cool. What kind are they?" I asked.

"Norwegian elkhounds. We're the top breeders in the area."

"Hmm . . . I've never heard of 'em."

"They come from Norway. Great hunters and herders."

"I like their silver and black fur, their rounded tails. They remind me of those sled dogs that live with the Eskimos."

"How would you like to pick out one of the puppies to take home?" she asked with a big smile. I raised my head, looking back at Mama, my face a question mark.

"Yes, *mijo*. I've been listening to the *Bargain Roundup* on the radio for weeks, waiting for someone to advertise puppies so I could surprise you guys."

I was so excited I could hardly stand it.

The lady led us into a pen where a litter of pups looked snug and warm, suckling on their mother's milk.

"How old are they?" I asked.

"Eight weeks. They were born on Thanksgiving, to be exact."

"Can I pick one up?"

"Of course, you can. That's why you're here, honey."

I grabbed the cutest one and rubbed it next to my face so I could feel her soft fur and the beating of her little heart. Her face was grayish black, and she had a silvery sheen that ran down her legs to her paws. Bobby and Lisa crowded around me, *oohing* and *aahing* at the adorable little pup and showering her with affection.

The lady's eyes lit up. It was clear we were all quite taken with her.

"She seems to really like you," she whispered in my ear. "That's a good sign, you know."

"It is?"

With a pink tongue that felt like fine-grade sandpaper, the pup suckled my finger so eagerly it made me laugh. Her blackish-blue eyes sparkled. I was a goner.

"How about this one, Mama?" I asked.

"She's really sweet," Lisa added, "and I like her little black nose too."

"Yeah, and I like the white pattern in the middle of her chest," Bobby said.

"If that's the one you like, then let me talk to the nice lady about it while you guys wait in the car."

While the women discussed the transaction near the veranda, we sat in the car, eavesdropping on every word.

"Fifty dollars?" Mama asked, slowly shaking her head.

"The parents are pedigreed, and I have all the certified papers, so you'll be getting a purebred elkhound."

Mama opened her purse and started counting, "Five, ten, fifteen, twenty," then stopped at twenty-five. She looked at the woman with a heartfelt gaze. "Is there any way you would consider taking twenty-five? And the difference in cookbooks?"

"What do you mean?" the lady asked with a furrowed brow.

"I have some brand-new cookbooks in the trunk that I just received from the Doubleday Book Club." Mama had always wanted to learn to be a better cook, and it had only cost ninety-nine cents for her first shipment of six books. At this point, even though she didn't want to part with her new stash, she was hoping the books would give her something of value to barter with.

"So . . . you don't have the other twenty-five dollars?" The woman was no longer smiling.

Mama sighed. "I'm not even sure I have enough gas to get home. This was a little farther out than I expected."

"Uh-huh. I see." The lady crossed her arms and tilted her head in frustration. "Well, the truth is I don't really need any new cookbooks."

Mama's shoulders slumped. There was an awkward silence. Then she looked at the woman pleadingly. "You see, ma'am, our dog, Duchess, was shot to death by some cruel neighbors. I promised the kids I would get them another dog somehow."

"Oh my god, I can't believe anyone would do such a horrible thing," the lady said with fury on her face. "What kind of people would shoot a dog? Makes me want to shoot those monsters myself!"

Mama nodded. "Call it a mother's intuition or what have you, but I felt compelled to call your number after I heard your ad on the radio. I was hoping to sell some things to raise the full amount, but I didn't have much luck. Of course, I don't want to disappoint my children. But I understand you may not want the cookbooks. Maybe we could pay the rest a little at a time?"

Just then we heard a man's deep voice coming from an open window in the house. "Ma, I think you could do with a few new recipes around here."

The lady chuckled.

"Just so you know," Mama said with a smile, "the collection is worth over fifty dollars if you bought them in a bookstore today. My children will take great care of the dog and give her lots of love. I assure you."

"Well, that's important to me. I always want my pups to go to a good home."

Mama stood in silence, awaiting the woman's response. In the car, Bobby, Lisa, and I held our breath.

The lady looked at my mother with piercing eyes, then glanced at us in the car. Finally, she said, "Maria, I am moved by your faith. You can have the puppy for twenty dollars and the cookbooks, but I want you to keep the other five dollars for gas."

I balled my hands and squeezed them, then whispered "yes," as if my team had just scored the winning touchdown. Bobby and Lisa looked at each other, beaming.

We were going home with our new puppy, and we were over the moon about it. Mama dished out the twenty dollars, opened the trunk, and handed over all the cookbooks. A few minutes later she came back with our puppy.

"Thank you, thank you, thank you," I said to the lady. Then I turned toward the house and yelled, "Thank you, mister!"

On the way home, Mama was so happy she began to sing the chorus of the Patti Page song "That Doggie in the Window."

"What are we going to name her?" Lisa asked.

I shrugged my shoulders.

"How about Lobo?" Mama suggested. "Means *wolf* in Spanish, and she was born in Wolf Creek."

I looked down and whispered, "Hi, my sweet little Lobo. Welcome to our family."

At home, Mama heated milk in a saucepan. Then we watched our little Lobo lap it up with her tiny pink tongue. We placed a soft packing blanket in a box and made a bed for her on the floor between Bobby and me.

A year came and went, and we loved every moment with our precious Lobo. On Thanksgiving we celebrated her first birthday, gave her a small plate of turkey, and presented her with a brand-new shiny black leather collar and a nickel-plated ID tag with her name engraved on it.

We took turns around the table and shared what we were most thankful for. Mama went first. "I'm grateful that God used the kindness of a stranger to blunt my anger toward our cruel neighbors. It felt as if the woman we got Lobo from was sent like an angel to demonstrate his love for us."

"I'm thankful Lobo protected Bobby and me from the porcupine at the top of Bolt Mountain," I said, petting Lobo, who was resting beside me under the table.

"Yeah, and I'm thankful she protected us from that rattlesnake too," Bobby added. "And that Boone hasn't shot her."

"I'm thankful Lobo gives me snuggles," Lisa said, giggling. My older siblings chimed in too.

We had a warm meal sitting in front of us, a mother who loved us, and a healthy, happy dog who would risk her life for us.

Who could ask for anything more?

Bobby and I were playing with our orange Nerf football in the yard one afternoon when Lobo approached us, hobbling and whimpering.

"Oh my god!" I screamed.

"What is it?" Mama called from inside the trailer.

"It's Lobo!"

She burst out the door. The only thing remaining of Lobo's right leg was a string of tendons and a dangling fragment of bone. It had been shot nearly clean off.

Mama put a hand across her mouth and shrieked, "Oh my god, no! Get Lobo in the back of the car right away, boys. Hurry. We have to get her to the vet before she bleeds to death."

We gently picked up Lobo and laid her between us on the back seat. While Mama raced through the back roads, Bobby and I pleaded, "Please don't die, Lobo," patting her on the head as she went into shock. With tears spilling down our faces, we thanked her for always protecting us. Her eyes told me how much she loved us too.

"If my father were alive, he would throw the book at those evil people," Mama said as she wiped her eyes, trying to contain herself. Then, in a broken voice, she lamented. "But he's not here to defend us."

At the animal hospital, we were instructed to leave Lobo with the vet, not knowing whether she would make it or not. The next afternoon, we went back and waited anxiously for the verdict. Eventually a nurse came out, holding a leash in her right hand. On the other end was Lobo. I was never so happy to see an animal in my life. With her tail wagging, Lobo limped over to me as best she could. I knelt down and hugged her, pressing her head tightly between my hands while she slathered my face with her tongue.

The backwoods of Oregon were fraught with danger, not only for us but for anything we loved. Yet like any other place, Grants Pass was filled with good as well as evil. After assessing our financial desperation and learning about our heartless neighbors, the kindhearted vet waived his fees. It was because of our neighbors' evil that we were left with a dead German shepherd and a three-legged elkhound. But because of the goodness of our God-fearing veterinarian, we got Lobo back.

Most of her, anyway.

CHAPTER 20

Listen to the Music

In the window stood the blue-sparkle drum set I had long fantasized about. I was smitten. Hopelessly. Deliriously. On a Saturday afternoon, Mama had dropped me off downtown to roam about for an hour while she took Bobby and Lisa for their flu shots.

Seeing me pining away in front of her Music Shop display, an attractive brunette with big, brown eyes stepped outside. "Well, why don't you come on in, son?" I froze. "You know, it doesn't cost anything to look around. I'm Pearl Jones. Let me give you a tour of my place."

Ms. Pearl's magnetic personality and the lovely scent of her perfume made it hard to say no. I nodded and walked in behind her. On a shelf up high, she'd arranged a row of colorful drum sets—red, green, silver, gold, and champagne. Those glittery finishes, sparkling in the light, made my heart race.

A clash of sounds reverberated throughout the shop, from customers strumming on guitars to an album playing on the turntable by a new band called the Eagles. But none of the noise seemed to bother Ms. Pearl, including the kids blowing on kazoos. "Those are just cheap toys," she said, "but it keeps them here. Then, one day, they'll buy a real instrument." She winked.

Ms. Pearl seemed like a smart businesswoman. On her desk, a metal spindle impaled a pile of yellow receipts, and behind it, an oval birdcage held her Macaw named Kizzy. The ornery old bird guarded the lesson rooms and repair shop, where Ms. Pearl showed me a variety of brass and woodwind instruments. "We rent to kids in the school band program," she explained. While she took in the expanse of the store, her mood shifted from lighthearted to one that was more reflective. "I bought this place a little over ten years ago, and it's brought a lot of happiness to the people of Grants Pass." She paused again, looking straight into my soul, or so it seemed. "There's nothing quite like the power of music, is there?"

I nodded, feeling like I had just been given the keys to a secret world I never knew existed.

"What kind of music do you like?"

"All kinds, but soul . . . soul is my favorite."

"Well then, let me take you to our record bins."

I thumbed through the albums, wishing I had a record player of my own. Then I glanced at the grandfather clock and saw it was time for me to head out. "I have to meet up with my family now, but thanks for showing me your store, ma'am."

"Oh, honey, I'm a lot of things, but I'm certainly no ma'am," she said, laughing again while handing me some catalogs. "Please call me Pearl. And if you need anything, you just ask. We're friends now. Come back anytime."

It felt special getting a tour from the owner, and I left with an almost effervescent sensation of possibility bubbling up inside me. I rehashed Ms. Pearl's words: *There's nothing quite like the power of music, is there?* She was right. Nothing had ever moved me like music, and somewhere in my heart, I believed music would find a place for me.

In the car, I could hardly contain myself. "Mama, Mama! I met a nice lady named Ms. Pearl, and she showed me all the instruments in her store. They sell records and record players with lots of fancy knobs to twiddle too. You should see all the music in there!"

A smile spread across her face. "That's wonderful, *mijo*. Just wonderful."

"Look," I said, waving the catalogs in the air. "She gave me these and a big hug before I left."

"Is *that* why I smell perfume on you?"

I blushed, and Bobby teased me relentlessly about it all the way home. Together, we rifled through the catalogs and talked about how great it would be to start a band one day. A week later, while we were in school, Mama paid a visit to the Music Shop, where Ms. Pearl set her up on a monthly payment plan for not one but two General Electric Wildcat record players with built-in speakers.

Mama surprised Bobby and me with a blue one and Lisa with a pink one, bringing a symphony of musical expression into our lives. Every song we played told a story, and every story connected with me deeply, inspiring me to imagine a better story for my own life. Like the instruments in Ms. Pearl's shop, those songs set my heart to dreaming.

When Armando heard we had new record players, he surprised Mama with *Fiesta Mexicana*, an album by Jorge Negrete, her favorite mariachi singer. Mama played the album so much she almost wore it out. Like me, nothing stirred her more than music. Especially music that evoked memories of her youth. She would laugh, cry, and dance all in one listening, taking us on the journey with her as we internalized her every emotion. Though I had no idea what Jorge was singing about, I felt the Mexican pride in his delivery, which was important for a boy who had experienced so much humiliation because of his heritage. By listening to that music, I could sense something of the sorrow, the struggle, and the triumph of the Mexican people. That's when I first realized that music is a universal language, and that despite the language barrier, Jorge sang with so much of his soul that his music touched mine.

"You're such a good singer, *Madre*," Armando told her. "It's a shame you never got to live your dreams."

Mama smiled. "I am living my dream. I'm here in America, surrounded by the people I love most in the world—my children. And we're all healthy, happy. That's my dream."

"But don't you ever wish you'd become an entertainer, like you wanted?"

"You guys are the best thing that ever happened to me, and I'm happy," Mama insisted. "Besides, my father never really wanted that. The profession of an entertainer was beneath the high hopes he had for me. Though he made it perfectly clear he did not approve of my acting, Conchita was twenty years younger than Papa, and she understood my passion for show business. She supported me fully."

"Your dad didn't want you to be in the movies?"

"It wasn't just the movies," Mama said, laughing. "When I was sixteen, I took a waitressing job so I could hang out with friends. When your grandfather found out, he became *so* angry," she said, her face portraying the kind of anger she had once witnessed. "He showed up on my shift in his suit and tie. Right there, in front of everyone, he pulled me up by the ears, peered down through his gold-rimmed glasses, and in a stern voice said, 'No daughter of a supreme court judge is going to be working in a place like this.' He drove me straight home, and neither one of us said a word the entire way."

With that, Mama turned up the music and cheered us all to our feet. The living room became a Mexican dance hall as we sang at the top of our lungs. Music of all kinds was making a deep impact on me. Aside from my family, I still had not met my herd, my tribe, my people. But listening to music proved they were out there, somewhere, waiting for me.

I just didn't know where to look.

CHAPTER 21

Come Fly with Me

Tony Bennett's resonant voice was doing little to drown out the torrential downpour one spring evening in 1975. The pelting rain, like an onslaught of angry ravens pecking on the tin roof of our mobile home, made it hard to hear the music through the living room speakers.

I pressed my face against the glass to get a glimpse of the swell of muddy brown water gushing down Sleepy Hollow Loop, and I wondered how long it might be before we went floating downstream in the aluminum torpedo we called home. This inclement weather, though, would not be the most memorable part of that night.

It was two months before Ricardo's high school graduation. In July he would be leaving to join the Air Force. Nothing would ever be the same, and at age twelve I was terrified of becoming the man of the house. Mama had been planning a special going away surprise for him but was keeping the details secret.

In spite of the jarring sound of thunder outside, my siblings and I were peacefully playing Monopoly while watching an episode of *The Waltons* as the smell of Hamburger Helper, a family favorite, made its way toward us.

"I have something exciting to share with all of you," Mama said as she stirred ground beef and noodles in the skillet. "But you have to clean up before I'll tell you."

In our household, bribery was always the best method to get us to work. We scrambled to put away our things while Mama turned down the burner on the gas stove, took off her floral apron, and pulled something from one of the kitchen drawers. With a gleam of *joie de vivre* in her eyes, she paced back and forth with one hand behind her back, zigzagging around us with a childlike grin.

Bobby and I tried to sneak behind her to see what she was hiding, but she quickly raised her arm above her head, waving a handful of tickets in the air with an ear-to-ear smile on her face. We circled her, trying to grab them from her hands, but she outmaneuvered us. "Guess what I'm holding?" she asked teasingly.

"Tickets!" Lisa exclaimed.

"Yes, of course, my darling, but what are they for?"

"The circus?" Bobby asked.

"No."

"The Ice Capades?" Patricia asked.

Mama shook her head, waving her index finger to keep the guesses flowing.

"I know! I know!" I yelled. "They're tickets to see Evel Knievel's big jump at King's Island."

"Keep trying."

Ricardo was the last to give it a shot. "I bet they're tickets to the Air Show."

Mama was having fun stringing us along, but she finally gave in to our impatience and said in a cheerful voice, "You're all wrong. They're for something much better than anything you guessed."

Like a proud poker player holding a royal flush, she slowly plunked down the tickets on top of the counter. I grabbed one and pulled it close to my face, reading it out loud from top to bottom: "Portland Memorial Coliseum. Jerry Weintraub Presents . . ." When I saw the next line, my eyes bulged, my jaw fell open, and I blurted out in disbelief, "*Frank Sinatra!*"

As soon as I uttered those two simple words, my siblings began jumping up and down. All our lives we had listened to Sinatra's records and watched his movies. We knew his blue eyes from the album covers, we had role-played scenes from his movies, we had learned the words of his many songs—and now we were going to see the living legend in person! For a family whose torch of hope remained lit by the lyrical stanzas he sang so eloquently, this was an epic shocker.

"I wanted to do something special together before Ricardo leaves," Mama explained.

She had socked away every extra penny for a long time, and, boy, had she delivered! Little did I know this would prove to be more than a special family outing. The concert would change my life.

At 4:00 p.m. on Friday, April 25, 1975, Ricardo declared himself the designated driver. Mama acted as copilot, while Bobby, Patricia, and I scrunched in the back seat. To get us in the spirit, Mama popped in her 8-track of *Frank Sinatra's Greatest Hits*. And just like that, we were on our way to Portland.

During the long 245-mile drive, I was consumed with the rhythm of the rotating tires, clocking in my head the milliseconds between each revolution. Whenever Ricardo flipped on his turn signal, I would play rhythms with my hands on the back of his seat, just as I had done years earlier when we had gone to see the Temptations in Long Beach. Drumming between each click, I drove my brother nuts, but we were all in too good of a mood to argue.

A couple of hours into the drive, we stopped at a rest area for supper. It was already beginning to get dark when we gathered around a picnic table to share a couple of bottles of 7 Up and the bologna sandwiches Mama had packed for us. Then we crowded back into the car for another two hours of travel. By then, we were eager to find a place to stay the night. Mama said we needed to find someplace just outside Portland since it would be cheaper than a room in the city.

I spotted a billboard in the distance that read, MOTEL NEXT EXIT. As we veered off the interstate, the motel's sign announced, "Let Magic Fingers Relax You," and flashing in pink neon under those words was VACANCY.

From the motel parking lot, we eyed the ghastly place with trepidation. "Where the heck are we?" Patricia asked.

Mama peered out her window suspiciously and shrugged her shoulders at Ricardo.

"We're low on gas," he said, "and I'm too tired to drive any farther."

Mama eyed the fuel gauge. "For fourteen ninety-five, the price is right."

"Yeah, but will we survive the night?" Bobby asked, trying to lighten the mood.

No one answered.

After Mama secured our lodging with the skittish manager, we tiptoed as quietly as possible up the concrete staircase to the second floor. Ricardo inserted the key slowly to open room 226. Then he pushed back the door for the big reveal—*va-va-voom!* Sitting on the nightstand was a cryptic machine. A placard next to it gave the following description: *Magic Fingers Relaxation—service featured in over 10,000 hotels and motels around the world. It quickly carries you into the land of tingling . . . relaxation . . . and ease.* TRY IT—YOU'LL FEEL GREAT.

The cost for this hedonistic pleasure? A mere twenty-five cents.

After being squished in the back seat for nearly four hours, we pleaded with Mama to give us a quarter. This seemed a just reward for enduring such an exhausting journey with virtually no complaints or fights, which was an absolute rarity for us. Mama caved and slid the coin into the slot as we all plopped onto the polyester bedspread. With a jolt, the bed began to vibrate, filling the room with its arrhythmic clunking, clanking, and buzzing. The magic fingers didn't relax us, but they sure did entertain us. We quickly learned that the advertising gurus had overlooked the most important selling feature of the whole experience—the absolute hilarity of it all!

The next day, we toured the Portland area, counting down the minutes until show time. At dusk on that clear Saturday evening, we drove across the Broadway Bridge, peering out over the Willamette River before pulling into the parking lot of Memorial Coliseum.

The venue had been previously graced by legends such as Glenn Miller, James Brown, the Beatles, Elvis Presley, and the Rolling Stones.

Now, "the Voice" (as Sinatra was known) would fill the hall with the irresistible charisma of an old-world saloon singer.

Mama shouted, "Look! Look, you guys!" She pointed hysterically to the red and white flashing lights that announced, "Frank Sinatra in Concert with Don Costa and Orchestra." It was a marquee we had been waiting to see all our lives.

Mama's giddiness was palpable, and it was touching to see her take in the moment with such childlike splendor. Despite how bad her arthritis could get at times, she refused to let the pain stop her from hearing the music she loved. She was about to immerse herself in an unforgettable evening with her favorite crooner, and she was glowing with glee. Even better, she was experiencing this entrancement while in her children's company, the ones she had so purposely reared on his music. It would be our last outing together for a while, and we understood the weight of that.

Minutes later, it was hard to believe we were entering this massive glass structure to hear Sinatra perform. We handed our tickets to the usher, who pointed us to our seats. Sitting next to us was an older couple with strange accents. The portly man with a wide jaw was fashionably dressed in a plaid polyester leisure suit with stripes going in so many different directions I had to look away for fear my eyes might become permanently crossed.

With a Camel dangling from the side of his mouth, he patted me on the head and said, "Sonny, youz in for a real treat. Where youz guys from?"

"Los Angeles," Ricardo said proudly.

"Long ways from here," the man remarked. He was also wearing a fedora, like Sinatra, and a powder-blue ascot. The epitome of cool.

"Yeah, but we live in Grants Pass now," Ricardo admitted with less enthusiasm. "Where're you from?"

"Weehawken—Jersey," the man said, blowing smoke in my face. "Five minutes from Hoboken, where Sinatra grew up. Made a foortuun there in the restaurant business, I did."

"But weez live in Lake Oswego now," his aging blond companion added, adjusting the mink stole around her neck.

Sitting next to this posh couple made me wish we could have arrived with a bit more panache. But with the cost of the tickets, motel, gas, and food, not to mention the quarter for the vibrating bed, we couldn't even afford the tour program we wanted so badly.

Of course, Mama was after something far more personal. While the audience was still finding their seats, she took me by the hand and walked me down to the ground floor, pushing through the pain in her feet. Then, with something hanging suspiciously from underneath her arm, she did the unthinkable. She approached one of the security guards near the backstage area and said, "Excuse me, sir. Would you please ask if Mr. Sinatra would autograph my book?" She showed the guard her treasured copy of *The Films of Frank Sinatra*. Considering how much she had spent on so many of his records, I figured Mama had earned that autograph, especially since she had always had to work extra jobs to splurge on any nonessential items through the years. That's how much Frank Sinatra had meant to her, to all of us. Maybe we couldn't afford his music, but Mama knew his songs would sustain us through the darkest hours. She understood there was no price too high for a dose of hope.

But that security guard just flat out said, "No."

Few things saddened me more than to see my mother turned away so rudely from something that meant so much to her. If only the "Chairman of the Board" could have gazed into her Ida Lupino eyes and felt her irresistible charm, he would have fallen under her spell. Only the guard seemed immune to her vibrant spirit.

By the time we returned to our seats, Mama was holding her head high once again. No amount of disappointment ever kept her down for long. Just as we settled, the lights dimmed and the timpanist swelled into a full roll on his copper kettledrum, signaling the orchestra to begin their rousing overture. Excitement was buzzing, and the atmosphere grew thick with anticipation.

At last, the moment we had all been waiting for. From out of the tunnel at the back of the venue, two spotlights followed a shadowy figure. Bodyguards surrounded the iconic singer as he made his way to the stage. Suited in his crisp black tuxedo, the debonair Sinatra took front and center. He grabbed his microphone and had us with his first five words, "Good evening, ladies and gentlemen."

The audience cheered.

He immediately went into his arrangement of Stevie Wonder's "You Are the Sunshine of My Life," followed by a cover of Jim Croce's "Bad, Bad, Leroy Brown."

I stared at my besotted mother's face when Sinatra broke into "Nice 'n' Easy." She looked the happiest I had ever seen, and we were tickled pink to be experiencing the evening with her. In the presence of the music that deeply touched her soul, her pain seemed to take a back seat, and I witnessed the evocative way in which music could make someone forget her troubles and woes.

Just when I wondered what melodious treasure I might hear next from the beloved Sinatra catalog, the mood shifted. The house lights slowly faded, and darkness overwhelmed the auditorium. A sweeping silence ensued. Then, ever so softly, the strum of a cherubic harp was accented by a single shaft of light. It shone from the highest point of the auditorium, falling directly onto Ol' Blue Eyes. "We will now do the national anthem, but you needn't rise," the singer from Hoboken said as he sat on a throne of confidence. Stealthily, the guitar and piano segued into one of the most poignant songs ever written, "My Way."

Frank's vocal prowess was astonishing. The tone and timbre were soothing to my soul, calming every agitation within me. Hearing him made me feel as if the fears and insecurities I carried would somehow vanish and that everything would be all right as long as I kept listening to that voice. With each rising crescendo from the explosive horns and counter melodies from the impassioned string section, the hair on my arms stood up. I had no way of processing what I was feeling. It seemed I had been touched by something otherworldly, something spiritual. Something I couldn't understand. I cried.

When the orchestra reached their final *fermata* at the end of the stirring arrangement, Sinatra held his final note so long I felt I grew an inch as I sat listening to it. The audience jumped to their feet, applauding. The couple from Jersey looked at me and smiled.

That evening with one of the world's greatest performers would be a turning point in my life. Something happened in the midst of that musical genius, something that seemed to alter my physiology. I was overcome with determination to rise to the world stage. The desire had come bursting forth from deep within me. There was no holding it back. I had no idea how I would get to that stage. I just knew I had to be on it. Somehow, someday, I would be on that side of the music.

The path from here to there was a mystery waiting to unfold. But a small piece of the puzzle fell into place as I listened intently to Sinatra's drummer, Irv Cottler, who had been swinging the orchestra all night. With an intricate balance of subtly and ferocity, he drove that big band, not simply with precision but with passion. His brilliant drumming, steady as a heartbeat and fluid as quicksilver, accentuated every vital transition in Sinatra's songbook with an impeccable elasticity that lifted the music—and me—to a euphoric state.

The show ended with "Put Your Dreams Away (For Another Day)." But I didn't want to put mine away; I wanted them on display for all the world to see. I wanted to feel the thrill that Sinatra's drummer felt in moving the audience.

As we slowly threaded our way through the exiting crowd, I couldn't get Frank and Irv out of my head or out of my heart, which was fuller than it had ever been. Back in the car, I asked Mama to pop in her 8-track of *Frank Sinatra's Greatest Hits* again. She happily obliged, glad that her favorite music meant so much to me.

In the wee hours of the morning, with Bobby asleep in my lap and Patricia out cold on my right shoulder, we came up over the mountain and down into Grants Pass. As the dense forests closed in around us, the gentle *glissando* of the oboe and bassoon moved gracefully into "It Was a Very Good Year." As Frank reminisced in the first verse about his seventeenth year, the clarinet section responded with a haunting melody that made me pensive. I was on the brink of manhood. My older brother was about to pass the torch to me. *What kind of man would I become? What would I do with my life? How would I find "my way"?*

With the strings plucking in unison, Sinatra continued sharing indelible moments of his twenty-first year. Again, I mused. Would my twenty-first year be as good for me as it was for him, with "city girls who lived up the stair"? Or would I end up hauling manure in a flatbed somewhere in the Rogue Valley?

Every line of that song stirred the hope in me that my life could bring me a very good year. A whole string of them, in fact. At least one worth singing about the way Sinatra did. He sang not as a man just reciting lyrics on a page but as one who had weathered many storms and seasons, his voice self-assured, full of unvanquished glory. Even though I was just twelve, I wanted to become a man like him.

I couldn't help wondering if at some point in my life I would be riding around with chauffeurs in limousines, with "blue-blooded girls of independent means," or would I be stuck in a ramshackle travel trailer on Sleepy Hollow Loop, burning with regrets?

Toward the close of that wistful song, the orchestra's strings played with fervor as Sinatra reached autumn, the final season of his life. He likened it to vintage wine, sweet and clear, being poured from the brim to the dregs. The imagery was so powerful and the sentiment so seductive that I sat in envy, longing for such a life.

What would it take to achieve it?

Was it even possible for a kid like me?

CHAPTER 22

Take Me Home, Country Roads

One hot summer Saturday morning, Mama asked me to fetch the mail. I did as she asked and handed her the pile of envelopes. "Look," she said, holding up one. "A letter from your grandmother." She opened it briskly, eager to read its contents. Inside was a small photo she gazed at for a minute. At first, she smiled. Then, suddenly her face began to droop. "It's a picture of your father."

I grabbed it from her and stared at it intently. My father and I had the same cheeks, nose, and mouth. But there was something very different about us. Something that stung. While he was sitting behind a ship's wheel somewhere in the tropical South Seas, looking happy as the breeze swept through his hair, I was sad and brokenhearted in jerkwater Grants Pass, wondering why he didn't love me enough to take me with him. *He'd really like me if he ever gave me a chance*, I thought to myself. "Why did my grandmother send that picture?" I asked Mama. "Was it to make me jealous or sad?"

"I'm not sure," she said, raising her eyebrows. A painful silence passed between us, but then she tried to console me by telling me how special I was—something she always did. Well, I wasn't feeling very special after looking at that picture. All it did was fester up my deep-seated wounds of abandonment.

Mama turned on the record player and dropped the needle on "Moonlight Serenade," a luscious ballad with a rhapsodic horn arrangement. "Come here, *mijo*," she said with such tenderness I couldn't resist. "Dance with me." I leaned my face against her harvest gold blouse while she draped her arms around me. While we danced, I glanced up to see the love in her soft brown eyes. One second, she was laughing; the next, she looked as though she would break down and cry. In those few moments that we danced, her message to me was how sorry she was that my father didn't want anything to do with me and how she felt it was somehow her fault.

The start of that summer stretched before us like a river of days, one flowing into the other, without the annoying sound of an alarm clock going off or a bus horn honking or the school bell ringing. There was nothing but the chirping of birds, the barking of dogs, Mama's record player going round and round, and of course, the soothing sound of Maria's children and grandchildren at play. Bobby and I were shuffling through our football cards, going over which cards belonged to whom. He was convinced the Roger Staubach card was his. I was certain he had traded it to me for his Terry Bradshaw card and yanked it out of his hand.

"Give it back!" Bobby shouted.

"It's mine!" I shouted back, whacking him on the arm with my knuckles. Bobby fought tears as he grabbed the leather football and threw it at me—hard. I ducked, and it crashed against the wall.

"Boys!" pleaded Mama from the living room of our mobile home.

I threw the ball back with all my might, grazing my little brother on the shoulder. He yelped, then lunged at me. We threw fists at each other so fast we became a blur of body parts. When a lucky punch found its mark, the one on the receiving end let out a yell or a string of the worst words he knew.

"You boys stop it right now!"

Of course, we didn't. We knew she couldn't stop us, knew she didn't have the strength to stop us. Mama's arthritis came and went, and this day was a particularly bad one. Her hands were in too much pain to hold a spoon or a skillet, let alone a belt. Her feet were too inflamed to chase us. After a while, she just cried.

Usually, that's what stopped us. Not the yelling. Not the threat of force. Her tears. We always felt bad when we made Mama cry. We didn't understand all the pain she had borne over the course of her life, but we knew enough. We had heard enough, seen enough. Knowing that we added to her pain was the worst punishment of all.

By now, Mama's rosary was tangled around her bent fingers, and tears were streaming down her face. Our words overlapped each other's. "We're sorry." "It was my fault. I started it." "No, it was mine." "We won't do it anymore, Mama. Promise." "Please don't cry."

I kissed her hands softly. "You want me to rub them, Mama?"

"Yes, please, Danny. That would be nice."

I gently massaged her hands while Bobby sat by the side of the bed. She looked at me and in a plaintive tone said, "Bobby needs an older brother to look up to. Lisa too."

I looked at Bobby and patted him on the shoulder. I said, "Sorry," and meant it.

He nodded, wiping away a tear.

Me? The big brother? How did that happen? And how did it happen so fast? The family had changed so much already and was changing still. Armando had left home years earlier after marrying Diane. Mary had left in '72 to go to college, leaving her daughter Lydia in Mama's care much of the time, which felt like having another sister. Patricia had moved to Ashland to live with Mary, and I missed her terribly. And Ricardo would be off to boot camp in less than a month. I didn't want him to leave. He was our head musketeer. Bobby and I would not be the same without him.

There would be no more working on his many construction projects or doing yard work for neighbors together. No more trips to Denny's restaurant to sip hot cocoa while sharing our hopes for the future. No more hikes up Bolt Mountain with Lobo hobbling along. No more lengthy battles of Monopoly, Billionaire, and Battleship. No more hiding in the trunk and sneaking into the Redwood Drive-In.

My life was changing yet again, whether I wanted it to or not.

The sun set early that evening. As Ricardo took me to the store to buy some groceries, the mountain range was silhouetted against the orange skyline. While we drove past Murphy Mill, the metal slash burners exhaled smoke like giant teepees. We called them wigwams. Out of their tops spewed sawdust and small cinders that covered everything nearby with ash and soot.

That smell of burning wood kindled my desire for a real-life campfire. I pined for a mountain excursion and a rite of passage that would let the world know I was no longer a boy now that I was thirteen. That opportunity seemed to come my way when we ran into Ricardo's older friends at the store and they asked us to tag along for a camping trip.

The next day, I went to Dirty Bird Sporting Goods across the street from the Music Shop to pick out a backpack. I decided on an orange nylon one that had every secret compartment I could hope for. Having spent some time in the Boy Scouts, I knew the motto Be Prepared, and I wanted to do just that since rattlesnakes were out in full force in the summer months.

I picked up a green rubber snakebite kit and envisioned this headline in the *Daily Courier*: "Young Boy Saves Hiker's Life—Grants Pass Parade in Hero's Honor." To step into Armando and Ricardo's shoes and become the family protector, I had to get to where the danger was. All that separated me from this excursion was Mama's permission. Since the older guys who had invited me were Ricardo's friends, I felt this would be a cinch. But for reasons that made no sense to me, she wouldn't let me go. I begged, I badgered, and I bargained, but she held her ground. Our Latin tempers flared, and we exchanged harsh words. Raging with anger, I decided to run away.

To survive in the wilderness, I would need food, but the only thing I could get my hands on without getting noticed was a box of Ritz crackers and Nilla wafers. I stuffed the boxes in my backpack, filled my canteen with water, and headed out the door. But as I ventured farther from home, I got an uneasy feeling. *How far can I possibly get on a box of crackers, cookies, and a canteen of water?* When I came to my senses, I walked back home with a better idea. I would hide in the woods behind our property, just long enough to make Mama worry about me. Instead of taking satisfaction in my revenge, I leaned against a tree and cried.

When I was all cried out, I used my backpack as a pillow and stared up at the patches of blue sky. I daydreamed about traveling the rugged wilderness like a mountain man, whitewater rafting down the Rogue, climbing the rocks at Hellgate Canyon, and killing rattlers with a single throw of my Bowie knife.

I had imagined myself halfway to the top of Wizard Island on Crater Lake when I heard Mama's voice calling, "*Dan-yell!*" She only called me this when she was either upset or wanted to get my attention. The longer I withheld my response, the more distraught her voice became.

In desperation, she phoned our Big Brothers Big Sisters mentors, Bill and Beverly Large. When the Larges arrived, they spotted me in the woods and said their baby kitten was stuck in a tree and they needed me to rescue it. I wasn't buying it. When the sun started setting, the thought of what lurked in the dark began to worry me. As my hunger intensified, my obstinacy weakened. The Larges eventually lured me out with an offer to take me to the Arctic Circle for ice cream as they had done on numerous occasions. I couldn't resist. After I devoured three large vanilla cones dipped in chocolate, they drove me home.

On the way back, they tried to convince me that Mama was just looking out for me, and that one day, when the circumstances were right, I would have the opportunity to go camping. As I listened, I sulked.

The next morning, I could see that Mama had been up crying all night. I recognized those puffed-up eyes from all the times she had cried through the night for my older siblings. She tried to hug me and kiss me, but I wouldn't have it.

Over the next few weeks, she made calls looking into various camps. At night I saw her on her knees, praying for the right opportunity to open up. By way of Reverend Ed Williamson at Faith Baptist Church, she found out about Wilderness Trails—a weeklong summer camp for underprivileged boys from difficult situations. Reverend Williamson was so determined to help that he bought Bobby and me the new hiking shoes we would need for the camp. It wasn't the first or last time he would help us, as he had already welcomed our family into his home for warm showers in the earlier days and had driven the big church bus to pick us up for youth events.

When the church van arrived to take us to the campsite, Bobby and I were beside ourselves. My backpack and canteen would finally be put to use! Mama hugged us both, then got a little choked up as we climbed into the van. We waved goodbye from the windows, and when I glanced back, she was still waving. I held back my tears because I didn't want any of the other boys to make fun of me.

The camp was set on a 160-acre parcel of land nestled in the Cascade Mountains. I had never seen anything like it. Conifer trees rose to the heavens. Purple lupines dotted the grassy knolls. I turned to Bobby, smiling from ear to ear, and said, "God Almighty. Would you look at this place?"

The sun shone in a cloudless turquoise sky. As we raced through the lush meadows, I spotted a rope suspension bridge spanning a rushing stream. At the top of the hill perched several Indian teepees. *Real* ones made of animal skins. This was turning out to be better than I could have ever imagined.

Once we finished taking in the surroundings, the staff divided the campers into assigned teams, then laid down the rules and the week's agenda. A competition was to take place, and the first-place team would win a plane ride over Table Rock plateau.

Like a drill sergeant, I rallied my team, the Cherokees, adding up points for each day's activities, determined to win the grand prize. If the competition and the awe-inspiring mountains weren't enough to make a man out of me, the camp leaders went to extra efforts to make the entire week a kid's paradise. Each team was given a donkey—*a donkey!*—to carry our supplies through the mountains in large aluminum canisters called panniers. The leaders taught us how to cook over an open fire, stressing the importance of keeping our equipment clean and serving as stewards of the earth. To top things off, cartons of ice cream, packed in dry ice containers, were dropped by parachute into the glistening Blue Lake from a tiny Cessna aircraft. We paddled out to the middle as fast as we could to retrieve our *scrumpdillyicious* treats, then devoured every finger-licking bite by the shore.

At night we performed skits and sang songs like "John Jacob

Jingleheimer Schmidt" and the hilarious "Sausage Machine" in the moonlight with the sound of crackling logs and the smell of roasting marshmallows.

When everyone left, I sat alone by the dwindling fire, gazing up at the stars, wanting to feel the same kind of faith Mama had. She always had hope when everything seemed hopeless, and I'd seen enough of her prayers answered to realize she might be onto something. I closed my eyes and said, "Dear Jesus, I've done some bad things and was wondering if you could forgive me." With my eyes fixed on the smoldering embers, I remained silent in pensive thought, and since I wasn't struck down by lightning, I figured I could continue. "Oh, and if you don't mind too much, can you help me make my dreams come true?" After that, I walked away in the coolness of night back to my tent, believing he would.

After we raced across the river on our final day, the staff inspected our panniers to see how well we had scoured them with the steel wool they had provided. I had stayed up late the night before, scrubbing our pannier by the firelight so it would gleam brighter than all the rest. When the official tally was done, we took first place. The plane ride would be ours!!

When we returned home, waiting for more information about the upcoming flight, Mama saw how happy we were to see her. The second she hugged me, things were instantly patched up between us. I apologized and thanked her for finding out about the camp. Something special had happened to all of us during that week—something that would forever remain in our hearts.

Mama had been vigilant during my childhood, watching to make sure I didn't fall in with the wrong crowd. As it turned out, one of those guys who had wanted to take me camping eventually ended up in prison, while the others became drug addicts and rabble-rousers. God only knows how my life would have turned out had Mama given in to my whining. Stalwart in every way, she had chosen the perfect place for Bobby and me to make our rite of passage. The camp meant so much to me that I even saved my *Trail Guide* booklet. Within those twenty-six pages were spiritual principles we had learned at camp that would help shape me into the man I wanted to be. It focused on God's love and how to trust in him, how to ask for forgiveness, and forgive others, and how to treat others the way you want to be treated. These were all the things Mama tried to teach us, but I didn't always want to listen. Now that it was coming from men I admired, somehow it seemed to matter more. These leaders carried themselves with an infectious sense of conviction and purpose. They knew who they were and what their purpose was. For a boy who struggled with identity, self-worth, and longed for a sense of belonging, they welcomed me with open arms. Given my less than noble track record, I knew I didn't measure up. But in spite of that, they showed me love and grace as if I had deserved it. Their actions served as a moral compass by which I would soon measure my character as a man. They inspired me to shed my old skin and become more like them.

Two weeks later, we were treated to our plane ride on the same Cessna aircraft that had dropped the ice cream containers into Blue Lake. It was my first time on an airplane, and I'll never forget the way it felt to get off the ground and soar. Suddenly the landscape seemed to open up beneath me, proving that the world really was a big place and that life existed far beyond the little town we called home. We flew on a crystal-clear day over Table Rock plateau, dipping in and out of the ancient ravines like World War II fighter pilots.

We continued soaring over the sumptuous Applegate and Rogue Valley regions. We even took a spin over our house on Sleepy Hollow Loop. As we flew the Oregon skies, I thought about the last team-building project we had done at Wilderness Trails—we had made an Indian war drum by hollowing out a log and stretching leather taut across the opening. Then we had carved out a pair of drumsticks from a couple of dead branches. The Cherokees had presented me with our team drum just after our victory, saying it was in recognition of my "great leadership." Drums were continuing to play a role in my life, beat by rhythmic beat.

Henry David Thoreau once wrote, "If a man does not keep pace with his companions, perhaps it is because he hears a different drummer. Let him step to the music which he hears, however measured or far away."

I was a long way from stepping to the music, but I could feel it all the way down to my toes, which were already beginning to tap to the beat.

On July 15, 1975, my entire family went to the Medford airport to see Ricardo off. He was headed to Lackland Air Force Base in San Antonio, Texas, for basic training. In his dark blue uniform and crisp flight cap, he looked sharp walking toward the aircraft. On his final step onto the plane, he turned around, gave us a big smile, and waved. After having put on a brave face through all the hugs and farewell wishes, he now looked choked up, which caused Mama to start sobbing. As the plane taxied down the runway and took off, we all huddled around Mama, clinging to her, to each other, and wept.

With their "Fly-Fight-Win" motto, the Air Force claimed to be the most elite branch in the military—a big draw for a meticulous young man who was determined to excel. Plus, Ricardo had always been fascinated with airplanes and had spent hours hanging out at various airports, naming each type of aircraft as it took off, enumerating details about all of them. He also loved old war movies. Whenever they came on TV, he and Mama would sit together and watch them.

While the US Marine Corps was looking for "a few good men," Mama would have settled for just one to partner with in life. Somehow, a man of virtuous character had always managed to evade her. At only seventeen, Ricardo had been the best man in our home. He was our resident handyman and the only other adult driver to help when Mama was too sick to drive. But now we would have to let him go.

As much as Bobby and I were sad to lose our best friend, we were equally happy to see him travel the world as he had always dreamed. We also believed that a victory for one of us was a victory for all of us. Besides, Ricardo had left us with a lifetime of memories and something very practical—his 1968 Chevy Malibu Super Sport. The old Chevy Nova had served us faithfully but finally gave up the ghost. We all welcomed the new wheels, especially with the souped-up motor that made my pulse race.

While Ricardo was preparing to fight outside our borders in Southeast Asia, Armando was still fighting the battles of injustice going on within our borders. He was quick to defend the rights of the poor and immigrants, as well as those on the fringes who had been marginalized by society. He and Mary would establish the first Latino Student Union at Southern Oregon College in Ashland, offering support to young adults like them. Like Ricardo, all my siblings were fighters, each willing to fight in a way that aligned with their individual ideals, believing with great conviction in the just battles they waged.

But fight or no fight, once again our big and crazy family was shrinking. I would miss those times in Compton with all of us laughing around the Formica dinner table in those wobbly chairs of ours. Or gathered around the black-and-white TV, sharing a bowl of Jiffy Pop popcorn. Or turning up the record player to dance to the Temptations or Supremes.

All that was now gone.

Now it would just be Bobby, Lisa, and me, with frequent visits from Lydia.

And Mama. *She* would never leave us. No matter how much our family shrank, she would always be there, in the center, holding us all together with her prayers and drawing us home by the gravitational pull of her love.

CHAPTER 23

A Change Is Gonna Come

The summer of 1975 in Grants Pass offered plenty of opportunities for a kid to roam. Our world was filled with green rolling hills, Boston ferns, sweet-scented pines, sparkling streams, and breezy skies. We filled our days with Boy Scout projects and nights at the Rogue Theatre with our family. In frayed cutoffs and bare feet, we tramped through overgrown places few had dared to explore. At home, we turned to comic books filled with tales of superheroes and ads offering freebies of one kind or another.

I even spent fifty cents to get a sixty-four-page booklet called *1001 Things You Can Get for Free.* Most of what they offered as *"free"* were useless pamphlets such as *Let's Collect Shells and Rocks.* What a sham. Bobby kept asking Mama to buy more Wheaties so he could save enough box tops to send away for a free Super Bowl poster. What came back was another dud. All proved to be cleverly designed acts of deception that ended up in the trash. Yet, the mailbox remained proof that a bigger and better world awaited. Maybe one day a letter from my father would arrive. I continued to write to him faithfully, month after month, year after year. But I got nothing. Not a letter, nor a card. Nothing on Christmas or on my birthday. Not one single check for child support.

Nothing. Maybe this was part of the reason I wrote away to companies with nameless, faceless people who *would* write back.

One day I went to the mailbox, hoping to find the X-Ray Specs I had sent away for, the ones that let you see through other people's clothes, but I found something better—a letter from the Farmers Home Administration. Our sister Mary had persuaded Mama to fill out a loan application with this government program for low-income families. If they approved our application, they would help us build a house on our property. Mama's forehead wrinkled as she began reading the FHA letter to herself, but then a few seconds later, her face brightened.

"We got the loan!" she hollered. "We got the loan. We're finally going to have our very own house."

Bobby and I were so happy we both started jumping up and down. Lisa and Lydia followed our example. "When?" I asked.

"According to the letter, they'll start building next month."

By the middle of August, a team of masons had laid the foundation. Every day afterward, plumbers, framers, electricians, and roofers did their part to construct a three-bedroom ranch-style house. It would be the first structure on the property that hadn't been built by us three boys. Seeing how intrigued Bobby and I were with the process, the contractor assigned us a few tasks, and we spent the last part of the summer helping him build our family's house.

Every evening after the crew left, we walked the construction site to see the progress. While the sun set, we sat in lawn chairs, imagining what our new house would look like when it was finished. Soon we would have a living room, dining area, kitchen, one full bath plus another three-quarter bath, a single-car garage, and appliances we could be proud of. Fourteen hundred square feet of living space—the most we had ever had.

The day we moved in was one of the most exciting of our lives. We all stood in front of the house with Mama, who held the keys in her trembling hands. Before she stepped inside, she dabbed olive oil above the doorsill and anointed it with a prayer of thanksgiving and protection as was Christian custom. Her face lit up as she pushed the door open. We followed behind in wonderment equal to hers, taking in the smell of fresh paint, carpeting, and cabinetry. I loved those smells—the aroma of new beginnings.

With the sun pouring through the front windowpanes, we explored our new home. Lobo followed, wagging her tail in approval. She sniffed her way to Lisa's room, where she buried her nose in the bubble gum pink carpeting. With the same level of curiosity, she checked out the royal-blue carpet in the bedroom that I would share with Bobby. The colors throughout the house were as different as each of us, as Mama had always gone out of her way to give each of us a say, even down to the choice of paint for our bedroom walls.

Mama opened the refrigerator door and ran her fingers across the glass shelves. Closing it, she beamed at the oven. "I can't wait to cook something in my new kitchen."

"Can you make your mac and cheese casserole, and your yellow cake with chocolate frosting?" I asked.

"I'll do it tonight. It will be our first official dinner here." Mama was so eager to have guests that within our first month she threw a Tupperware party, packing the house with friends from church. That night, she sold enough to earn a new set of bowls, a pitcher, a cake holder, an orange peeler, and some Popsicle molds, which we were all looking forward to using. Mama took pride in our new house, and we all stood with our heads held a little higher throughout the evening as friends came and went.

But a new house couldn't change the fact that junior high was just around the corner. On the first day of school, the smell of new clothes filled the halls of Lincoln Savage Junior High, where I was starting eighth grade. My clothes, of course, didn't have that new, store-bought smell, because they were hand-me-downs from my brothers. That had never bothered me before. Now, suddenly, it did.

Without Armando and Ricardo to stick up for me, I would have to fend for myself in these hostile halls, where the tormentors picked on me because I was skinny or half-Mexican or fatherless or poor, or for no other reason than wanting to appear tough.

Now *I* was the big brother. I would have to be the one to protect Bobby and Lisa when they were harassed by bullies. I would have to be the one to stand up for our mother when someone made fun of her accent or some perv tried to hit on her. I would have to be the one to defend our family, our honor. The responsibility was overwhelming.

I was just a ninety-seven-pound weakling with the weight of the world on my shoulders. Throughout the years, I had faced one loss after another, one challenge after another, one transition after another, not the least of which were the changes going on in my body. Girls, in general, terrified me, but I was taken with a drop-dead gorgeous blonde named Joni. I wrote about her in my diary. Dreamed about her at night. And every time the Frankie Valli song "My Eyes Adored You" came on the radio, I sang along, thinking of her.

Though she made me dreamy-eyed, I could hardly look her in the eye, let alone carry on a conversation with her. We were in math class together, and I felt flustered every time I saw her, every time I smelled her perfume.

I felt so insecure, so inferior, so invisible. I wasn't a member of any club. I wasn't a jock, wasn't a party kid, wasn't a popular kid. *Who am I?* I wondered. *Where do I fit in?*

Maybe if I made the football team, maybe then I would have some kind of identity. I loved watching football on TV, especially whenever the Miami Dolphins played. After each game, I would coax Bobby outside to try out my moves, faking him out like fullback Larry Csonka, then running untouched into the end zone to the thunderous cheers of everyone in the stands. I was a natural. *Yeah, football. That's it. That's what I'll do!*

As always, my mind was playing a soundtrack of my life. In 1975 my favorite song was "Shining Star" by Earth, Wind & Fire. I would recite the lyrics over and over while waiting for the school bus.

The song insisted that everyone in some way is a shining star, even me. So that day, fully stoked, with the song playing in my mind, I was ready to shine. I went out for the team. After realizing what a natural I was on the field, the coach . . . cut me. I checked in my equipment but not my delusions of grandeur. Later that evening, I scrawled one sentence in my journal: "*I love football, and I'm about the best player around.*"

CHAPTER 24

I'll Be Home for Christmas

Before I knew it, fall had come and gone, leaving no evidence that I was a star, let alone a shining one. But the Christmas of 1975 would be memorable, as they always were with my family. By the first week of December, a few inches of snow had already fallen, blanketing the trees in the Rogue Valley.

Mama came home one afternoon with an early holiday gift—a Lowrey electric organ she had picked up on extended credit from Ms. Pearl at the Music Shop. To the left of the keys were colored plastic levers you could flip to play different beats at various tempos—Latin, rock, swing, polka, and waltz. It was like having a one-man orchestra, and the mind-blowing technology housed in this wooden console stirred our passions, keeping the spark of music alive in all of us.

The most exciting thing about that Christmas, though, was Ricardo coming home from Keesler Air Force Base in Biloxi, Mississippi, where he had been stationed after basic training. On a chilly winter's day, Mary drove us younger ones to the airport in Medford to pick him up. We stood in the cold, watching the plane as it taxied down the runway. As my brother made his way toward us, I could see that his mustache had matured. So had he.

Only six months had passed since he had left us, yet it was clear he had become a man. I watched him in awe and wondered if that would ever happen to me. On the drive home, he shared his latest adventures with us. We sat glued to our seats, soaking up every last detail as snow pelted the windshield.

Bobby asked what it was like to be in boot camp. I asked what it was like to be on his own, all the way in Mississippi, and whether he liked it or not. We bombarded him with questions until we turned up Sleepy Hollow Loop, where we sat quietly waiting for him to get his first glimpse of the property.

A look of astonishment came over his face the moment we pulled in front of our new house. It was painted a butterscotch color with cream trim. Below the living room window, we had planted a few bushes, filling the empty space with bark mulch, just like the nice homes with actual landscaping. With each step toward our new home, Ricardo's eyes grew wider and beamed brighter.

Mama had gone all out for his homecoming and bought a real Christmas tree. We decorated it with colored blinking lights and a gingerbread-man ornament Lisa made at school. We finished it off with a gold garland and strands of silver tinsel. Underneath was a ceramic display of the nativity and a stash of wrapped presents.

Like a butler, I held the front door open for our honored guest. When he crossed the threshold, Mama was there, ready to embrace the son she had missed so dearly. After giving him a big hug, she grabbed his hand excitedly and took him on a tour.

I followed closely, not wanting to miss out on all the fuss. The house meant so much to all of us, especially to him, because he had worked so hard over the years to improve our living conditions. Now that he was witnessing Mama's dream come to life, his face was filled with sheer delight.

The entire family was back together that Christmas Eve, which warmed my soul in a way I can't put into words, even now. With the fragrance of Douglas fir filling the room, we gathered around the electric organ. Mama plunked out a few carols, while the rest of us joined in the singing.

Following our annual tradition, Mary handed her our family Bible, and Mama read the Christmas story. Ricardo added a reading of *The Night before Christmas*. Afterward, he reached into his duffel bag and handed out small gifts to everyone, saving the last one for me. It was a slightly larger box wrapped in shiny red paper.

I tore off the wrapping, opened the heavy box, and found myself staring at a slate-gray BB gun. Bobby and I looked at each other in disbelief. The expression on Mama's face was one of terror. "*Ay, Dios mío,*" she said while making the sign of the cross.

"He's the man of the house now," Ricardo said to her. "I want him to feel that way."

I couldn't stop smiling.

Mama had set the thermostat to a cozy temperature as the smell of Pillsbury cookies sweetened the air. With Perry Como's Christmas album playing, then *Miracle on 34th Street* showing on television, we spent the rest of the night in our soft flannel pajamas, sipping Nestlé's hot chocolate and playing Monopoly in front of the shimmering Christmas tree.

While everyone else was busy adding up their assets, from Boardwalk to Park Place, Mama set down a plate of warm cookies. For years we had played the game, dreaming of the day we would own a real home, a day when we would all be warm and fed. Now we were living that dream. It was better than Park Place. It was *our* place. How far we had come from living in our car, rationing slices of Wonder Bread.

The house bubbled over with love and laughter, just like the old days, all of us talking over one another, trying to gain the attention of the room while playing with Mary and Armando's young children in the middle of all the chaos. On account of Mama infusing our lives with sentimentality, we spent much of the night reminiscing as we flipped through one photo album after another. With the snow falling softly in front of the bay window, Mary pulled out her Super 8 projector. As images flickered on the screen, we lost ourselves in the wistful nostalgia of days gone by.

Memories were everything for us. At that moment, though, I had no idea we were making new ones. No idea this would be our last Christmas together. No idea of the depth to which it would entrench itself. In us. In me.

While the lights twinkled from the tree and the star we made from tinfoil glistened, Mama watched us from the couch. Her chicks had come home to roost, and it seemed she couldn't possibly be more fulfilled. The house was saturated with her love, reminiscent of her past, and redolent of the hopes she held for our future.

As long as Ricardo was home, I felt the weight lift from my shoulders. I savored every moment I had with him. I didn't want him to ever leave. But he would soon fly to Thailand for his first duty assignment. And I knew this lightness of being would not last. I would have to go back to being the man of the house. I knew that too. Already I felt something of the weight returning to rest on my shoulders.

The day Ricardo left for Asia was one of the saddest of my life. Early that morning, before the sun was up, we had a man-to-man talk in the kitchen over a bowl of Apple Jacks.

"It's your job to protect Mama and the family now," he said, grabbing my new BB gun off the table and placing it in my hand. "Keep this by your bed and be ready to pull it out at any time."

"But it's only a BB gun."

"It looks like a real handgun. No one will know the difference. Hopefully, you'll never have to use it, but you have to be ready just in case."

I was hoping I would never have to pull it out for anything other than shooting at cans with Bobby. After my hypervigilant brother gave me some final instructions on what to expect as head of the household, he placed a military medallion around my neck. With his hand on my shoulder, he spoke a blessing over me the way they did in Biblical times. It was a special moment between us. With that blessing, he passed the family baton to me. I felt empowered.

At the airport, I clung to him, not wanting him to go, but I held back my tears until he walked through the gate. Then I ran to the bathroom, where no one could see, and let it all out.

That snowy evening, as we drove past the somber woods toward home, I wished we could go back to the way it was at Christmas. I wished the Rockwellian gathering of our family would never end, that we would all stay together, gathered under the new roof of our new house, which felt like a home, with fir-scented air and the taste of Mama's cookies.

My mother, Maria, came from a powerful diplomatic family in Mexico City. But one fateful day, her family went from riches to rags. *From author's collection.*

My grandfather Antonio Islas-Bravo served in the Mexican Army and fought in the Mexican revolution alongside Pancho Villa and Emiliano Zapata. Later he battled over many important social issues as one of Mexico's most revered supreme court justices from 1941 to 1947. *From author's collection.*

My father abandoned me when I was six months old. The only thing he left me was a set of bongos. Here, my destiny dangles beneath my feet. *From author's collection.*

The only family portrait with Mama and all seven of us kids taken in 1967. I'm the little tyke in the bottom right-hand corner. From left to right, top to bottom: Mary, Armando, Mama, Patricia, Ricardo, Lisa, Bobby, and me. *From author's collection.*

Mama and "the magnificent seven." I'm the one front and center with the Grinch Who Stole Christmas look on my face. I was up to a lot of shenanigans back then. *From author's collection.*

My fierce and fun-loving family shortly after arriving in Grants Pass, Oregon. Through all of life's battles, we were there for each other. Our bond was unbreakable. I'm the one on the right, wearing a baggy shirt. *From author's collection.*

Wearing the T-shirt I won at the watermelon-eating contest in Riverside Park with Bobby and Patricia. *From author's collection.*

Celebrating Ricardo's fourteenth birthday during our first fall in Grants Pass, Oregon, in 1971. From left to right: Lisa, Bobby, Patricia, Ricardo, Mama, and me. *From author's collection.*

Giving Mama a kiss on Christmas morning. The holidays were a fun and chaotic time for our family, and Mama always scrimped and saved to get us the best gifts she could. *From author's collection.*

Bobby and I atop Bolt Mountain on one of our many boyhood adventures. *From author's collection.*

Bobby, Lisa, and me with our three-legged dog, Lobo. Our malicious neighbors shot her leg off. Then she gave birth to pups. Nothing could stop Lobo. *From author's collection.*

Mama and me with our rooster Brutus at the rooster-crowing contest in Rogue River, Oregon. I'm about thirteen years old here. *From author's collection.*

On your first day as a high school senior in rural Oregon, make sure you arrive wearing a fur coat. You'll fit right in. Promise. *From author's collection.*

Meeting my father for the first time, the day before my high school graduation in 1980. *From author's collection.*

For years one of Mama's dreams was to become a US citizen. She finally achieved this in 1999 at the age of sixty-nine. *From author's collection.*

The last photo of Mama and me in 2003. Her bright light from within is still shining. You never know when it will be your last photo with a loved one. *From author's collection.*

Six years after Mama passed, "the magnificent seven" posed in the same order as our original 1967 family portrait. *From author's collection.*

My amazing and vivacious sister Patricia has been one of the great blessings in my life. She is beautiful inside and out. *From author's collection.*

Maria's legacy continues, as shown by this 2010 family reunion. Her ethnically diverse family continues to grow and make positive contributions to this great nation. It's much larger now! *From author's collection.*

Undeniably the best part of my life: my wife Renée, daughter Jordan, and son Jarod. Family is everything. *From author's collection.*

My mother, Maria, in her glory days in Mexico. She was a budding actress before my six siblings and I came along and changed the trajectory of her life forever. Her spirit lives within my heart every day, and I still wear scarves to honor her memory. *From author's collection.*

Performing with Stevie Wonder. *From author's collection.*

Behind Philip Bailey of Earth, Wind & Fire during our soundcheck. *From author's collection.*

Ready to lay down the beat with New Edition at the National Mall in Washington, DC, before a sea of humanity. *From author's collection.*

Mama, all smiles backstage with Ricky Bell, myself, my niece Lydia, and my nephew Anthony after our New Edition concert in Los Angeles. *From author's collection.*

One of my teen pinups from a fan magazine in the mid-1980s. I imagined a lot of things as a kid, but never being a teen idol. Life is full of surprises! *From author's collection.*

Backstage with New Edition for a photo op. *From author's collection.*

Live with Bobby Brown on the Don't Be Cruel tour at the height of his career. *Photo by Chris Mackie.*

5 BIG PRIZES:
Here's your chance to enter the

WIN A DATE WITH ZORO CONTEST!

Wanna find out what it's really like being the drummer for one of America's hottest groups? Now here's your chance to find out from none other than Zoro himself!

The winner will spend a fun-filled evening with the young Gemini drummer that won't easily be forgotten! And don't worry—you don't have to live near Hollywood to win this date. Zoro travels all over the country and your date (if you win) will be coordinated near the city he's visiting while on tour.

Zoro has a wonderful evening planned for the winner and, if possible, it will be played out something like this. First you'll attend a concert by another famous group with Zoro, then out for a night on the town and, finally, off to dinner for some conversation where you'll get to find out just what it takes to make it in show business. The memories of the evening will linger on long past that magical evening.

FOUR OTHER GREAT PRIZES for runners-up in the contest:

1) A pair of Zoro's specially lighted drumsticks with signature on them.
2) An autographed picture, poster and T-shirt of Zoro and FREE membership to Zoro's personal fan club.
3) One of Zoro's prized hats from his personal collection; and his favorite Spanish earring.
4) An autographed poster of New Edition along with a copy of the *All For Love* album and their new book *Cool It Now, The Story of the New Edition*.

Sound too good to be true? Well, it's for real and you may be one of the lucky 5 winners if you send in your entry today. (Please don't delay as the drawing will take place the next time Zoro's in Los Angeles.)

To enter, simply fill out a postcard with your name, address, city, state, zip code, age, and phone number and send it **immediately** to; Zoro Contest, FRESH!, P.O. Box 91878, Los Angeles CA 90009.

5 winners will be chosen at random by Zoro himself sometime during the month of September (his schedule permitting). —Good Luck—

FRESH! 37

Fresh! magazine ran a "Win a Date with Zoro" contest. Another surprise in a life filled with twists and turns. *From author's collection.*

A young Lenny Kravitz and me in Central Park at the start of his 1989 Let Love Rule tour. *Photo courtesy of Stephen Salmieri.*

Ready to hit the stage with Mick Jagger and Lenny Kravitz at Wembley Stadium in London. *From author's collection.*

Mama in front of the Frankie Valli and the Four Seasons marquee in Las Vegas. She was thrilled I was playing for one of her favorite groups! *From author's collection.*

With Frankie Valli just before a show. *From author's collection.*

Rocking out with Lenny Kravitz somewhere in Europe. *From author's collection.*

CYRUS BOLOOKI • GET UP KIDS

MODERN DRUMMER

The World's Most Widely Read Drum Magazine

September 2004

Lenny Kravitz & Zoro
Let Drums Rule!

CLARENCE PENN
JAZZ MASTER

WOODSHEDDING WITH
HORACIO "EL NEGRO" HERNANDEZ

JEAN-PAUL GASTER OF CLUTCH

THE DRUMMERS OF CIRQUE DU SOLEIL

PLUS
METRIC MODULATION, LISTENING FOR OLD K'S, AND 16 ESSENTIAL TIPS FOR TEACHERS

www.moderndrummer.com

$4.99US $6.99CAN

0 74808 01203 9

I've been fortunate to grace the covers of numerous drum magazines worldwide, but *Modern Drummer* with Lenny Kravitz was a dream come true for both of us. I was thrilled Mama saw it just before she passed. She was so proud! *Photo by Alex Solca, courtesy of Modern Drummer magazine.*

Seafaring with Microsoft cofounder Paul Allen aboard his megayacht, the *Octopus*. *From author's collection.*

In 2013 I was honored at the White House for promoting responsible fatherhood and mentoring as part of President Barack Obama's "Champions of Change" initiative. *From author's collection.*

Backstage at *The Tonight Show* with Jimmy Fallon before performing a drum solo. Jimmy is one of the nicest guys you could ever meet. He offered me his pizza, but I didn't have the heart to take it from him. *From author's collection.*

A blissful moment in the heat of battle doing one of the things I was put on this planet to do: bring people joy through the gift of rhythm! *From author's collection.*

Another passion of mine is being a motivational speaker who inspires others. *Photo courtesy of Protiusmime Photography.*

Lenny Kravitz and me today. Our forty-four-year friendship is still going strong! *From author's collection.*

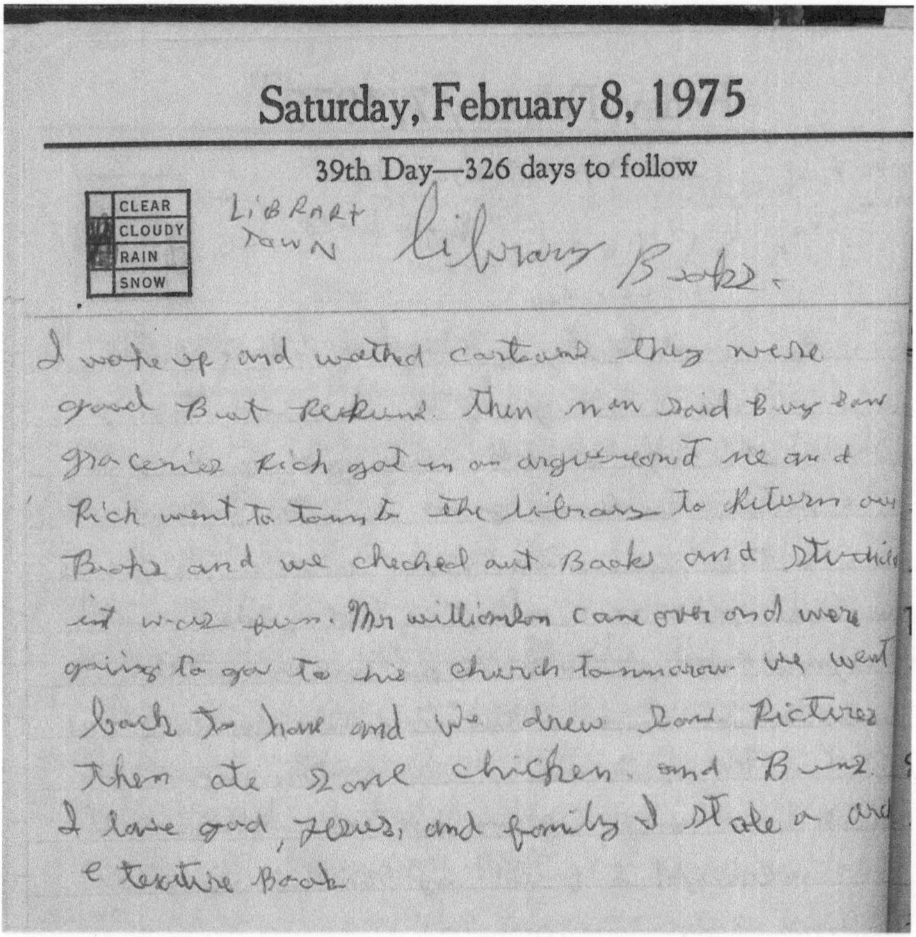

Saturday, February 8, 1975

39th Day—326 days to follow

CLEAR
CLOUDY
RAIN
SNOW

LiBRARt TowN library Books.

I woke up and watched cartoons they were good But reckun Then mom said Buy som groceries Rich got in an argument me and Rich went to town to the library to Return our Books and we checked out Books and studied it was fun. Mr williomon came over and were going to go to his church tommorow we went back to home and we drew some Pictures then ate some chicken and Buns. I love god, Jesus, and family I stole a an e texture Book

A page from my 1975 diary. The last line is the most telling: "I love God, Jesus, and family . . . I stole an architecture book." *From author's collection.*

Ads like this lured me with the hopes of winning a bicycle! *From author's collection.*

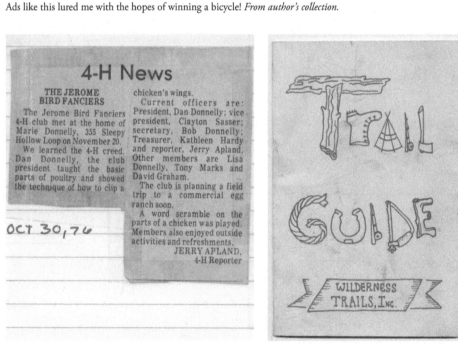

Grants Pass Daily Courier clipping on the Jerome Prairie Bird Fanciers. Seeing my name in the newspaper for the first time was exciting! *From author's collection.*

Trail Guide booklet from the Wilderness Trails camp. I still have it after nearly fifty years! *From author's collection.*

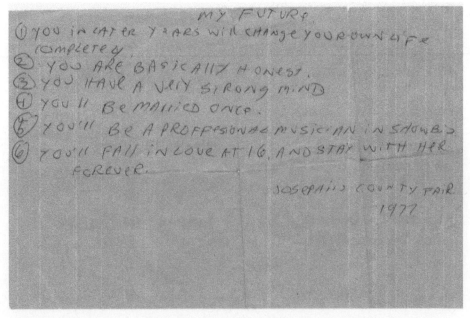

DEATHS OR LOSSES							ACCOUNT No. POULTRY	
DATE	ITEMS	POST. REF.	DEBIT	DATE	ITEMS	POST. REF.	CREDIT
5/4/76	CORNISH X 2 PULLETS SET+inG	3	LOST	10/2/76	PULLET WHITE LEGHORN	1	UNKNOW
5/21/76	1 N.H. PULLET	1	LOST	10/2/76	COCK+2 ARAUCANA	1	UNKNOWN
7/1/76	1 W.L. PULLET	1	STEPPED ON KILLED				
7/19/76	1 W.L. PULLET	1	NEW MONIA				
8/4/76	1 CORNISH X COCK	1	HEART TROUBLE				
8/19/76	1 R.I.R PULLET	1	UNKNOWN				
9/16/76	1 ARAUCANA COCK	1	UNKNOWN				
9/9/76	1 WHITE LEGHORN	1	SMASHED				
9/9/76	1 ARAACANA	1	NEVER CAME OUT OF EGG SHELL				
9/11/76	2 ARAANA	2	not UNDER DEVELOPED				
9/22/76	1 ARAUcana Chick		UNKNOWN				
9/28/76	1 ARAUCANA Chick		UNKNOWN				
9/28/76	ARA CANA Chicks		UNKNOWN				

The "death or losses" column from my chicken ledger, affectionally known as "the Chicken Diaries." I misspelled pneumonia as "New Monia." *From author's collection.*

MY FUTURE

1. YOU IN LATER YEARS WILL CHANGE YOUR OWN LIFE COMPLETELY.
2. YOU ARE BASICALLY HONEST.
3. YOU HAVE A VERY STRONG MIND.
4. YOU'LL BE MARRIED ONCE.
5. YOU'LL BE A PROFFESIONAL MUSICIAN IN SHOWBIS
6. YOU'LL FALL IN LOVE AT 16, AND STAY WITH HER FOREVER.

JOSEPHINE COUNTY FAIR
1977

A vision statement I wrote at age fifteen while working at the Josephine County Fair in Grants Pass, Oregon. *From author's collection.*

The

ROGUE RIVER
ROOSTER CROW

Contest

"Last Saturday in June"

**You're Always Welcome
in
Rogue River
Oregon**

NATIONAL ROOSTER CROWING CONTEST

Sponsored by the Rogue River Jaycees

Brochure from the Rooster Crow Contest we entered in Rogue River, Oregon. It still happens every year! *From author's collection.*

RECEIPT Date 2-28 19 81   2006

Received From DAN DONNELLY

Address

Dollars $ 10.00

For DRUM LESSON

ACCOUNT		HOW PAID		
AMT OF ACCOUNT		CASH	10.	
AMT PAID		CHECK		
BALANCE DUE		MONEY ORDER		By Ralph Johnson

8K808 REDIFORM®

The receipt from my first drum lesson with Ralph Johnson of Earth, Wind & Fire. *From author's collection.*

★★★

Disco Dan shoots for stardom

By Bryan Osterhout

"The drums are my life," says senior Dan Donnelly better known as "Disco Dan".

Donnelly a transfer from Los Angeles has been playing the drums for a year and a half, and many feel this is quite an accomplishment in such a short time.

Oddly enough Donnelly first got interested in the drums when superstar Elvis Presley died. "He really inspired my drum playing," said Donnelly. "I believe Elvis's dedication to music has rubbed off on me." Donnelly presently practices about three hours a day. Although these practice sessions will last as long as five hours this summer.

Donnelly's favorite music is Jazz. He also likes Rock n' Roll, but believes progressive music is his first love. Dan has an interest in disco too. "I like to play disco music, but I'd much rather dance to it," said the energetic drummer.

Donnelly doesn't suggest playing the drums, unless you have some money to spend. "I first started out working sixteen hours a day," he said with some relief. "But now I've got almost all my equipment paid for." When asked what his total cost for his equipment was, Donnelly silently answered. "About $8,000."

Dan believes his biggest problem was coming from Los Angeles and adapting to the different styles of life; "Many people believed I was weird," he said disappointedly. "But once I got a few friends, I felt a lot better," he said smiling. "Although many students think he is different, we all really like him," said senior Darren Rice. "He's just different," said Bonnie Muncie. "But I like the fact that he is so nice to everybody," she said.

When asked what his plans are after graduation, Donnelly says, "I hope to tour the United States this summer, then go on to college and major in music and percussion." He plans to tour the U.S. with his father, another well respected drummer.

Many people believe the chances of becoming a successful drummer are small, but not Donnelly. He says, "Hey maybe it's going to be hard but isn't that what it's all about." "If I work hard I'll make it," he said with a certain confidence.

It might be that his professional career is a dream. But if you asked Donnelly he'll say that you're wrong.

Senior Dan Donnelly shows the students of North that he really knows how to make his set of drums hum during a recent one man concert in the student lounge.

★★★

My first feature article appeared in my high school newspaper during my senior year at North Eugene High School in Eugene, Oregon—a sign of things to come. *From author's collection.*

Fantasy Productions

Proudly Presents

WAVE
IN CONCERT

FRIDAY, DECEMBER 3, 1982 — 8:00 P.M.

BEVERLY HILLS HIGH, K. L. PETERS AUDITORIUM
421 SOUTH MORENO DRIVE, BEVERLY HILLS, CALIFORNIA

ADMIT TWO

№ 2051

A ticket stub from my performance at Beverly Hills High School with Wave, a band I was in with my pal, Lenny Kravitz. This was our first concert together, with many more to follow! *From author's collection.*

CHAPTER 25

Ain't Nobody Here but Us Chickens

One day Mama drove Bobby and me out to John and Bruce Donovan's house in Williams, near the Applegate River. These classmates of mine had gained quite a reputation by raising show birds. I had always thought a chicken was a chicken—good for eggs and for frying but not much else. They seemed dirty and messy to me, all scraggly and feathery, and far too nervous to be much of a pet.

All that changed when I saw the Donovans' menagerie. With over two acres under wire and more than two hundred species of exotic fowl, it was like the United Nations of birds. Every shape, color, and nationality was represented, like dignitaries from all around the world convening to discuss matters of importance to the avian world.

As the boys proudly showed us their compound, Mama leaned over and whispered to me, "You and Bobby could do this. I know you could." When she saw the spark of excitement in my eyes, she started asking them questions. "How much does chicken feed cost? How often do they lay eggs? How much do you sell a dozen eggs for?"

While she was learning from the brothers, a dream was being hatched in my mind. Out of the eggshells came dollar bills!

We bought a hen and a rooster from them that day, which set in motion a new obsession. With the same affection people name a cat or dog, we dubbed our feathered friends Henny Penny and Sergeant. Henny was a butterscotch color, almost like a tabby cat. Sergeant was all scratch and strut, a beige and bronze military man from comb to claw.

It was no mystery that hens laid eggs, and we couldn't wait for Henny Penny to present us with her first offering. But after feeding her for a good month, our malfunctioning bird had yet to lay a single one. We decided to sell our money pit to someone who would make an eight-piece McNuggets special out of her. On a drizzly fall day, we set out to catch her. But chasing chickens was not as easy as we thought, and for ten minutes she outran both Bobby and me.

Chickens are considered animals of low intelligence. I would have agreed, until something happened that changed my opinion. With the fierceness of a bounty hunter, I pursued Henny Penny in the pelting rain. Eventually I managed to grab a clump of her sopping feathers and pin her down. I was about to hand her over to our buyer, when she looked back at me with her beady eyes, and *voil*à! She laid an egg. It was one of the most freakish things I had ever witnessed. It was as if she had a sixth sense. Like she knew she was about to be a chicken sandwich if she didn't produce.

Her egg was shaped like all other chicken eggs, but instead of being white or brown, the shell was deep olive green. Despite its odd color, we were thrilled to get our first egg. Of course, after such an ineffable moment, we couldn't just get rid of her. From then on, Henny Penny became the star of the show, laying an egg every day.

We were eager to learn more, so we went to see Mrs. Dubaroy, a local chicken whisperer with gray hair and a red face. She taught us how to keep our birds healthy and sold us two more hens and another rooster. This rooster had a lustrous black neckline with a green sheen, piercing black eyes, and striking multicolored tail feathers. He pranced around like a proud Indian chief, so we named him Cochise after the famous Apache war leader. The two hens went nameless, but they followed Henny Penny's example and laid eggs every day, which increased our sales.

With our meager profits, we went to Albers Feed and Farm Supply and bought some baby chicks. At home we put them in a tall box in our bathroom and attached a brooder light to keep them warm. We ripped open the bag of chick starter, which smelled of ground corn, grabbed a scoopful, and scattered it in the box. In no time they were able to fly to the top of the box and roost on the edges. Now it was time to send them into the chicken coop to meet the five birds who ran the place—Henny Penny, Sergeant, Cochise, and the two unnamed hens.

Noticing our devotion to this new adventure, Patricia gave us thirty-two dollars to buy an incubator from the *Sears Farm and Ranch Catalog*. We quickly learned it took twenty-one days for the fertilized eggs to hatch, and we eagerly watched three baby chicks peck their way out of their shells and into our lives. We wanted to learn more, so we started a 4-H club with some of the kids from our area.

At the county extension office, we learned that the four *H*s stood for *Head, Heart, Hands*, and *Health*. The club's motto was "To make the best better," and its slogan was "Learn by doing." We wanted to do both, so we checked out a movie projector, a screen, and a few short 16 mm films to show at the first meeting of the Jerome Prairie Bird Fanciers.

Tony Marks, who raised homing pigeons, brought a few of his birds to a meeting and let them loose. We couldn't believe they knew how to fly back to his house. Tony shared a wealth of useful information and gave us a catalog from "*Murray McMurray Hatchery: The World's Rare Breed Poultry Headquarters*." Together, Bobby and I pored over the listings of more than sixty-seven varieties of chickens. The first one that caught our eye was so fluffy even its claws were covered in white fluff. "Cochin Bantams," I read aloud.

"We got to get us some of those," Bobby said.

I agreed as I dog-eared the page and turned to the next one. With their full, feathery crests, the Golden Polish were the most fascinating to look at.

"They gotta be kidding!" Bobby remarked. "Easter Egg Chickens?"

"Ar-au-cana," I said, having trouble pronouncing the name. "Says they're from an Indian tribe in Chile."

"Look at 'em!" Bobby said, his eyes wide with awe as he pointed to the drawing of pink, blue, and olive eggs. "Henny Penny must be one of those Araucanas."

That was it. The wheels in my head started churning. As soon as we earned enough money, we were going to place our first order with Murray McMurray. Then the world would beat a path to buy our colored eggs, and we wouldn't be poor anymore. And once we were successful, no one would look down on us.

I took out a piece of paper and sketched a sign with my pencil that read, "D&B Poultry Produce Co."

I pointed to the D and said, "Danny." Then to the B. "And Bobby." I smiled and extended my hand. "Partners?"

Bobby shook my hand as I pulled him to his feet. "Partners," he said with a smile, then hugged me.

We spent the rest of the afternoon making a sign from leftover plywood. Then we painted our company logo on it, along with the prices of our eggs. We were officially in business.

In preparation for our expansion, we built bigger coops, relying on the methods Ricardo had taught us for salvaging scrap materials and constructing the buildings on our own. Every night we thumbed through the catalog and placed check marks by all the breeds we wanted to buy. The cost of each chick ranged from twenty-five cents to upwards of a dollar for the more exotic breeds. After we made our final selections, we sent in the yellow order form with a down payment of $5.45. Then we eagerly awaited the arrival of forty-six baby chicks.

Soon, the mailman came to our door carrying a cardboard box with little holes punched in the lid. A high-pitched chirping sound came from inside, where all forty-six baby birds clustered together. Breeds with exotic names like Salmon Faverolles, Blue Andalusians, Egyptian Fayoumis, and many more. We paid the mailman the balance of $34.25 in cash. Then we took our fluffy little treasures inside the house, where we had prepared a brooder for their homecoming.

Nearing fifteen years old, I was finally going into a legitimate business. No more swindling the greeting card and seed packet companies.

No more conning kids out of twenty-five cents for fake judo lessons. No more sending for get-rich-quick schemes in the mail. I would make my millions in chicken commodities and do it with good, old-fashioned, honest, hard work.

Given over to the idea that I would one day become the world's greatest chicken farmer, I immersed myself in the study of poultry husbandry. Two books, *Raising Poultry the Modern Way* and *Commercial Poultry Raising*, became my life manuals, with earmarked pages and highlighted facts.

I also kept a detailed ledger with organized columns to track the livestock inventory and the cost of supplies, as well as tallies for the number of eggs laid, eggs sold, and chicks hatched each day. Periodically I would conduct a census of each breed. But the most illuminating entry of all was my "death and losses column."

According to my childhood ledger, which affectionately became known as "the Chicken Diaries," the causes of death included the following:

Lost. Some disappeared into the woods and never came back.
Stepped on. Occasionally, someone would accidentally step on a baby chick.
Smashed. Mama accidentally ran over one she couldn't see.
Never Came Out of Eggshell / Underdeveloped. A baby chick who never fully hatched.
Unknown. Occasionally, one of my chickens would go from cackling to croaking, and I had no idea how they bought the farm. It was a conundrum.

As a self-proclaimed veterinarian, though, I once diagnosed the cause of death in two of my esteemed birds as heart trouble and pneumonia, only I spelled the latter "New Monia"—no doubt a result of my frequent school absences.

Although I loved each of my birds in the same way one might love their horses, my personal favorite was a muscular rooster with rich mahogany plumage named King. The Adonis of Rhode Island Reds, his shiny saddle feathers shimmered in the sunlight as he strutted around with his large red comb and wattles. But despite his outward beauty, King had a slight character flaw: he was vicious, so much so that his previous owner had kept him bound to a metal stake with a thick, long chain. We eventually discovered that King had attacked the neighbor's three-year-old daughter, which is why he had offloaded his enraged jailbird on us.

King had a rap sheet about as long as his tail feathers and was rumored to have survived a dog attack by fighting off a stray with his three-and-a-half-inch spurs. "That dog went away limping and never came back," the neighbor said, sure he had raised the toughest bird around. To feed our savage beast took a bit of military planning. Every day, I would enter his private cellblock and beat him back with a broom while Bobby put feed and water in his bowl.

Bobby and I were so enthralled with our fine feathered friends that after cleaning out their coops, we would lie on our stomachs from a distance and just observe them. Then later, with a pair of binoculars, I would sit up on the roof and observe the politics of the henhouse, scoping out which birds were doing what and trying to figure out why.

Even though she was happy that I had found so much pleasure in raising chickens, Mama began to worry about my fowl play. "*¡Ay, Dan-yell!*" Why are you staring at those birds all day long? At your age, you should be chasing after girls instead of chickens."

The truth was that I was out-of-my-mind crazy about girls. Infatuated with a few at school, in fact. But I was so insecure I lacked the confidence to pursue any of them. Chasing chickens was hard, but chasing after girls with expectations of dating one seemed impossible.

In addition to every other form of awkwardness known to junior high boys, looming over me was the low opinion that most kids had of me at school, a fact that further undermined my self-esteem. The time for girls had not yet come. It was also hard for me to believe that one would ever love me for *any* reason. People were complicated; chickens were easy.

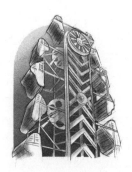

CHAPTER 26

Take the Money and Run

In small-town America, people have to dream up a variety of pastimes to keep from going stir-crazy. We had the Rooster Crow Contest. The game was simple. The rooster who crowed the most in thirty minutes was the winner. Since 1953, eager contestants would flock to the quaint town of Rogue River to enter this regional event.

After Mama told us about it, Bobby and I looked at each other and blurted out at the same time, "Brutus." Brutus, our Barred Rock rooster, woke us up bright and early every morning. We figured he had a good shot at winning the contest since he crowed incessantly and could beat the long-standing record of Beetlebaum, who crowed 109 times in thirty minutes. No one had broken his record since 1953. If Brutus did, we would win the trophy and $150, which we could use to buy more chickens.

Around 8:00 a.m. on the last Saturday of June, we put him in a cage and threw him in the back of the car. On our way to the event, he crowed nonstop. "Good boy, Brutus, keep up that crowing," Bobby said.

At the park, Mama filled out our entry form while we unloaded our superstar and carried him through the park. Along the way, people pointed at us and stared. With his sharply defined zebralike feathers and a chest like Arnold Schwarzenegger, Brutus was a mighty hand-some bird. But when it came to crowing, size and looks didn't matter.

At 3:30 the bell rang. Now Brutus would show the world what he could do. With his neck stretched into the air, he was off to a great start, crowing proudly. With all the roosters egging each other on, it sounded like a store full of cuckoo clocks going off at the same time.

While we stood cheering Brutus on, I wondered how the judges could keep track of their tallies with all the noise. But amid the cacophony, I began to discern the intricacy of compound rhythms. Rhythms within rhythms. Like a military drum line, the symphony of percussive crows became pleasant, at least to me. The crowing no longer sounded like random noise; it was ordered chaos, and as I attuned my ear to their patterns of communication, I felt as if I had been given the key to understanding a secret language. Lost in the cock-a-doodle-dooing of the roosters, I failed to notice that our rooster was showing signs of fatigue.

After the whistle blew, the judges tallied up the crows and announced the winner. It wasn't Brutus. One of the main judges, a short man with a limp, came over to us. "Boys, I take it this is your first time entering the contest?"

Bobby and I both nodded.

"Well, how about I let you in on a little secret?"

We nodded again.

"First off, you have to get your rooster in his cage when it's still dark outside—four thirty in the morning is best."

Bobby and I lobbed glances at each other. This was news to us.

"Then you throw a blanket around the cage so he still thinks it's dark."

We looked at each other again, this time with bigger eyes.

"Most importantly, don't remove the cover until the contest starts. As soon as the bell rings, yank off the cover so your rooster thinks it's sunrise. Then he'll start crowing like he usually does. You're just tricking him, really."

"No wonder everyone was staring and laughing at us," I said. "Our cage didn't have a cover."

"Oh, well, don't take offense to it," the man said. "They meant you no harm."

"Now that you boys know what to do, maybe next year you'll win," Mama said to us, ever hopeful.

With the county fair fast approaching, we had only two months to learn everything we needed to place well. Up to this point, the Donovan brothers had taken home all the top honors and prize money. We were determined to break their winning streak. I drilled Bobby and Lisa on the parts of the chicken, we practiced the proper way to show a bird, and we went over what the judges would be looking for. We even took a field trip to a commercial egg ranch to learn more. By the time August rolled around, we were eager for the Jerome Prairie Bird Fanciers to squawk louder than our rivals, the Crows and Quacks.

The Josephine County Fair was rated number one in the state. To celebrate its sixty-seventh birthday, the organizers went all out with teen dances, live music, a horse show, a greased pig contest, a livestock auction, and even a logging show. Clear blue skies and hot temperatures greeted us as we walked through the black iron gates on opening morning with the dense and suffocating crowds. Colorful flowers filled the planters of the entryway, and fragrant cedars lined the A-frame exhibit halls, where red, white, and blue bunting hung on display.

After weaving through booths filled with jellies, jams, and jars of every food imaginable, we were drawn to the commercial exhibit building by the hums of an electric organ. We followed the sound past a fleet of brand-new John Deere tractors to a balding man playing "Summer Samba." I quickly became hypnotized by the percussive nature of the Brazilian patterns. After his final crescendo, we made our way past a corridor of quilts to the fruit and vegetable exhibits, where we gazed upon the biggest pumpkin and tallest sunflower we had ever seen.

With the smell of cotton candy and hot buttered popcorn tempting our taste buds, the competition for our affections was thick. But it would be the sugary smell of funnel cakes that ended up extracting our loose change from our pockets. While devouring our sinfully sweet confections, we walked the hot asphalt midway toward the cows, hogs, horses, and sheep—animals we hoped to raise someday too.

Each of those creatures had its own distinct odor. So did the food they ate. Some chewed on grain. Others munched on freshly cut hay. There were many smells and so many sounds, with a cadence to them all. The scrape of shovels against the pavement. The powerful spray of water hosing down livestock. The swishing of grain as it spilled into metal troughs. An entire concerto of harmonious rhythms.

Part of my responsibility as 4-H leader was to sell corn dogs at our booth as a fundraiser. I took the shift at dusk. From the back side of that little white building, I could see the shadowy outlines of people scrambling to get their seats in the grandstand, where Ricky Nelson was scheduled to perform. Even though I was happy just to be at the fair with Bobby and our chickens, there was a longing in me to be up on the stage too.

As the sun set, the rides began to glimmer in various pulses of pink, white, red, blue, and green. The Radar, the Scrambler, and the old classic Tilt-a-Whirl came to life. The more adventurous teens screamed on the Zipper, while others took in the view from the neon Ferris wheel. And safely on the ground, parents proudly watched their precious little ones galloping on the merry-go-round.

With the electric sparks flying, the bumper cars beckoned, and I wanted to try my hand at the ring toss too, but I was stuck working the booth, watching all the other kids having fun. I envied them, but I envied the musicians on stage even more.

When the band kicked in, my bones hummed with the reverberation of the speakers. As the drums pounded in the distance, my spirit soared. I grabbed a small piece of scrap paper from between the relish and mustard. In a moment of inspiration, I wrote out some decrees about my future. When I finished, I folded up my future and tucked it in my pocket.

At the end of that first night, I lay in bed grave tired, but my mind wouldn't shut off. Our chickens looked fabulous, and we were well prepared. Still, I worried whether we stood half a chance to beat the Donovans. I remembered them showing me their newspaper clipping from the previous year that said, "Donovan Brothers Take All." With their experience and vast resources, was it possible to beat them in any category? Or was I entertaining delusions of grandeur once again?

The new school year would start in a few weeks. I would be in ninth grade, my last year at Lincoln Savage Junior High, and if I didn't win anything, my classmates would have yet another reason to make fun of me. So much was riding on the outcome. I just wanted to be a normal kid at the fair, but the pressure of needing the prize money, coupled with the intense desire to win something, was all-consuming. I was nervous and excited at the same time, eager for the fair to be over, yet never wanting it to end.

Despite my anxieties, we took in the splendor of the fair all week. Mama stopped by daily to encourage us with my niece Lydia, who also loved our chickens. They looked so proud, walking the aisles of the poultry hall, surveying all the chickens we had entered. Those four days went by so fast it felt as if they had never happened at all. But they did. And I would never forget them.

On closing day, I took home twenty-five first-place ribbons, two seconds, one third, and one fourth. Bobby and Lisa won a bunch themselves. Bobby even brought home the gold for showmanship, and Lisa for naming all the parts of the chicken. The Donovans stood stupefied, with their arms crossed, as we received our awards. Henny Penny's olive eggs earned a blue ribbon. Best of all, King managed to steal the blue ribbon for best Rhode Island Red rooster. Of course, the proud bird didn't look at all surprised.

I walked away with $75.50 in prize money, a handful of certificates and shiny satin ribbons, and a vision statement for my future. With the success of the poultry venture and our strong placement at the fair, life in the country was finally taking root in my heart. I was beginning to prosper, and I could see a future as the world's greatest chicken farmer. With any luck, maybe one day I would end up on the main stage at the fair, rocking out on the drums. And then, maybe my father would find me. I imagined he would beam with pride and pat me on the back with a hearty, "Way to go, son. Way to go!" After beating the Donovans, anything seemed possible.

I took out the crinkled piece of paper, unfolded it, and read it aloud.

My Future:
You in later years will change your own life completely.
You are basically honest.
You have a very strong mind.
You will be married once.
You'll be a professional musician in show biz.
You'll fall in love at 16 and stay with her forever.
I was fifteen, and as Ol' Blue Eyes would say, it was a very good year.

CHAPTER 27

I Will Survive

One day I stayed home from school to reattach some loose chicken wire to a fence post when a couple of hens slipped through the opening and strutted past Manny, a stray Saint Bernard we had recently taken in. Manny yanked his chain so hard he pulled the stake it was attached to out of the ground and bolted toward the chicken yard. I clung to his long chain and dug my heels into the ground, trying to hold him back, but he was too strong.

He found the breach in the fence and forced his way in. The frightened flock flapped their wings in a frenetic blur, trying to fly the coop. Manny dragged me behind him as he slaughtered chickens left and right until I could no longer hold on.

As dust and feathers filled the air, I wiped dirt from my eyes and turned to find Henny Penny clenched in his jaws. My number one egg layer was dead. Next, Manny went after Sergeant and Cochise. I managed to grab his tail for a second, but he quickly pulled away. After finishing them off, he barreled into the woods after the other escapees. I stood, looking at a battlefield of carcasses strewn about, then fell to my knees and wept.

When Bobby got off the school bus, he ran toward the war zone, his mouth agape. "What happened?" he yelled.

"That stray dog went ballistic," I said, wiping the dribble from under my nose.

We heard rustling from the woods behind our house as we sat on the ground, sobbing and trying to console one another. It was King. He stumbled out of the forest with a clump of feathers missing, but he was alive. Barely. The next sound was a familiar crowing, and out waddled a frazzled Brutus, bobbing and weaving his way toward us.

At the sight of those two bedraggled roosters, we burst out laughing. In the evening, Manny returned with claw marks across his face from his killing spree. Bobby and I looked at each other and smiled. We knew that could only be the work of King.

We sold King and Brutus along with our few surviving birds and equipment the following week. It was the end of D&B Poultry Produce Co. The end of the Jerome Prairie Bird Fanciers. And the end of my short-lived identity as the world's greatest chicken farmer.

Despite my mother's heritage and my older siblings, I didn't feel Mexican. And despite my father's blood, I didn't feel Irish. The luck they claimed as part of their culture certainly hadn't rubbed off on me. Growing up in Compton, I had felt more Black than anything. But I wasn't Black either. At least outwardly. I also wasn't white enough to be accepted by whites, nor Mexican enough to be embraced by Mexicans. Now that I was no longer a chicken farmer and had failed to make the football and wrestling teams, I was having an identity crisis.

Who was I?

My mother sensed my confusion. Like always, she rallied to my side, showering me with attention, affection, and affirmation. For once, though, her encouragement wasn't enough. She saw that I needed something to fill the emptiness, something that would build my self-assurance and put me on a new path. She came to my bedroom to try to tease a smile out of me. When I didn't budge, she said, "Now, don't forget the words to your favorite Earth, Wind & Fire song." Then she sang the four lines from the chorus of "Shining Star" to me.

I had no idea what my next adventure in life would be. No idea if I would find my true identity. No idea if I would ever become a shining star. All I knew was that I was grieving the loss of my chickens and feeling out of sorts over the passing of Elvis Presley, which had hit us all hard. I was desperate for something to lift my spirits. So I took a trip to the Music Shop to see Ms. Pearl.

Understanding my search for something more, she hired Bobby and me to do a variety of work. We spent our weekends helping her with yard work and polishing the spokes of her Jaguar and Lincoln Continental. One day she noticed me eyeing the drums in her store, as I had done so many times before. As if reading my thoughts, she said proudly, "Did you know Steve Miller buys his guitars from me? He lives right down the road in Williams and has a recording studio in his house. Maybe you'll run into him in the shop sometime."

"Wow! That would be so cool to meet him," I said. "'Fly Like an Eagle' is such a great song."

Ms. Pearl looked at me and smiled. "You're gonna make it big someday, Danny. I just know you are. You've always been such a hard worker, and you have more determination than any kid I have ever known. And trust me, I've known a lot of them in this town. Once you find your path, you'll go all the way."

"You think so?" I asked. Once she gave me a second boost of confidence, I was almost ready to believe her. "Well, you know what, Ms. Pearl? When I make it big, I'll get you front-row tickets for one of my concerts. I promise."

"Oh, I know you will." She laughed lovingly.

I was now in the tenth grade at Hidden Valley High School in the spring of 1978 when I saw one of the school drummers in the library. Out of the blue, I asked him, "Hey, Eden, you have any drums you want to sell?"

"Naw, not at the moment. But check with John Perkins."

John was another drummer from school. The next day after class, I waited for him outside the band room. "Hey, John, do you have any drums you'd be willing to sell me?"

"Maybe an old four-piece. But you'd have to wait until I get my new set in a couple months."

"How much?"

He hesitated, then said, "I don't know. Maybe a hundred bucks."

I had been saving up to buy my own drums. A hundred dollars would sting, but it was far less than the blue-sparkle drum set at the Music Shop. More importantly, it was a price I could afford. "Deal," I said, and we shook on it.

The first week of May, John and his mother dropped by our house to deliver the drums. I handed him $100, which was a large chunk of my hard-earned money. Then he and his mom helped me carry the set from the back of their truck into the garage. With the sunlight shimmering through the open door, I threw down a dusty throw rug on the concrete and began setting up. There were four drums in all, three wrapped in a tiger stripe covering.

I had waited so long for this moment. How many days had I stood at Ms. Pearl's window, dreaming of owning that sparkling blue drum set? How many hours had I worked in the Music Shop, beating out rhythms while other customers got to take the drums home? Now, finally having my very own felt like being reunited with a long-lost friend. After throwing the cymbals on the stands and attaching the foot pedal, I took a good long look at the drums. *My* drums. I sensed the significance of what was about to take place. I paused to relish the moment.

I remembered when I had banged on cans on the streets of Compton, when I had broken the toy drum set Mama had given me for Christmas, when I had played on the cardboard box at the talent show, and when I noodled around on Jeff's drums at Beverly and Bill's house. With my drumsticks in hand, I closed my eyes and smiled.

Then I pulled out the *Saturday Night Fever* album, dropped the needle on "Staying Alive," and began jamming along with the Bee Gees, trying my best to mimic the beat of their drummer Dennis Bryon. My spirit came alive. The feeling was so deep, so satisfying, so transcendent. So *me*! In the strangest way, though, I was afraid to fully give myself over to it. I feared it would be taken from me—like so many other important things in my life.

In an attempt to push back those fears, I put on the song "Shining Star" by Earth, Wind & Fire. Somewhere in the middle of that funky R&B jam, I found my groove. Even though it was my first day on the skins, I could see myself on stage, drumming my heart out for audiences around the world. I sang the lyrics with all my heart and soul, believing in their power to forge my destiny.

I felt powerful, weightless, like I was floating on air. My body knew what to do as if I had been doing it all along, and in the blur of arms, legs, and sticks, as I was grooving to EWF, it suddenly dawned on me, *Oh my god, I am playing the drums!*

CHAPTER 28

Gonna Fly Now

Now that I was able to envision myself as a star, the hard part was finding a way *to shine*, a way to rise above the crowd and take the stage. I spent hours staring off into space, imagining what it would be like under the bright lights. Much of this escapism took place on the long bus rides to and from school. The stunning landscapes of the Rogue Valley in springtime made for an easy drift into a world of wonderment as my hands drummed against my legs, the seat in front of me, the window—anything within reach.

One day my reverie was broken when I suddenly remembered my appointment with my guidance counselor, Mr. Baker. I wanted to see if he could help me find an after-school job to supplement my hours at the Music Shop.

Once at school, I darted past the other students to get to his office.

"What are you passionate about?" he asked. Mr. Baker was a stocky man who smiled a lot.

"Music, sir. I would love to do something that puts me around music."

"Give me about a week, and let me see what I can come up with."

A week later we met again.

Mr. Baker wasn't wearing his usual expression when he said, "I'm sorry to say, but the only job available is for a custodial position."

I had absolutely no interest in the job, but I needed the work and didn't want to appear ungrateful. "Where would it be?"

"Here at the school."

"Are you kidding me?"

"No, Danny. I wish I was." He strummed on his desk with one hand while he thumbed through his paperwork with the other. "Looks like it's a two-hour shift," he said, looking directly at me. "Can you start after school today?"

"Yes, sir, I can."

"Check in with Clarence Stone, and he'll go over everything with you. He's the head custodian here."

My first responsibility was vacuuming the library with an industrial-sized machine I called "Big Red." I felt embarrassed pushing it around the room while my peers studied. Scrubbing the toilets and urinals in the boy's restroom was even more humiliating, but at least there were no girls to see me do it.

The jocks were always loitering there during their breaks from practice, and they loved to torment me. Especially Hank Anderson, a linebacker with sullen eyes and a vacuous laugh, who found great pleasure in demeaning me every time he got the chance.

"Get used to cleaning up after our mess," he said in his deep and throaty voice. "That's all you spics are good for, anyhow."

I wanted to clock him with my wet mop, but I also didn't want to get fired. As usual, I resorted to what I always had—my words. "Go ahead. Laugh all you want, Hank," I said, swirling my mop in circular motions. "When I'm famous, you'll be pumping gas on Sixth Street."

His splotchy face flushed with anger. He grabbed the gray trash can and hurled garbage all over the floor.

His cronies chimed in with their own verbal attacks and spat loogies onto the mirrors on their way out the door.

After they left, I determined I would do whatever was necessary to make Hank and his fellow troglodytes eat crow. Every time they spewed more disparaging remarks, it motivated me to work harder to formulate my plan.

The last half hour of my shift was spent tidying up the band room, which I could do in twenty minutes. Mr. Kantola, the band director, was never there at that time. With the room to myself, I could steal the opportunity to jam on the drums and fantasize about Hank pumping gas into my Italian sports car as I passed through town.

One late afternoon, I was pounding away as usual when Mr. Kantola popped out of his office and startled me. "Stop what you're doing and wait right there," he said.

As he headed out the door, I waited nervously, knowing how hard it was going to be to find another job. He returned with Mr. Talluto, the choir director. Was I about to get interrogated by the two of them for messing with school property without permission?

"Play like you were when I walked in on you," Mr. Kantola said.

I picked up the sticks and did as told. They mouthed words to one another over my drumming and occasionally raised their eyebrows. Mr. Kantola yelled, "Okay! You can stop now!"

The room went quiet.

"Where have you been hiding?" Mr. Kantola asked, scratching his head. "You have some real talent, son. You play with conviction, and I sure could use you this fall in my ensembles."

"And I need a good drummer playing behind my swing choir," Mr. Talluto added.

"How about it?" they asked simultaneously.

On the bus ride home, I got lost in my thoughts. *They believe I'm a good drummer? They* need *me? They* want *me? Me!*

When I told Mama the news, she nearly cried. "You see, *mijo*, you just have to have faith in the Lord. I know you didn't want this job, but since you were willing to take it, God used it to change your destiny. I'm so excited for you."

As a freshman, I had missed sixty-two days of school. Before my sophomore year was over, I was up to sixty-one. With those kinds of numbers,

I held the distinction of being the school's all-time record holder for the most absences. But now that I would be playing drums in the school's stage, marching, and symphonic bands, I would have a reason to show up every day. The first thing I did over the summer was to take a few lessons from a senior named Eric Christianson, the best drummer in the school. He taught me some basic beats and how to read drum music. Then I studied on my own a lot.

The second thing I wanted to do was to get new drums to mark the beginning of this milestone. The set I had bought from John Perkins was a used beginner kit. I wanted a top-of-the-line model that professionals played. My heart had moved on from the sparkly blue set at the Music Shop to one in my Slingerland catalog—a five-piece maple set, complete with hardware and cymbals. My hero, Buddy Rich, played Slingerlands. If they were good enough for the world's greatest drummer, they were good enough for me. Ms. Pearl didn't sell Slingerlands, but Music West in Medford had exactly what I wanted, and I was hoping they wouldn't be gone by the time I could save up the $1,300 to buy them.

With Mama's prayers and a lot of hustling, I managed to land two full-time jobs that summer. From 7:30 a.m. to 3:30 p.m., I worked at Rogue Community College for $2.35 an hour as a groundskeeper—watering, mowing, weeding, sweeping, and whatever else my boss asked me to do. Every morning I rode my bike there, ready to do my best work. During my shift, I occasionally ran into Mama, who was taking summer classes there in child psychology, US history, and English.

From 4:30 p.m. to 12:30 a.m., I trudged it out at the Hellgate Jet Boat Excursions, a tourist attraction on the scenic Rogue River. The fare included a dinner stopover at the OK Corral, a restaurant situated along the banks of the river. Under the shade trees, we served barbecued chicken and ribs. I set the tables, cooked, and washed dishes. It was summertime, but the living proved to be anything but easy. By the end of each night, I was dog-tired.

Working sixteen-hour days left me with little spare time, but I spent every available second of it drumming with slavish regularity, practicing on tables, dashboards, even on my thighs. By the end of the summer, I gave Mama some money to get our car fixed. I bought myself a black-and-white television with a foldaway antenna for $80. With what I had left—which was more money than I had made in my life—I drove down to Music West in Medford with Bobby and plunked down the $1,300 in cash for those Slingerland drums. After browsing through some instructional books, I asked the salesman if he knew a good drum instructor in the area. "Sure do. That guy standing over there with the brown hair and glasses is Kent Clinkinbeard. He's one of the best."

I introduced myself to him and asked if I could take lessons. "I'd be delighted," he said.

Kent lived in Medford but played in Grants Pass with Chuck Wade, an R&B keyboard player and singer who held a steady gig at the Red Baron, a nightclub at the north end of town. "I'll swing by your house when it works out with my schedule," he said.

I couldn't wait.

CHAPTER 29

Bang the Drum All Day

The fall of my junior year was bursting with promise, and I was finally looking forward to school for the first time because I was playing the drums every day, three times a day. When spring rolled around, our stage band was gearing up for a statewide competition. I was psyched because Mr. Kantola had given me a drum solo in Maynard Ferguson's arrangement of "Pagliacci."

Since I had resumed my janitor position when the school year started, I still had keys to the band room. The night before our concert, I planned an all-night practice session, telling Mama I was spending the night at a friend's house because I didn't want her to talk me out of it.

That evening I let myself into the band room and worked myself up to a fever pitch. Looking up at the clock, I couldn't believe four hours had passed. Sweat drenched my face and dripped onto the drums. With only one pair of drumsticks, I wasn't sure they would get me through the night at the speed I was whittling them down. Stopping to catch my breath, I eyed the scant wooden shavings scattered on the floor.

I turned off the fluorescent lights and flipped on the other set of lights to soften the room. The blue sparkle on the drums shimmered like the Las Vegas strip, filling my head with a kind of dreamy abandon. By the time I checked the clock again, it was midnight.

In pursuit of perfection, I kept practicing until blisters surfaced on my thumbs and on the sides of my index fingers. Once more I glanced at the clock. It was 3:00 in the morning. My hands felt numb. Impervious to the time, I kept going. By 5:00 a.m., my T-shirt was soaking wet and my hands were bloodied. Like a horse with blinders on, I was on a mission.

Mr. Kantola believed in me, and I figured the best way to show my appreciation was to shine for him as brightly as possible. I refused to stop until my solo felt like second nature. My eyelids were heavy as I squinted up at the clock one last time—7:00 a.m. I knew I had to catch a quick nap in order to give a good performance.

At 8:30 a.m., the sousaphone player found me cocooned in my sleeping bag next to the drums. "What are you doing here?"

"I've been here all night," I said, yawning and stretching, "practicing my solo."

His eyes bulged. "Unbelievable."

I stood up slowly, wiping the sleep from my eyes as the students whispered among themselves.

At the competition I came out blazing, and Mr. Kantola looked on with a sense of pride. With my heart slamming against my chest, I played not only passionately but flawlessly, which made every second of those twelve hours of practice worth it. In the midst of that cathartic moment, a sudden burst of applause thundered as if I had broken a world record.

One of the judges told me what an impressive solo I had played. He asked Mr. Kantola if he was a drummer. "No, I'm not," he answered. "I play the saxophone, actually. Why do you ask?"

"The way your drummer plays, I thought he might be your protégé. The kid has an impeccable sense of time and really knows how to drive the band."

When the judge walked away, Mr. Kantola thrust his arms into the air and gave me two thumbs up. At that moment, all my insecurities about my identity washed away. And for the first time in my life, I knew who I was. I wasn't a half-Mexican, half-Irish outsider with a Black soul. I wasn't a rejected boy whose father had abandoned him to live a life of poverty and heartache. I wasn't a skinny misfit who had to scrub toilets for school nimrods.

I was a drummer.

My luck was also changing too.

The kismet continued when stage band members Bill Newman and Cory Graper asked me to join them for a performance at our school cabaret. Bill and Corey played guitar and bass for the most popular band in our area—White Lightning. After our electrifying performance of Led Zeppelin's "Stairway to Heaven" and the Beatles' "Come Together," I was no longer invisible. In fact, I was in the spotlight.

All of a sudden, I was one of the cool kids, and people began treating me with respect. After being a nobody all my life, it felt some kind of wonderful to be seen. To be appreciated. To be liked.

By the time May rolled around, I felt confident enough to attend our spring dance. I had never attended one before. From the edge of the cafeteria, I spotted Marley Madison standing alone in a faded rose crop top and bell-bottomed jeans. Brimming with self-assurance as the budding rock star I believed I was, I wore one of Mama's scarves and a polyester disco shirt with a wide lapel.

Marley was a freshman from a well-known family with lots of cousins. All the Madison girls were attractive, but with her soft brown wavy hair, rosy cheeks, and the kind of face you couldn't stop looking at, Marley was the one who made my heart sing.

Gazing at her with lovesick eyes, I worked up the nerve to ask her to dance. To my surprise, she said yes. After we danced for a while, we ditched the crowd and walked to the parking lot in the back of the school, where we sat in the evening breeze on the hood of Ricardo's Chevy Malibu, which I now had a license to drive.

"I just love the way you play the drums," she said, batting her eyelashes.

"I love playing them more than anything. One day I'm gonna be a famous drummer."

"Well, aren't you the confident one?"

"You have to be. If you don't believe you can make it, you never will."

She giggled. "I suppose you're right."

"What do you like to do?" I asked, scooting closer to her.

"Ride horses."

It was all I could do to focus on her words. "Sounds fun."

"You should come riding with me sometime at our ranch in Williams," she said, touching my elbow.

Sparks were flying. I tried to act as if I wasn't on fire. "I've never ridden before."

"Don't worry, silly. I'll teach you." She took off her glasses. It got quiet as we stared into each other's eyes. Then she brushed her lips against mine as her fingers caressed the back of my neck. We kissed under the soft light of the moon, and we kept kissing until it was time to go. After that moment of bliss, any notion of carrying on the work of the blessed Saint Anthony by doing good deeds (as Mama had hoped) went right out the window. On our walk back to the courtyard, I asked her on a date. She went silent, looking at me with those dazzling eyes of hers, and then she said, "Yes."

The sound that hit my ears was too thrilling for words. It was the best sound I had ever heard.

I left the dance like a boy in blue suede shoes, walking in Memphis, my feet ten feet off of Beale Street. I drove home over the dark country roads, lost in the magic of that moonlit night. I tossed and turned in bed for hours with an intense longing to gaze into her eyes again, to feel those soft lips against mine, to smell her smooth neck. Intoxicating! I couldn't wait to tell Mama the next morning that I had a date with one of the cutest girls in school. When I told her, she was ecstatic.

On Memorial Day weekend, I played the snare drum in the marching band at the Boatnik festival—the same festival where we had won all the eating contests when we first moved to town eight years earlier. It was a wonderfully sunny day full of pleasure and pageantry as I marched down Sixth Street, exactly as I had once dreamed. When we walked past Marley, I hoped she would notice me. I made sure I would be easy to spot as the only kid wearing fake turquoise stage jewelry and Ray-Bans with my orange shirt and white pants uniform. I saw her smiling and cheering from the side of the road.

After the parade, Marley and I strolled through Riverside Park. She squeezed my hand and said, "I think I love you."

My heart thumped wildly. I knelt down, picked a handful of dandelions, then handed them to her. "I think I love you too," I said nervously.

She blushed and put her arms around me, pressing her chest against mine as I breathed in the floral smell of her hair. While I held her close around her waist, her breath on my neck gave me shivers. She blinked her eyes at me, inciting feelings I had never known. All the ecstasy I had ever hoped to find in the world, I found in those eyes, those lips, that embrace.

Until . . .

Two weeks later she took up with a heartthrob named Dave Rogers, who drove a spiffed-up red Mustang. It was an imponderable twist of fate that cut me to my core. In a matter of seconds, I spiraled from the pinnacle of bliss to the valley of shame. Too embarrassed to tell Mama, I kept the devastating news to myself.

At school I hid behind a fake smile, as if the breakup were no big deal. Anyone with an ounce of perception, though, could see beneath my false bravado that I was drowning in a sea of despair. Even though he wore an outdated pompadour, Dave was a nice guy, and I didn't hold it against him as all was fair in love and war. Still, I was crushed.

To cheer myself up, I stood in long lines at the Rogue Theatre to see *Grease* over and over again. Though my savings dwindled, the escape was well worth the price of admission. I was so obsessed with the movie that I smuggled in a portable cassette player in a paper bag and recorded the entire film.

Each morning before school, I listened to the dialogue while primping my hair in the mirror. The day the soundtrack was released, I raced to the Music Shop to buy an official copy. I loved every song on that double album, especially "Grease" by Frankie Valli. The drumbeat was so infectious I took the time to learn it, note for note.

Early one evening, Kent finally came over to give me a drum lesson. The first thing he showed me was how to hold the sticks properly. "A good drummer uses mostly wrists and fingers. This is where the finest motor skills in the human body are housed," he said as he rolled his thumbs across the tips of his fingers. "Everything that requires great precision is executed from these nerve endings: painting, writing, carpentry, even surgery. It's the same for every instrument. Every musician must develop finger control, so it's no different for a drummer. If you want speed and finesse, you have to strengthen your fingers. You can also get a lot of power and thrust from your fingers."

"You can?"

"Sure," he said, walloping the stick onto the drumhead like a ninja warrior. "Now, for bigger backbeats and getting around the drum set, you'll also need to develop your wrists. Think of the wrists as four-inch paintbrushes for the big strokes and the fingers as thin paintbrushes for detailed trim work. These are your tools," he said, making nimble and quick movements with both his wrists and fingers and then effortlessly blazing around the drums at the speed of light.

Midway through the lesson, I asked Kent who his favorite drummers were.

"For big-band jazz, I love Buddy Rich, and for jazz fusion, it's Billy Cobham and Lenny White," he said. "For contemporary studio drummers, I love everything Steve Gadd, Harvey Mason, Jeff Porcaro, and Bernard Purdie have recorded. They're on tons of hit records with some of my favorite artists—Boz Scaggs, Steely Dan, Toto, Paul Simon, Tom Scott, Grover Washington Jr., and the Brothers Johnson."

The only drummer I had heard of was Buddy Rich, but what did I know? I had just started playing. Since these drummers were Ken's favorites, they would soon be mine, and I wanted to learn about each one. When the lesson was over, I was determined to work as hard as possible to be as good as possible. Maybe even as good as Kent someday.

Later that evening, Bobby and I drove to the Red Baron, where we stood outside the club's doorway, listening to Kent perform with Chuck Wade. Kent had proved to be an affable and patient teacher. He taught me the fundamentals of keeping time and how to play with an ensemble, and he worked with me on some of the music I had to play for the school bands. But he quickly became more than a drum teacher, taking on the role of mentor and friend. His family owned a lovely beach house in Brookings on the Oregon coast, a region known for its rugged coastline. One weekend he was playing there with his own band and invited Bobby and me to tag along.

At night we hung out at their gig. Later that evening, when Bobby and I were in bed in the next room, I eavesdropped on their late-night, musical conversations about tightening up on their songs, their set lists, and how much they loved Earth, Wind & Fire, George Benson, the Crusaders, and Chuck Mangione between the sound of shuffling cards. During the day, Kent took us boogie boarding at Harris Beach, which was home to Bird Island, the largest on the Oregon coast. Sea breezes brushed our faces as waves crashed all around us, a complete contrast to the crowded city beaches we had always known.

After a full day of exploring the mysterious rocks, caves, and inlets, Kent treated us to ice cream at the harbor. Seated at the edge of the dock, we were rapt by the crimson sun sinking behind the massive rock islands, highlighting each silhouette that jutted from the surging waters. As I was immersed in the shifting hues of sunset, the scent of the sea, and the sound of seagulls, slowly the enchanting color of Marley's eyes, the flowery smell of her hair, and the alluring sound of her voice began to fade. In fact, all of life's problems seemed to fade.

What I didn't know then was that another change would soon be upon me. An unexpected one brewing back home.

CHAPTER 30

New Kid in Town

In an effort to expand their employment and educational opportunities, Armando and Mary had decided to move a couple of hours north to Eugene, home to the University of Oregon. With its substantially larger population, a mall with real department stores, and more activities for people their age, the prospects for them were promising.

Family was everything to Mama, and she wanted to keep us close for as long as she could. And so, in July 1979, despite earlier promises that we would never have to move again, she sold our place on Sleepy Hollow Loop. With the equity from the sale, she put a small down payment on a modest house in the Santa Clara suburb of Eugene. Our place on Kirsten Street sat just a few miles from North Eugene High, home of the Highlanders, where I would be attending my senior year. Having won several state championships in football and other sports, the Highlanders were known as rather big, bovine athletes who roamed the school in herds.

The thought of transferring there was both frightening and liberating. No one knew anything about me in Eugene, so I would be free to be whoever I wanted, not a hick from the rural woods of Grants Pass, but I would miss my bandmates from school and playing for my band director, Mr. Kantola. I would miss taking lessons from Kent and Ms. Pearl at the Music Shop. I would especially miss Beverly and Bill Large from the Big Brothers Big Sisters program. Still, I was a city kid at heart, a musician, and part of a creative tribe whose chief aim in life was self-expression. I wanted the chance to do that without anyone having any preconceptions about me. Somewhere between Grants Pass and Eugene, I took ownership of my true identity once and for all.

To help me "get into character" for my new school year, I picked up some threads from a secondhand store and then got a perm. My hope was to look like Barry Gibb of the Bee Gees with his iconic lion's mane, but I ended up with a bad Afro instead. On the first day, I strutted onto the schoolyard wearing a rabbit fur coat and tight pleather pants tucked into platform boots. I cruised the hallways with my boom box cranking Michael Jackson's *Off the Wall*. As heads turned with my every step, I was finally getting what I had craved for so long: attention.

"Where're you from?" one student asked.

"Los Angeles," I said proudly. LA sounded glamorous. Mysterious. Intimidating. And it wasn't a complete lie. I did transfer from there—only with an eight-year detour through Grants Pass. I saw no reason for anyone to know that, though, since I was now reclaiming my South-Central roots.

Most of the students despised me right from the start, especially the jocks. Every morning as I walked from the parking lot to the school, pimply-faced athletes would rev their engines, threatening to run me over with their souped-up cars. Running in platform boots was no easy thing, but since my survival depended on it, I learned fast. A particularly large brute named Rocco Rivera came after me at every turn, usually surrounded by his posse of Neanderthals from the football team. When a few cute girls took an interest in my bad boy image, their disdain grew more intense. With all that prehistoric testosterone flying around, I worried for my safety.

If the chasm between me and the jocks was not already obvious, the day I wore my white canvas boots with acrylic see-through heels made it crystal clear. Evidently, my new classmates had never tuned into *Soul*

Train or had subscriptions to *Right On!* or *Jet* magazines, the epicenter for all things Black. Roaming the hallways with my silver herculean cuff bracelets, I looked more like my idols Philip Bailey and Maurice White of Earth, Wind & Fire than a high school student from Eugene, Oregon. As a result, I became a human landing strip for paper clips, rubber bands, and paper airplanes with nasty messages written on them.

I may have found myself in one of the least diverse areas of the Pacific Northwest, but I remained steadfast in my allegiance to those who laid down their lives for the almighty groove—Elvis Presley, James Brown, Aretha Franklin, Barry White, Al Green, Rufus, L.T.D., and so many others. It was their music that lifted my spirits during my darkest days. So if I was forced to choose teams, I was going with the syndicate of soul.

When I needed an escape from the turmoil at school, I spent hours downtown, flipping through the vinyl bins at Play It Again Records. One day while I was perusing the jazz section, I came across a striking purple album cover called *Virtue*. Below the slick lettering was a hip Black cat named Alphonse Mouzon, wearing an applejack hat, red shades, and a fur. My kind of guy.

I flipped it over to find another image of him seated behind a massive set of drums. Underneath, in all caps, it read, "IF POSSIBLE, PLEASE, LISTEN TO THE 'DRUM SUITE' IN STEREO!" I had no idea who Alphonse Mouzon was, but I was gripped by his appearance enough to buy the record.

The second I heard his drum solo, I was blown away. It propelled me in a new musical direction. But at the same time, there was another development taking place at North Eugene that no amount of jazz could remedy.

I don't remember who first started calling me "Disco Dan," but the nickname quickly gained momentum. One day, I was grabbing my books for my next class when Homer Wadsworth, the last putz in the known universe with a flattop hairstyle, blasted me for what I was wearing and gyrated his pelvis as he taunted me with "Disco Dan! Disco Dan!" Like Rocco, he had been trying to start a fight with me all year, but I had managed to avoid it.

Now I was in a corner, and it was a tight one. If I let him belittle me without defending myself, I would look like a wuss. If I fought and lost, I would pave the way for others to rail on me without fear of retribution. There was a lot riding on this moment—mainly my future treatment at school.

Giving him a contentious glare, I slammed my books to the ground, signaling the start of battle. A crowd encircled us like a mob ready for a show. "Homer, Homer, Homer," they chanted, goading him to draw first blood. With a blue vein bulging from his milky white forehead, he lunged forward, throwing a punch. By some miraculous twist of fate, he missed my face, grazing me on the shoulder instead.

A panic came over me, and the muscles in my jaw tensed. I had a flashback to page 12 of my *Boys' Judo* book and pumped out a Bruce Lee–inspired high kick, nailing him straight in the pie hole with my four-inch heel. Blood splattered everywhere. The crowd booed me with unabashed abhorrence.

Homer slunk down the hallway with his hands over his stubbled cheeks. My heart rate shot up. Anger coursed through my veins like jet fuel. Before I could catch my breath, it was over. In the afterglow of the moment, with my adrenaline pumping full throttle, I yelled out, "Who's next?"

I wanted to gloat. News of my bloody conquest spread rapidly, which I was most happy about until it traveled to the front office, and I was summoned by the principal, Mr. Essig.

Sitting behind his cluttered desk, he waved me in. My stomach was in knots, my mind was racing, and I wondered what my punishment would be as I took a seat. Suspension? Expulsion? Juvenile hall? I leaned forward and pleaded my case. "I'm sorry, but Homer's been trying to pick a fight ever since I transferred here."

"So," Mr. Essig said as he clasped his hands behind his head and leaned back in his swivel chair, "you kicked him in the face?"

"He was making fun of me in front of everyone."

"And you knocked his teeth in?" he said, as if baiting me to incriminate myself further.

My throat tightened. "I never wanted to fight him, but he threw the first punch. What was I supposed to do? Not defend myself? If I didn't, everyone would run all over me."

The principal leaned forward, thrusting his hands on his desk. "Look. I've had my own share of dealings with Homer. I can't say I blame you, really. Truth be told, he's had this coming for a long time."

I couldn't believe my ears. "Does this mean I'm not in trouble?"

"No. In fact, you did me a favor. That's one bonehead I'm pretty sure won't be giving me any more headaches," he said with a sigh of relief. "Now get back to class and try not to kick anyone else's teeth in for the rest of the day."

As I walked the long hallway back to class, I felt vindicated, but the longer I walked, the more I began to worry whether I'd be hailed as a hero or a hooligan. Surely there were others who'd be pleased to hear Homer finally got what he had coming. But I wasn't exactly positive about how things would pan out. I was a dreamer and a survivor, and I knew I couldn't leave it to chance. I would have to brainstorm a bigger, bolder, and bodacious plan.

CHAPTER 31

Stayin' Alive

If necessity is the mother of invention, then surely desperation is its father. Out of that desperate state, and the will to live, an idea came to me. But to execute it would hinge on Mr. Essig's permission. In his office, I unveiled my plan to cure the students of their animosity toward me. It was a method that had been used to sway teenagers for generations.

"Mr. Essig, most of the kids here hate me. The way I dress. The music I play on my boom box."

"I'm well aware," he said.

"That's why I need your help to win them over."

"I can't wait to hear this." He rubbed his hands together with almost devilish delight.

"I'd like your permission to put on a solo drum concert. At lunchtime."

He leaned forward, pulling off his glasses. "Well, you've got chutzpah, kid. In all of my years as a principal," he said, rocking in his chair, "no one has ever made such an outrageous request."

"Well, it's just that—"

"Hush . . . I'm not finished yet."

"Sorry."

"I know you've had a hard time here, and since I don't want to attend your funeral," he said laughingly, "I'm giving you permission to do your thing." He put his glasses back on and flipped through his calendar. "How's Friday, March fourteenth?"

"Perfect, sir. You won't regret this."

"Last I checked, music never hurt anybody. Good luck, pal. I admire your . . . gumption."

Drums had become my saving grace at Hidden Valley High in Grants Pass. I was hoping they would come to my rescue at North Eugene. If the students could see me as a performer, they might finally come to accept me for the artist I was or, at least, was *trying* to be. The lunch concert was my last card to play. If that didn't win them over, I was finished.

In preparation for the big day, I asked a classmate what songs he thought would go over big. "Most of us are rockers," he said. "If you play 'Rock and Roll' by Led Zeppelin and 'Walk This Way' by Aerosmith, you'll be a hero. We love that stuff."

I took his advice and added those songs to my set list, then relentlessly practiced my show from the opening piece to the finale.

The night before my performance, Bobby and my friend Ken helped set up my gear in the student lounge with its Scottish shield and bagpipes hanging over the fireplace. This was going to be my time to shine before my fellow Highlanders.

I went all out to make it a full-blown production with a PA system and my new Sony cassette deck. I had even rented some electronic drums and brought my turntable to play background music in advance of my premiere.

Since attending my performance was not mandatory, I played a fifteen-minute teaser set during the first break to get a buzz going, then invited everyone back at lunchtime for the full concert. It worked. By show time, the place was crawling with students and faculty, including Mr. Essig. A few minutes before downbeat, I was greeted by Misty Gattis, a stone-cold fox if I ever did see one.

"Here, I made these for you," she said with an alluring smile as she handed me a bag of cookies.

"How'd you know I liked chocolate chips and M&Ms?"

Her dimples deepened. "You look like a chocolate chip and M&M kind of guy."

My heart melted. As did the cookies from the heat of my hands. After envisioning our wedding ceremony, honeymoon, and what our children would look like, I shifted gears and got my head back into performance mode. Butterflies swirled inside me as I peered out at a slew of onlookers, many of them the very guys who had been threatening my life.

As the crowd gathered on all sides, Misty sat front row center on the carpet, her smile beaming up at me. Do or die, I was determined to play my heart out for her.

I grabbed my sticks, let out a sigh, then signaled Ken to hit the play button on my cassette deck. I opened with "I Want to Be Your Lover" by Prince, then segued into Michael Jackson's "Rock with You." When I kicked into "Refugee" by Tom Petty and the Heartbreakers, there was a noticeable shift of energy in the room. After playing "Rock and Roll" by Led Zeppelin, the crowd went bananas. I nailed every track with intense precision and riffed some short drum solo vignettes between songs.

My entire family had come to watch me play. Seeing them in the audience took me back to the fifth-grade talent show. Seeing Mama way in the back wearing one of her signature scarves inspired me to kick it up a notch. I was also happy to see John Bishop, a drummer from the University of Oregon who had given me a couple of lessons.

Saving the best for last, I put everything I had into my final push. I pummeled back and forth on the tom-toms, hammered through some lightning-fast rolls on the snare drum, then sizzled into some flashy cymbal work I had learned from watching Buddy Rich on *The Tonight Show*. Then I modulated into some escalating crescendos that led to my grand finale, thrashing my drumsticks down on the cymbals with one final thunderous blow. The room stood to its feet in ovation as sweat poured down my face.

Then I looked up to find Rocco Rivera cheering me on and Misty gazing at me with adoring eyes. Even Homer Wadsworth was grinning with his remaining teeth. I stood to take a bow, and the applause grew.

It was a dizzying moment, a near-perfect performance. But the one person who wasn't at school that day was the person whose approval I wanted more than anyone else's in the world: my dad.

John Bishop came up to me afterward. "How the heck did you get permission to put on something like this?"

With a shrug, I said simply, "I asked."

"Never in a million years would I have had the audacity to ask for something like that when I was in high school. You've got true grit, man."

My performance proved to be my final rite of passage. By the end of it, I went from being reviled to being revered. Even our school newspaper, the *Caledonian*, published a full-page feature on me with the headline "Disco Dan Shoots for Stardom." The copy read, "Disco Dan shows the students at North that he really knows how to make a set of drums hum during a recent one-man concert in the student lounge."

The article catapulted me into a campus celebrity. From there, I joined the marching band and played at all the pep rallies. There was still a faction of foes, though, and occasionally a confrontation ensued. Only now, Rocco Rivera and his wrecking crew came to my defense. Flanking me from all sides with an impenetrable wall of protection, they were ready to pulverize anyone who so much as looked at me the wrong way.

During one of those confrontations, Rocco stared down several of my antagonists with those steely eyes of his. His look was so menacing, the jut of his jaw so unnerving, that you could almost see beads of fear drip from their foreheads. Then Rocco spoke. "If you mess with our boy, Disco here, you better be prepared to take on me and the rest of the football team."

My challengers wilted under Rocco's glare, mumbled apologies, and dispersed. As they turned to leave, Rocco high-fived me.

I had always believed anything was possible, because that's what Mama had taught me. But for a guy who was once my arch nemesis to become my avenger bordered on the miraculous. A conversion of this scale was proof of music's power to break down walls. And if it could erase the wall that once separated Rocco and me, I had a feeling there would be more miracles to come.

CHAPTER 32

I Just Called to Say I Love You

There were plenty of things I didn't like about life as a Highlander at North Eugene. But in two words, I could tell you exactly what I liked most—Korin Hughes. A junior with exquisite poise, Korin was the most enticing creature I had ever seen. She had a regal way about her as she strolled the campus with her perfectly feathered flaxen hair, and whenever she cheered in her red skirt and white knee-highs, I would fall into a trance. Hardly a night passed when I didn't dream of traveling with her to some exotic destination for a romantic getaway.

Along with her tantalizing figure, Korin had a smile that could melt ice. And she had teeth so white they could almost blind you, thanks to her father, a prominent orthodontist in town.

We didn't have any classes together, which gave us few opportunities to talk, but I took advantage of every chance that came along. Before winter break, she told me she was going to Austria with her family to go skiing. Here she was, jet-setting off to Europe to hit the slopes when the only slopes I had ever seen were on the *Wide World of Sports*.

I didn't have money or a successful father like she did, but I had a lot of heart and ambition, and I wanted her to know that. So much so that I was tempted to get my teeth cleaned at her father's practice just so I could try to impress him, though it would be hard to carry on a conversation while he probed my teeth with his sharp instruments. Afterward I'd only have the bill to show for it, not a step closer to being his son-in-law.

The day I saw Korin holding hands with a junior from a well-to-do family, I was wrecked. After that, I focused my energies on becoming rich and famous so I could one day win her affections. But there was no chance of hitting the big time in Eugene. To do that, I would have to go out into the world and make a name for myself. There were heavier things weighing on my heart besides my obsession with Korin. Painful things. Hidden things. Secrets lurking behind the masks I so cleverly wore.

I was now seventeen and had never met my father or had a single conversation with him. Never received a card, letter, or present. Nothing. His total disregard left a hole in my heart that gave birth to an endless yearning. A yearning to prove to him I was worthy of his time, attention, and ultimately his love. I wanted these things more than anything in the world. Even more than I wanted Korin.

Despite his indifference, a burning desire to meet him began to well up inside me. I wanted him to share the secrets of being a man with me, even though he had not displayed any traits of a man worth imitating—a fact I had suppressed. I was eager for a relationship with my father.

Nothing I had tried granted me an audience with him, so I was determined to accomplish something so unbelievable he could no longer ignore me. Something to make him realize I was worth more than the value he'd placed on me. Something to make him regret abandoning me. Though we never discussed it, my siblings and I seemed to share this longing in common. I could see it in their eyes whenever we played our favorite Motown song, "I'm Gonna Make You Love Me," and sang it at the top of our lungs. I sensed they were channeling the words to their fathers, just as I was. The only thing I could think of to make him love me was to become a better drummer than he was and make it all the way to the top.

But I had to find him first.

We had maintained contact with my grandmother, Marion, who

knew his whereabouts at all times. But asking her to divulge her son's contact information was off-limits. He hid behind her, and she protected him fiercely. Nothing was going to change that.

Mama knew how much I wanted to meet him and worked vigorously to track him down. After months of good old-fashioned detective work, she learned he now worked for Union Steel Products in Santa Fe Springs, California. I was surprised to find out he was living on the West Coast again, near me, and not back in Chicago, where his mother had said he was living when she had visited us in Compton years earlier.

With this vital information, it came time for the big moment—the moment I would make the call and hear the sound of my father's voice. It was February 11, 1980, four months before my high school graduation, when I decided to give it a try. Before I dialed the number from the avocado-green telephone on Mama's nightstand, she hugged me and said a prayer. Then, sitting next to me with her ear near the phone, she waited while I called the number.

"May I speak with Dan Donnelly?" I said as I tried to steady my shaky voice.

"Let me put you through to his secretary," the receptionist replied. She patched me through, and I asked again to speak with him, this time with a more assertive tone.

"I'm sorry, he's out to lunch," his secretary said. "Would you like to leave a message?"

"Well, actually I'm an old friend, and I really want to surprise him. When do you expect him?"

"Call back in half an hour. I'm sure he would love to hear from you."

Don't be so sure, lady, I thought. I had no idea what his response would be once I revealed my identity. I only knew I was willing to take the risk.

Exactly thirty minutes later, I called back.

"I'll put you through to him," his secretary said cheerfully.

My heart raced. A lump in my throat formed as I waited. Mama gripped her hands nervously too.

Finally, a man's voice came on the line. "Dan Donnelly."

I paused for a second, taking in the sound of his voice. Mama leaned against me, hyperventilating, "Hello, um . . . *this* is Dan Donnelly," I said, pausing. "Your son."

He chuckled, then went silent.

My heart raced faster, and my hands grew clammy. I wondered what he was thinking. Wondered if he believed it was me. Wondered what he was going to do. When I could take it no longer, I broke the silence. "How are you?"

More silence. Mama looked at me with nervous eyes. The second hand of the clock ticked off time as if the entire room was waiting for his response.

"I'm great," he finally said. "How the heck are you doing?"

I took a deep sigh of relief. "I'm doing okay."

As we continued the conversation in stilted fragments, I wondered how long we could go on like this.

"Let me call you back so you won't have to pay for the call," he said.

My stomach knotted. Was this a ploy to ditch me? Would he really call back? Would this be my first and last conversation with him?

I didn't want to hang up, but I did as he had requested, imagining him scolding his secretary for not properly screening the call.

I waited.

Then waited some more . . .

Then a little longer . . .

My heart sank.

Finally, the phone rang.

I picked up the receiver before the first ring was finished.

It was him.

This was the first time my father had ever called me, and I reveled in the magnitude of the moment. He began asking me superficial questions about my life, when I really wanted to connect in a deeper way.

I told him I played the drums like he did. That piqued his interest. As soon as we started talking about our favorite bands and drummers, the awkwardness waned.

For as long as I could remember, people would say to me, "Man, you sure can talk." Listening to my father carry on, I realized where my gift of gab came from. It was eerie to discover how similar we were, considering we hadn't spent a single day together since I was an infant.

Once we broke through the ice, I found him easy to talk to. But for some strange reason, it didn't feel as if I was talking to my father, even though I had no idea what that was supposed to feel like. Our conversation seemed more like talking to an older friend who had common interests. Sadly, the hole in my heart was still there.

I asked about his personal life. "Are you married?"

"I sure am."

"Children?"

"A nine-year-old daughter. Megan."

"I have a little sister? Sweet."

He quickly turned the tables, probing deeper into my life. "Where do you live?"

"Eugene, Oregon."

"How are your brothers and sisters doing?"

"They're doing really well, actually. Mary and Armando are right here in Eugene. Ricardo's in the Air Force, and Patricia's working as a model out of LA." I had almost forgotten he had known my four older siblings since he had been in their lives for a couple years when they were young. "What kind of work do you do?"

"I'm the western regional manager for Union Steel Products, in their Materials Handling Division."

"You still play the drums?"

"Oh, man. I haven't pulled them out in a while, but I do love to play. These days, I'm really into Latin Jazz, and I play the congas. They're not as loud, so I can play them without disturbing the neighbors. What grade are you in?"

"I'm a senior."

"You're graduating soon?"

"June fifth."

"Tell you what. I'll try and arrange my schedule so I can make it out there for that."

Mama's eyes filled with tears as she sniffled into a tissue. The dark hole in my heart felt as if a bright light had penetrated the center of it.

"It'll be great to finally meet you."

After talking a bit more, he shared his love for the sea and said he wanted to take me sailing on his boat sometime. We exchanged contact information. I was relieved he didn't ask how I had tracked him down. My voice shook again as I said the words I had been longing to say for seventeen years. "I love you, Dad." I don't know why I said it, but I did. It just slid out, and there was no way I could take it back.

I guess I wanted to hear him say it so badly that I figured if I said it first, he would say it back. But when he replied with, "Okay, we'll talk again soon," that sudden burst of light in my heart just as suddenly vanished, bringing back the darkness and the longing that had made their home there for so long.

Life had kicked Mama and me down so many times that we chose to celebrate even the slightest victory, savoring every morsel of goodness that came our way. And so, when I hung up, we hugged and cried, then talked about the miracle that had just transpired. To rejoice, she made my favorite dinner—her delicious Velveeta macaroni and cheese casserole and a Betty Crocker yellow cake with chocolate frosting. The taste of home.

Even though I was happy to finally talk with my father, deep inside I was still reeling from the years of rejection. One phone call couldn't suddenly make that pain go away. He had missed out on my entire life, and I knew we could never get those years back. During the months leading up to graduation, a barrage of questions whirled around my head.

Would he have ever called me if I hadn't called him? Why didn't he answer any of the countless letters I had sent in care of his mother? Why hadn't he taken the slightest interest in me? How could he so easily disregard me when all I wanted to do was love him?

And the million-dollar question was . . .

Would he really show up for my graduation?

CHAPTER 33

I'm Gonna Make You Love Me

A week before my graduation, I drove to Portland to pick up a new outfit from Mario's, a stylish men's clothing store. I wanted to make a good impression on my father, who had promised to arrive the day before the ceremony. I settled on a tweed sport coat, brown wool gabardine trousers, and a pair of beige lace-ups. I'd look more like a Wall Street executive than a high school senior.

Late afternoon on June 4, I pulled into the airport parking lot. The closer to his arrival time, the more my stomach churned. In a few moments, I would be standing face to face with the man I had longed to see all my life. I was excited. Yet apprehensive. *Will he like me? Will I like him? How will he interact with Mama and the family?* So many thoughts spun around my teenage brain as I mulled over the weight of what was about to happen.

When his plane touched down, my heart raced. As passengers disembarked, I kept a watchful eye out for him. One by one, they passed me by. The crowd thinned. Still, no sign of Dan Donnelly. I paced back and forth. *Did he change his mind at the last second?*

I poked my head in the doorway to see if anyone else was coming. No one.

My stomach sank.

Suddenly, the sound of heavy footsteps, then a glimmer of a man about six feet three in the shadows of the jet bridge. *Can this be him?* When the light finally shone on his face, I caught my breath. It *was* him. Dan Donnelly, my father, was the last person to deplane. I remembered what he looked like from the picture my grandmother sent me as a kid.

Just outside the door, our eyes met. I greeted him with a firm handshake and a smile. "Hi, Dad. Long time no see," I said, turning to my sense of humor to ease the tension, a defense strategy that had gotten me through many hard times.

His comb-over shook as he gave a hearty laugh in his brown polyester suit.

On our way to baggage claim, as we idly chatted about the flight and the weather, I found myself staring at him. As he stood by the conveyor belt, looking out for his bag, I studied his physical appearance and mannerisms, wondering what parts of him had been passed down to me. He had strawberry-blond hair, baby-blue eyes, and pale skin. My hair was brown, my eyes were hazel, and my skin was olive. He was bigger boned, with lanky arms and substantial wrists. I had Mama's smaller and slenderer frame. I was six feet even. He stood a few inches taller. After grabbing his bag, I walked behind him, noticing we had the same gait. We jumped in my car, and he yapped away as we headed to the Howard Johnson's motel, where he had booked a room.

With his obvious charisma and sparkling sense of wit, I could see how he had wooed his way into Mama's heart all those years ago. With the exception of his overgrown mustache, his mouth was the spitting image of mine. I liked him immediately. I hoped he liked me too.

The next morning, I attended senior breakfast. After the speaker gave a short pep talk, Mr. Essig jokingly mentioned how I had asked for more graduation tickets than anyone in the school's history. My entire family was coming out, including all of my nieces and nephews, and I was excited Patricia was flying up from Los Angeles just for the occasion. I missed her so much. Everyone was eager to meet my father.

Achievement awards were given to highly accomplished seniors, of which I was not. But to my surprise, I was named "Best Dressed." *Suddenly, the people who despised the way I dressed all year are now handing me an award for the very thing they hated about me in the first place?* The irony was laughable, but I accepted it graciously, feeling proud to be acknowledged for my colorful sense of style.

After breakfast I went to the Valley River Mall to buy my dad a Father's Day present. I sprang for an expensive bottle of cologne, then picked out a few Buddy Rich albums I knew he would love. Back at the house, Mama asked me to put on my red cap and gown so Bobby could take photos of us together. Afterward she gave me a big hug under the mulberry tree.

"I know you're going to do something amazing with your life," she said, looking up at me with great expectation. "But I'm going to miss you so much."

I held her close, trying to console her. "Don't worry, Mama. I'm not leaving just yet. Besides, I have no idea where I'm going."

Before the ceremony, my father greeted my family members, who were dressed to kill in their Sunday best. He was cordial to Mama and seemed happy to see my older siblings, who shared some of their childhood memories of him. I was glad they never mentioned how much it hurt when he had abandoned them. Instead, everyone was kind and respectful, welcoming him with open arms and a spirit of grace.

With my entire tribe seated in their designated bleacher section, the festivities commenced. There were only four letters ahead of me, and I waited for each of them with increasing anxiety, wondering all the while what kind of response I would get when my name was called. Even though I had won over most of the students, a remnant of haters still troubled me. The last thing I wanted was to be humiliated in front of my father. As soon as they started announcing the Cs, I began shivering underneath my gown. After the first D, the pressure intensified. My entire senior year was to be defined by the moment my name was announced.

Finally, that moment came. "Dan Donnelly."

I was breathless. Light-headed. As if I were having an out-of-body experience in slow motion. I stood up and looked around. Then suddenly I was back in real time. It was hard to fathom what my eyes were taking in or what my ears were hearing. Students had jumped to their feet from every corner of the gymnasium to cheer me on. As I made the long walk to the podium, the crowd continued to hoot and holler. "Disco! Disco! Disco!" they chanted in sync as they stomped on the bleachers.

With my father and family there to witness it all, I almost floated across the stage to accept my diploma. It was surreal.

After the band finished playing "Pomp and Circumstance," a gang of students lined up to congratulate me and sign my yearbook, sending me off with words of admiration.

"You refused to cower, and you showed us class. Much respect."

"Congrats on not letting any of us change you."

"You were kind to us even though we all gave you hell. Kudos to you, bro."

"We were all just jealous you had the boldness to be unique and we didn't."

The challenges I had faced throughout the year had been nearly insurmountable, but the pinnacle of that evening certainly made the climb worthwhile. Mama looked prouder than ever, and my father appeared to be confounded by the fanfare directed at me. Outside the auditorium in the cool of the evening, he said with a sparkle in his blue eyes, "No one else got a standing ovation."

"I guess a few people like me," I said humbly, with a smile.

He had no idea all I had gone through to earn that respect. How could he? He had just met me the day before. I think he would have been proud if he knew, but I chose to keep the details of my struggle to myself. I was thrilled he took notice of how well I was liked. Maybe after that, he might even like me himself. After all, it was his acceptance and praise I wanted most.

Before leaving campus, I introduced him to Mr. Essig, who knew we had never met before. The kindhearted principal had never wavered in his belief in me, and in that moment, he seemed to know what I needed most. He shook my father's hand and said, "You have a terrific son, Mr. Donnelly. It's been such a pleasure getting to know him."

A quizzical look ran across my father's face, leaving him speechless.

Mr. Essig continued. "I've known a lot of students over the years, and I can tell you that your boy has stood out among them, distinguishing himself as a young man of conviction and character. I'm certain he'll go far in life. You should be really proud of him."

I was so moved by his words, hearing them aloud and having them spoken in front of my father, the man I most wanted to see the worth in me. From the start, Mr. Essig had stood with me, and I was grateful for the support he had shown.

We took pictures with my father, Mr. Essig, and my family, then went back to the house to celebrate. In the living room, I caught myself glancing at my mother and father chatting, observing their interactions with one another with almost childlike curiosity. Seeing them in the same room was another surreal experience for me. It was hard to imagine they had once been husband and wife, hard to imagine we were all a family, living together. But for that one night only, that one providential night, we appeared to be a family again.

After dessert, I opened cards and small gifts from Mama and my siblings. Then my father handed me a leather drumstick bag and a $100 bill.

The next afternoon, I picked him up from his hotel and brought him back to the house so we could play drums for each other. In my bedroom loft above the garage, I threw on "Toad's Place" by the Jeff Lorber Fusion, playing along with it for him. He seemed impressed.

"You got any Buddy Rich records I can play along with?" he asked.

"Sure, what song would you like?"

"It doesn't matter, as long as it's Buddy Rich."

Can he really do that? I thought. He would have to know the entire Buddy Rich catalog to pull that off. I threw on *The Roar of '74* and chose "Time Check," which was a blistering song that featured a couple of rip-roaring drum solos. I figured this would be a good number for him to strut his stuff, if he had any. Standing over his shoulder, I marveled at how well he could emulate the Buddy Rich style. He was a fireball.

Mama snapped a few pictures and shot some Super 8 footage while we exchanged our favorite drum licks, talking shop until it was time to take him to the airport.

At the gate, I shook his hand, hoping he would pull me in for a hug as we said our farewells. But he just kept shaking my hand vigorously. On the drive home, I replayed the past three days in my head, wondering if there was anything else I could have done to win his affection.

He was the only one who didn't give me a graduation card, which I wanted more than the drumstick bag or the hundred dollars. I was desperate for anything that showed how he felt about me, what his dreams for me might have been, or how glad he was to finally meet me. I left the airport feeling saddened that the hole in my heart was still there. I don't know exactly what I had been hoping for, but at that moment, I realized the hurt might never go away.

After I pulled into our driveway, I turned off the ignition and sat in the car for a while, looking up at my bedroom window, where a momentous reunion between father and son had just taken place. It triggered something in my subconscious. I ran into the house and rifled through the family photo albums in search of that picture of me as a toddler— the one with his bongos dangling beneath my feet in my stroller.

When I found it, I stared at it intensely. How was it possible that something he had left behind only by accident would play such a pivotal role in my life? No one could have guessed, when he left me as an infant, that I would someday become a drummer like him, or that seventeen years later we would finally meet and play drums for one other.

Life had proven to be full of surprises. At least *my life*. If something as impossible as our meeting could take place, then perhaps what I had said in my *Caledonian* interview might also come true: "When asked what his plans are after graduation, Donnelly says he 'hopes to tour the US in the summer with his father, another well-respected drummer, then go on to college and major in music and percussion.'"

That was the dream anyway.

But as he boarded the plane to return to *his* home, *his* wife, *his* child, I knew the dream of touring with my father would never come true. It was a brutal coming-of-age moment. I wasn't a child anymore. I was seventeen, a graduate on the cusp of becoming a man. It was time to put away childish things, such as my delusion of ever having a dad who longed for his son as much as that son longed for him.

CHAPTER 34

California Dreamin'

After graduation I kept working various jobs, practicing drums, then found some success by launching a mobile DJ business that I called "Disco Dan, Inc." A couple of months later, a friend of Mama's told her about an ad she had seen in the *Register-Guard* for a family band looking for a drummer. When I came home from work, I immediately dialed the number.

After I talked with the musical director, Vinnie Romano, he scheduled an audition at his house, which sat atop a steep hill in one of the more well-to-do neighborhoods of Eugene. Vinnie was charismatic, with dark hair, a nasally voice, and a nose that looked as if one too many wise guys had laid into it. His brother Gino, who had thinning curly hair, played saxophone and sang backup. And the other brother, Tony, with his matinee-idol good looks, played bass and sang lead. It was obvious they weren't from Eugene from their singsongy New Yorkese. Vinnie had a peculiar way of elongating certain words. "How are youuuuuuuuuuuuuuu doing?" What's Haaaaaaaaaaaaappening?" The longer he held his vowels, the higher his pitch rose.

After an exhaustive audition in their garage, they took me out on the veranda, where we took in the view of the city. Beneath the stars, they sipped from miniature white porcelain cups. "Would you like a cappuccino?" Tony asked.

"Maybe. What is it?"

Vinnie spewed out whatever he was drinking, and they all wheezed in laughter.

"What's a cappuccino? Boy, you don't get out much, do you?" Gino said. "But you're a natural on those drums, and we can't teach you that. Dat's sometin the good Lord above gave you."

"But we can show you the rest," Vinnie said, lifting his little cup to his mouth. "How'd youuuuuuuuuuu like to join our band?"

I couldn't hold back my smile. "I'd love to!"

"Dat's good. Because we got a lotta work," Vinnie continued, handing me a jam-packed calendar of their upcoming shows while all three explained their plans to "make it big."

For the next couple of months, the Romano Brothers and I played nonstop throughout the state—at bars, hotels, restaurants, and high schools, including my alma mater. Returning just months after graduation with a professional band filled me with a sense of pride. On the afternoon of our concert, I dropped by the front office to say hello to Mr. Essig. He was as happy to see me as I was to see him and delighted that things had worked out so well for me with the Romano Brothers.

While roaming the corridors, I bumped into Korin Hughes and lit up like a firefly. She was a senior now and more ravishing than ever. I was looking pretty dashing myself in my tight white pants, fitted T-shirt, shades, and tilted fedora.

"Well, hello there," she said, surprised to see me. "How've you been, Disco?"

"Fantastic." I was so eager to impress her I never bothered to ask how she was doing. "I'm in the best band in Oregon, and we're working all over the state."

"That sounds incredible. I'm so happy for you. You're certainly doing what you were born to do."

"And this is just a stepping stone. I'm going to be one of the greatest drummers in the world and play for top recording artists."

This was my only chance to show her I was a man of vision. A man of determination. A man she could count on to be a success. As we moseyed down the hallway toward the auditorium, I finally asked about *her* dreams.

"I'll be going to Portland State," she said.

"I heard that's a great school. What are you majoring in?"

"Accounting."

"You'll do great, I'm sure."

"I hope so. I'd like to become a CPA."

"Then you can help me count all the money I'm gonna make," I joked.

A giggle slipped between her soft lips. "I'd be happy to," she said in her genteel manner. "You can be my first client."

Once in the auditorium, I walked her to a seat I knew would give her a clear view of me on stage. Then I dared to ask for her number and address so I could stay in touch. She scribbled her contact information on a piece of notebook paper, tore it out of the binder, and handed it to me with a smile.

"It was great to see you again, Korin," I said, heading toward the stage. When she wished me luck, I turned back and said, "Good luck in college too. I'll drop you a line sometime."

"Please do."

All I thought about during my performance were her words, "Please do." Despite being distracted by her, the concert was a big hit, proving to the students at North Eugene that I was on my way.

Playing with the Romano Brothers was vital to my development as a young musician. Not all the gigs were illustrious, however. One night we played a seedy joint called the Pump House. This smoke-filled, rural roadhouse didn't even have a floor, so we played on dirt. And even the dirt was dirty! The place was packed with smoky-voiced buxom ladies stubbing out their cigarettes while eyeing grizzled bikers with big bellies, most of whom were loitering around pool tables as they threw back tequila shots and bottled beer. I was in the middle of my drum solo in "Wipeout," when a heckler pushing 350 pounds with a bulbous nose jeered at me.

"You think you can play them there drums, sonny boy?" he slurred as he stumbled closer.

Gino laughed while the buffoon circled my drum set, trying to intimidate me. He then did the unthinkable. He dropped his trousers and mooned me!

In the parking lot after the show, I tried to shake it off with laughter. "One day, when I make it big, I'll tell this humiliating story to the world. It'll be funny then."

Tony scolded, "You mean when *we* make it big, don'tcha?"

"Yeah, yeah, of course. When *we* make it big."

Two months into playing with the brothers, we decided to audition for a house band position at Disneyland. It rained incessantly in Eugene, and I was dying to return to the land of sunshine where I had spent the first half of my life. The thought of playing several shows a day on a stage that rose out of the ground by a hydraulic feat of engineering was exhilarating, not to mention how fun it would be to ride Space Mountain as many times as I wanted. For free! I was still a teenage boy, after all.

For the trip down to Disneyland, I gave Ricardo a down payment in exchange for his Oldsmobile Omega. It wasn't exactly a chick magnet. Actually, with its boxy design and mustard color, it was more of a chick repellent. But I was in the market for reliability, not flash.

When November 14 finally arrived—the day I would leave home for the audition—Mama was heartbroken, especially with Thanksgiving around the corner. She always got emotional when one of us left. I was as torn up as she was, but I held back my feelings, acting manly, as I had seen Ricardo and Armando do when they left the nest. Outside, with my car packed to the gills with drums, clothes, and everything else I could shove in it, we said our goodbyes.

Bobby and Lisa were the last two children remaining home with

Mama, and all three were there to see me off. Bobby threw his arms around me and squeezed tight.

"The BB gun is yours now," I whispered in his ear while I held my best friend close to my heart. "I stashed it under your bed with a carton of BBs. I never had to use it. I hope you won't either."

"I'm gonna miss you, bro."

"Gonna miss you too, Bobby."

"It won't be the same without you," he said nervously. "The thought of having to go back to North without you . . ."

"You'll be fine," I said, trying to bolster his confidence.

His eyes drooped, and I worried about how the students would treat him with me no longer there. "You should keep the DJ business going. I made some good money with it, and so can you. At least until I need my equipment back at some point."

Bobby and I had always been inseparable. I would miss him terribly, and I knew my absence would be tough on him as well. I looked him in the eye, putting my hand on his shoulder. "You're the man of the house now. It's up to you to look after Mama and Lisa."

"I know," he said, his voice quivering.

"It's okay to be scared, Bobby. I was, too, when Ricardo left. But I was thirteen. You're sixteen, so you'll grow into it quicker than I did, for sure."

He removed his black crucifix from around his neck. "I want you to have this," he said, handing me the cross Mama had given him for his first Holy Communion.

"You can't give me this. I know how much it means to you."

"It does, but you mean more. Take it. So God will watch over you, Danny."

His gesture touched me deeply, and it was all I could do to hold myself together. My voice broke with emotion as I tried my best to thank him. "We've been through a lot together, and you've never left my side. I couldn't have asked for a better brother."

Lisa nudged her way over to give me a hug, then planted a big kiss on my cheek.

"Who's gonna laugh at all my stupid jokes now?" I asked her.

"Are you kidding? All my friends think you're hilarious. You won't have a problem making people laugh, wherever you go."

"I love you, Lisa. You're a sweet sister," I said, hugging her tight. "Make sure to help Mama with whatever she needs."

"I will," she said, tearing up.

The three of us had grown so close after Ricardo and Patricia left the house. Now we would have to make yet another life adjustment. It would be hard for all of us, and Mama was overcome with emotion, watching us share our love for one another.

"Thank you, Mama, for taking such good care of me. You've been the greatest mother a son could have. One day I'm going to make you real proud."

"I'm already proud. Proud of how you've handled all the adversity in your life. Proud of the man you've become without a father. Proud of what a hard worker you are and for staying true to yourself."

I could no longer speak without shedding tears. So I just gave her a big hug instead.

"You're a fighter like me, *mijo*, and I know you're going to make it," she whispered in my ear.

I held her while she cried, trying my hardest not to break down. After she finally let go, she pleaded with me, "Please drive safe, and call me the second you get there."

"I will, Mama. I will. Don't worry. I'll be fine."

As I sat behind the wheel of the Omega, ready to embark upon my journey, a flood of emotions washed over me, from sadness and fear to doubt and worry. What if *this* happens? What if *that* happens? What if *nothing* happens? So many what-ifs ricocheting around in my head. But I was also fired up about my prospects in California, a place that had never left my heart. A place that had always felt like home.

After the fourteen-hour drive, I arrived in Anaheim. I called Mama immediately, and she was relieved to hear I was safe and sound.

A couple of days later, the Romano Brothers and I pulled up to Harbor Pointe, the main entrance for Disney cast members. In a building that looked like an employee cafeteria, we gave our best performance for the talent bookers. All the while, I imagined good-looking girls from around the world watching us perform, clamoring to get our autographs next to the Tomorrowland Terrace. If we could just land the gig, who knows, maybe Korin Hughes and her family would come to see me play at "the happiest place on earth."

A week passed before the talent booker called back. I was in Vinnie's motel room when he got the call. He listened quietly before responding. "Uh-huh . . . Okay. Yes, of course. Thanks so much." He hung up, then just sat there. Finally, he turned to me with a face that said what he couldn't bring himself to say. He shook his head. He stood and squeezed me on my shoulder regretfully. "They passed," he told me.

How could this be? We had worked so hard. The show was tight. We had even cut our hair to meet the ultraconservative standards Disney required.

I was devastated. And I wasn't the only one.

Vinnie and Gino tried to convince us backup musicians to stay in the area to give them time to regroup. I didn't need any convincing. The last thing I wanted to do was go back to Eugene with my tail between my legs. I was willing to do anything to stay in Southern California.

Well, *almost* anything.

I wanted to call Mama to tell her we didn't get the gig, but I didn't want to break her heart. I wavered between dialing her number one minute and hanging up before she answered the next.

After some more thought, I decided it was best to wait and see what the Romanos were staging for a comeback. I couldn't bring myself to tell anyone that Disney had passed on us. Because of that, I felt terribly alone. Frightened. Uneasy. I had left the security of those who loved me for the uncertainty of a world where no one knew me at all. I imagined the countless musicians who had dreamed of making it big, who had been down this road before me, meeting it with this same grave disappointment and loneliness.

How did they bounce back from such a devastating blow? My guess was that most never did. *Would I become one of them? Had I been kidding myself all along?* This defeat was a hard pill to swallow for a kid who was so sure he was about to be handed the keys to the kingdom, a kingdom he wanted entrance into more than anything.

But wanting something desperately wasn't enough to make it happen.

Even with all the resolve, all the passion, all the dedication, all the blood, sweat, and tears . . . it wasn't enough. *I* wasn't enough. It was the same old battle I had been fighting all my life.

CHAPTER 35

Dazed and Confused

While the Romanos took a couple of days off to reboot from the Disneyland setback, on November 27, I took a fifteen-minute drive to La Habra in LA County to visit my father. This would be our second time meeting in person. He was at work when I arrived, but his wife, Annette, and my nine-year-old half sister welcomed me. Megan practically leaped into my arms as I walked through the door. "I always wanted a big brother," she said, hugging me with all of her might as she looked up at me with her big blue eyes. She had only learned about me the night before.

Though we shared the same father, it was clear we came from different worlds. In reality, we had never actually *shared* him. He had always been a father to her but never to me. She was celebrated and cared for. For some reason, unbeknownst to me, I was a dark secret, left to fend for myself. But I didn't hold that against her, because I knew it wasn't her fault.

My grandmother Marion was living in Southern California near my dad at this time, and she came over that evening to visit. I hadn't seen her since her one and only visit to Compton when I was six years old. During dinner, Megan, who had fawned over me since my arrival, innocently blurted out, "I used to ask Dad and Grandma, 'Who is that little boy in those pictures in the photo album?' Then Grandma would ask me if I wanted a cookie or some ice cream, and I would forget all about that little boy."

My grandmother's face flushed with shame, while my father and his wife looked mortified. An awkward silence swept through the room.

I tried bringing some levity into the atmosphere by joking about how good that ice cream must have been, when what I really wanted to do was cry. I kept it together, though, hiding my broken heart behind my usually buoyant smile. While eating, I wondered about what I had just heard. Why had he saved all the pictures I had sent him as a kid yet never acknowledged me? I just couldn't make sense of it. It wasn't like I was an illegitimate child or someone he had fathered from a one-night stand. He had been married to my mother, for God's sake, even if it *was* just to avoid the Vietnam War. But I didn't dare bring that up.

On my second night with him, he played his congas for me and continued sharing his love of Latin music, giving me a deeper glimpse into the musical DNA I had inherited. By the end of my weekend visit, though, he still seemed like just another man, and the father-son bond I was hoping to experience had evaded me once again.

When we parted the next morning, I made sure *not* to say, "I love you, Dad." This time I withheld those words, hoping he might say them first. He didn't. He didn't give me a hug either. He just shook my hand and said, "Good luck." Once again, I felt disheartened by his refusal to show more emotion. I guess I was used to the way Mama expressed her love so openly, and I was hoping for the same from him. Whether he realized it or not, he was already teaching me some valuable lessons. The more I learned about my father, the more I knew I didn't want to turn out like him.

I drove off wondering if I might have been better off had I never reached out to him. At least I had found ways to manage those painful emotions I had known all my life. These new feelings were confusing, and I didn't know how to process them. They just made me feel worse about myself, even more unwanted. More unworthy. More unloved.

After returning to Anaheim from the weekend break, the band argued about what to do next. The Romanos' long-term objective was to secure a recording contract and become the next family act to make it big. But without a Disney contract, we were reduced to gigging at local bars and restaurants to keep us afloat. Good paying gigs for a show band our size had receded like Gino's hairline. The few places we did play were filled with people who couldn't care less whether we were there. Belligerent boozers heckled us about our puffy green and white checkered shirts, which were better suited for a Saint Patrick's Day parade than trying to win over a bar crowd. With nothing but kitschy outfits holding us together, rumors of desertion spread among the backup musicians.

One night at Salvatore's Italian Restaurant, I shared my dream of becoming a world-renowned drummer. Tony, our chiseled-face bassist, burst out laughing, then said, "I hate to tell you this, little buddy, but you won't amount to nothing without us."

I swallowed my pride, but I'm sure he could see the scorn on my face. From then on, he berated me every time he got the chance, reminding me how lucky I was to share the stage with the likes of him. He started positioning his six-foot-two-inch frame in front of my drums so no one could see me on stage. It was hard to believe I could go from liking to loathing him in just a few short months.

The tension between us became palpable. In the middle of one rehearsal, with a flush of bravado, Tony was hell-bent on extinguishing my flame. "Hey, Vinnie and Gino," he said, glancing at me smugly, "since we need to shorten the show, why don't we just cut the drum solo?"

His flippant remark was the last straw. And my last meal, too, since Salvatore's paid us in the form of pasta and meatballs. While the cooking was good, the pay was nothing I couldn't walk away from. I quit the band that night. As a result, I found myself stranded in Anaheim, with my dream of making it onto the world stage dissipating before my eyes.

There was only one person who could lift my spirits. I found a pay phone and called Mama. "I blew it," I confessed, explaining that I would be driving home. I knew she would be happy to have me back. Bobby and Lisa would be excited to see me too.

Her response was not what I expected. "I'm so sorry about all of this, *mijo*, I really am, but whatever you do . . . don't come back home," she said sternly. "If you do, you'll never leave Eugene again. Trust me. I know what I'm talking about. I know it's tough, but you have to find a way to stick it out down there. You have real talent, but there are no opportunities for you here."

I slowly pulled the phone away from my ear. A steady stream of cars rushed by on Katella Avenue. *How many of them are going home?* I couldn't believe she had just told me to stay in LA. It was all I could do not to say, "Who is this impostor? Give me back my mama."

My mother would have said, "Don't worry about anything. Come back home, son. I'll make your favorite mac and cheese casserole and a yellow cake with chocolate frosting. Afterward, we can sit together and figure out your next move."

But that's not what *this* woman said. At this point it didn't seem worth mentioning that the Romano Brothers had already kicked me out of the motel and that I had no place to stay. The conviction in her voice was resolute.

With headlights flashing past me in both directions at the busy intersection, I knew she was right. Besides, the thought of having to face my old school mates was unbearable. Haunting me was the headline from my high school newspaper: "Disco Dan Shoots for Stardom." I didn't want to go down in the Highlander record books as a falling star.

I had read that article so many times that I had it memorized. Especially the last couple of sentences, where I had said in a self-assured tone, "Hey, maybe it's going to be hard, but isn't that what it's all about? If I work hard, I'll make it."

Now my moment of truth had arrived. I could fall flat on my face by staying in Los Angeles, but I could just as easily fail at home. And if I had to fail, I would rather it be in the pursuit of my dream.

At the end of my long silence, I said to her, "You're right, Mama. You're right. I'll stay in LA. I'll figure something out."

Suddenly, her tone changed, as if some great revelation had just dawned on her. "Call Patricia," she said excitedly. "She just rented an apartment with a girlfriend in Beverly Hills. I don't know if she's in the country right now, but it's worth a try."

"Really?" My beautiful sister Patricia had just signed a contract with a prestigious modeling agency, and things were really taking off for her. She had been traveling the world for photo shoots, proving to all of us that dreams really could come true. This was just the break I needed. "I'll call her right now!"

"Yes, right now, Danny. I'm praying for you. Don't give up."

This was the response I had expected when I called. I was glad to have Mama back. I thanked her, admitting I could use all the prayers I could get.

After we hung up, I put another quarter in the phone and dialed Patricia. The phone rang several times, my heart sinking lower with each ring. Finally, someone picked up, and as my sister's sweet voice greeted me, I exhaled and told her about my plight.

"Why don't you come stay with me at my place on Oakhurst and try your luck in this part of town?" she asked. "You're only about an hour away."

"Really? You'd let me do that?"

"Of course! You're my little brother."

Once I arrived, I unpacked my few possessions, including my drum set. Patricia explained she would be traveling a lot for work and would rarely be home. Thankfully, her roommate Judith didn't seem to mind having me around, even though they had a small, two-bedroom apartment.

I had only been to Beverly Hills once in my life, when Mama took us there on the bus to show us how she used to live and to give us that pep talk about dreaming big. I was eight years old that day when I had stared up at those exquisite homes. Now, here I was, ten years later, living with Patricia in the middle of it all, both of us drawing closer to our dreams.

Mama had been right all along.

Anything *was* possible if we worked hard and had faith.

CHAPTER 36

The Great Pretender

The last time I had lived in Los Angeles, I was a kid using wagons, tricycles, city buses, and my own two feet to get around some of the roughest parts of the city. Now I had a car, and I spent that first week driving around to get a feel for the ever-changing landscape. I quickly realized that the path to becoming a world-renowned drummer was nothing like becoming a lawyer or doctor. There was no instruction manual, no curriculum, no clear path to success. For a teenager trying to unlock the mystery of the music industry, it proved to be a disorienting labyrinth, and without a map to guide me, I felt lost.

I turned to the *Los Angeles Times*, hoping to research the local music scene. When that proved useless, I popped into a variety of bookstores, looking for anything I could find about how a backup musician could land gigs. I found nothing. Nada. Zippo. I needed a break, just one. If I could only find a band in search of a drummer, I was certain I could deliver the goods. After more research, I came across two places worth investigating.

First stop—the Professional Drum Shop in Hollywood on 854 Vine Street—the place where the top drummers in the world bought their equipment. When I entered, black-and-white photos of all the greats greeted me along the walls of this legendary store. I was standing on holy ground, where Buddy Rich, Gene Krupa, and Frank Sinatra's drummer, Irv Cottler, had all stood. The shop smelled of metal drum hoops that had been heavily lubricated, and mountains of used hardware crowded the entrance to the bathroom. Just knowing my favorite drummers had been here made me feel one step closer to seeing my picture on the wall with theirs.

The owner, Bob Yeager, a graying percussionist, was refurbishing a vintage snare drum, one I would learn belonged to the great Louis Bellson, who had played with Benny Goodman, Tommy Dorsey, Harry James, Duke Ellington, and many other jazz luminaries.

"What do I need to do to be as good as those guys?" I asked, pointing at the wall of fame above his head.

He looked up from his worktable. "Don't practice what you already know, kid." He unthreaded a lug from the topside of the drum. "Practice things you *don't* know, and you'll become a better drummer." His pithy advice was simple yet profound.

"Thank you, sir."

"Sure, kid. Drop by anytime."

From there, I walked across Vine Street to the Musician's Union Local 47, a building that looked like the Department of Motor Vehicles. Despite its dingy appearance, every professional musician in LA belonged to this union. It was inspiring to stand in another sacred space. At this point, I hadn't met the criteria necessary to join. But even if I had, I didn't have the money for the initial membership dues. I took my time, looked around, and promised myself I would walk back into that building one day to become a member. Even though I hadn't taken ownership of my heritage, unwittingly I was being led by the ancestry of my genetic code. The Irishman in me was just brash enough to believe I could succeed. The Mexican in me was a fighter from a long line of warriors, willing to lay my life on the line for anything I was passionate about.

By the beginning of the second week, I was eager to make something happen. Running out of time and options, I concocted a crazy idea that would take a lot of gall. Never lacking in nerve, I decided to go through with it.

When I shared it with Patricia, she stepped up to help. "Listen, Danny. I've learned a lot the hard way, and if there's anything I know, it's that you've got one shot to make a good impression when you're trying to break into something." She eyed my unimpressive attire. "I'm taking you shopping."

While making her way in the fashion industry, Patricia learned to carry herself with the utmost class and sophistication. But it wasn't a game to her. Nothing about my sister was fake. She had always walked with that presence of mind. Her gregarious personality was larger than life, just like Mama's. Now, after she bought me some designer clothes and a sleek Monceau Swiss wristwatch with a mother-of-pearl face, she spun me around in my new duds and said, "Look at you now. Ready to take on the world. You look so sharp!"

"I feel like an actor, playing the part of a rich kid," I said, grateful but hesitant.

"That's what's holding you back. You gotta own it. If you don't believe you belong here, your doubt will come across."

"I suppose you're right."

"Listen. Half of the successful people here are immigrants who came from dire straits. They crossed these borders from all over the world with nothing but a dream and a willingness to work hard. Like our grandfather, they pulled themselves up from their bootstraps and made something of themselves. That's nobler than having it handed to them like the other half, who lack character because they didn't earn it. How are we any different?" she asked, peering at me with arched eyebrows.

I shrugged my shoulders. "We're not?" I answered meekly.

"And how are they any better than us?" she asked.

"They're not?" I said, as if it were a question.

"That's right. They're not!" Patricia said sternly. "We're entitled to the same opportunity to make a name for ourselves as anyone else. That's what makes this country what it is. It's made up of immigrants, dreamers, and go-getters. You and I are going after our dreams with all we've got. We're not asking anyone for anything. We're doing it with hard work and using the gifts and talents God gave us. Who can fault us for that? Don't forget our refined heritage from Mexico. Don't forget your grandfather's legacy. We belong here just as much as any of those other people."

Patricia was never one to mince words, and she was right about our grandfather. We both knew it. But was she right about *me*? "Look, Danny. I can buy you all the clothes in the world," she continued, "but if you don't see your own worth, they won't either."

There it was. My deepest wound. That feeling of not being good enough to earn anyone's love or acceptance. It was all rooted in being abandoned by my father. But Patricia's father had abandoned her too, and she not only had overcome that wound, but she had grown stronger as a result. She was a proud lioness who knew the power of her roar. Now she was using that might to set me up for success and teaching me how to believe I belonged in this world of privilege and excess as much as anyone else.

I still had a lot to learn, but hearing her speak with such conviction, emboldened me to give this preposterous idea my best shot.

It was a warm December day in 1980 as I cruised the west end of Beverly Hills for a parking space. I planned to make a day of it, so I plugged the parking meter with a ton of change and grabbed my Panasonic boom box and satchel. I bought this newer model because I had seen the members of Earth, Wind & Fire promoting it in a *Rolling Stone* magazine ad that read, "Get Platinum Power." Even though I barely had enough money to cover it, I wanted to have the latest technology to make an impression.

So, with my new platinum power, I walked down Olympic Boulevard, took a right on South Spaulding Drive, and passed an oil derrick towering incongruously over a football field. Then I veered left onto South Moreno. It was so peaceful strolling along the resplendent street, nothing like the south-central part of LA where I had grown up. Both sides of the street were lined with crepe myrtles. Fallen leaves blew in the wind. I imagined a camera taking sweeping shots of the picturesque scene. When I panned left, I got my first glimpse of Beverly Hills High School.

With its pristine white buildings, the sprawling campus looked like an Ivy League university. I made my way toward the front entrance, thinking, *Why couldn't I have gone to a school like this?*

I walked up the first set of concrete stairs and sat on the well-manicured emerald lawn in the most visible spot I could find. Dressed in canary-yellow pants and a silk shirt, I tilted my Panama Jack straw hat and tweaked the angle of my sunglasses to channel the ultimate state of cool.

As students spilled onto the lawn during lunch break, I cranked up Earth, Wind & Fire's *Greatest Hits* on my boom box, pulled out a set of sticks, and began jamming along with the music on my practice pad.

At age eighteen, I hoped to draw the attention of the school's serious musicians, thinking maybe someone would want to form a band. I jammed through to "Fantasy," the second song on side one, but no one came to check me out. By the time I double-stroked my way into "Can't Hide Love," I was starting to lose hope that anyone would approach me, other than perhaps the head of security. But I kept going. While I was pounding out my sixteenth notes in "Getaway," a wide-shouldered Black kid wearing a pink short-sleeved polo shirt approached me.

"You're new here, aren't you?"

"Sure am," I replied while continuing to play one press roll after another.

"Where you from?"

"LA originally, but I just moved down from Eugene, Oregon."

"Well, welcome to Beverly," he said with a grin. He stuck out his hand to give me a shake. "I'm Kennedy."

"Great to meet you, Kennedy." I put my drumsticks down to give him a firm handshake. "My name's Danny."

"You play the drums for real?"

"Sure do."

"Right on. I play bass."

"Awesome. We should jam sometime."

"Yeah, I'm down with that for sure."

The cassette tape abruptly clicked at the end of side one.

"Catch you later, my man," Kennedy said and then took off.

Not wanting to lose my mojo, I flipped the tape to side two. I was grooving my brains out on "September" when a slender Black kid with bronze skin walked up to me. With an intense look in his eyes, he said, "Yo, homie. You got some mean skills with those sticks."

"Thanks, man. You play?"

"You know it!" He smiled. "Guitar, bass, drums . . . and I sing up a storm too."

"That's tight. I dig your confidence, bro." I stopped playing in order to give him my full attention. "What's your name?"

"Lenny. Lenny Kravitz. Yours?"

"Danny."

"Well, Danny, you're obviously new around here, because it would be impossible to miss a cat like you."

"My first day," I said, smiling as the school bell rang.

"I can't be late again," Lenny said. "What class you got next? Maybe we can walk together?"

"Go ahead," I said, feigning an excuse. "I have to put my stuff away."

"Cool. Let's hook up after school, then. Meet me in front of the swim gym?"

I nodded, playing it cool. "See you then."

By the time he left, lunch hour was over, so I walked back to my car to feed more change into the meter and put my boom box and satchel in the trunk. I was excited to meet musicians my own age, but as I walked around the area, killing time until school let out, I realized I had just told those guys I was a new transfer student. How was I going to keep up *that* charade? And what would they think of me when they found out I wasn't?

When my new watch ticked to 3:30, I made my way back to the court-yard near the swim gym. Lenny tapped me on the back and said, "There you are! Sorry, man. I actually have to jet, but . . . let's hook up tomorrow."

"Here?"

"Sure," he said, giving me a high five and hurrying off.

If there was any hope of building this friendship, I would have to come back and pretend to be a student. Again.

Later that night, I went to Thrifty's on North Cannon and picked up a cheap school backpack. Since I couldn't afford the all-day parking meters, I woke early the next morning to secure a seat on the city bus, choosing the route that would drop me off near the school. Then I strolled across campus, ready to play my part. This time I dressed more low-key.

Despite my fears, infiltrating Beverly Hills High proved easier than expected. I simply walked into the school as if I were one of the students, navigating the hallways with my canvas backpack. I had only graduated a few months earlier, so age-wise I fit right in. And with Patricia's encouragement, I convinced myself that I belonged there. No one questioned me, and with a diverse mix of Middle Eastern, Black, and Jewish students, I didn't stand out the way I had in Eugene.

A friendly-looking red-haired girl was walking next to me, so I asked her for directions to the library. She kindly pointed the way, and I headed for the stacks. While the other students went to class, I pretended to be studying. Actually, I was—just not any subjects the school offered. There were no calculus, history, or biology books in my backpack. Instead, I pulled out the latest issue of *Modern Drummer* magazine, which I read cover to cover.

When the lunch bell rang, I slipped back into the hallways, heading out to the lawn to look for Lenny.

"Hey, Danny," he said, adjusting his black aviator shades. "How's it going so far?"

"I love it!"

"Who'd you get for math?"

"I can't remember his name," I lied. "It's all a little overwhelming." And that was true. It was.

"I get that for sure. This school is massive. Follow me. I've already been bragging about you." We walked down the concrete steps and made our entrance into the band room, where a few guys were shooting the breeze. "Danny," Lenny said, "meet Vadim Zilberstein, a ridiculous jazz guitarist. Osama Afifi, the fastest bass player around. And Donn Wyatt, the funkiest keyboard player at Beverly."

"Great to meet you guys," I said, giving them the soul brother handshake. I couldn't believe my luck. Mama's prayers were definitely working.

"Lenny tells us you have some sick chops," Osama said, casting his Egyptian eyes toward the drums. "You wanna jam?"

"Sure." He had no idea how much I had wanted him to ask. With the sun peeking through the open door, I hopped onto the school drum set, pulled a pair of sticks out of my backpack, and began playing my best stuff. The musicians in the room looked dumbfounded.

"Whoa! You really do have some chops," Vadim said in a thick Russian accent.

Donn clapped his hands. "That was grooving, man!"

We had a blast jamming together through the rest of the lunch period. Then we exchanged numbers and went to class—everyone, that is, except me.

From that day forward, I continued going to school. I acted as though I belonged there, because I managed to convince myself I did. This seemed the perfect place for a starry-eyed young man to get headed in the right direction. Before I knew it, I was reliving my senior year—only this time without having to do any homework!

Soon I became a familiar face, and everyone, including the security guard, was under the impression that I was legitimately enrolled. Consequently, I was given a free hall pass.

Lenny, Kennedy, and the rest of my new musician pals began recommending me for gigs around town. My first television appearance was filmed at Beverly High on KBEV Channel 6, a student-run public access show, with Vadim and Osama. We called ourselves the Jazz Trio and performed a few jazz standards on the broadcast. The guys cut me loose for a drum solo on "Spain" by Chick Corea.

After our smashing performance, they (along with Lenny) talked the music teacher Mr. Farmer into letting me sit in with the school jazz band. Though I wasn't enrolled in his class, I told him I was a transfer student and that I would be willing to spend my "free period" playing drums in his ensemble whenever he needed me since he had a few drummers he rotated through regularly.

Whenever I felt I had been seen in the library too long, I would sneak into one of the small practice rooms in the band building and play on my drum pad while listening to Patricia's Sony Walkman. It was the perfect hideout. But as I spent more time there, I sensed that Mr. Farmer might be on to me. Ironically, now that I didn't *have* to go to school, I was terrified I might be kicked out.

Attending Beverly Hills High—a school where the graduation rate was nearly 100 percent, the ethnic diversity unparalleled, and the honor roll ginormous—had opened my eyes to an entirely new side of life. After discovering that some of my friends had wealthy fathers, I wished I had one too. Then I could have been a real student at Beverly instead of having to keep up this sham. I was envious that they were being groomed for success by fathers who loved them, who weren't ashamed of them, and who were giving them a leg up in the world.

Against their pedigrees, contacts, and net worth, I didn't measure up. But if I couldn't be one of them, then I would do my best to be one *with* them. To do that, I would have to win them over with the only thing I had: my dogged determination and two wooden drumsticks. With that, I would solo my way into their hearts as I had done so many times before—with music.

In the most audacious of ways, I managed to sneak into one of the most prestigious public high schools in America without detection. It was a place where I was finally being celebrated for what I *did* have—my God-given musical talent and my ability to make friends laugh until they cried. Friends with swimming pools. Friends with mega-homes. Friends with fathers. Friends with futures. Only seven years earlier I had been living in our family's old car, with no running water, no electricity, and no place to bathe. Secrets no one at Beverly High ever needed to know.

Somehow, I knew my destiny was connected to that school and that fulfilling my dream depended on claiming this new identity as my own.

I wasn't trying to pull off some mischievous prank. I was just desperate to rise above the circumstances foisted upon me throughout my childhood. I was eighteen, and the thought of failure was abhorrent to me. After years of dreaming of unencumbered flight, this seemed my only chance to soar. Day after day, I kept going to school, praying that my true identity would not be discovered.

Every time I ran into Mr. Farmer outside of the band room, I avoided eye contact for fear he might know I wasn't really enrolled. Despite my best efforts, one afternoon he spotted me during class time. I acted as if I was on my way to a classroom. As I ambled down the polished corridors, I could feel the band director's eyes burning a hole in my back. The bell had just rung, and the door was already closed, so I peeked through the narrow vertical window. When I thought he was gone, I made a U-turn and headed back toward the library. But there at the front entrance, I came face to face with Farmer.

He stood silently, his red face peering through my deceptive teenage soul. *Was the jig up?* Finally, he broke his silence. Not with his words but with something deeper than words. As he gazed into my eyes and saw my trembling face, a smile emerged from the side of his mouth. His message was clear: *Your secret's safe with me, kid.*

After that heart-stopping encounter, I went on my way. To my good fortune, he never did broach the subject. Perhaps he turned a blind eye because he knew we were on the same team. I wanted to make good music. So did he. We were both determined to create something—something meaningful, something beautiful—and because of that mutual desire, he let me stay. And because he did, I was able to navigate the halls of Beverly Hills High, which, little did I know, would lead to opportunities beyond my wildest dreams.

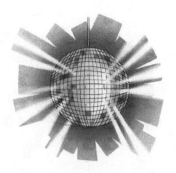

CHAPTER 37

Hollywood Swinging

One Friday after school, Lenny asked if I would give him a ride to his house in Baldwin Hills, an affluent Black community about thirty minutes from Beverly Hills. On the way there, he saw something from a distance and got excited.

"Have you ever had Golden Bird?" he asked.

"No. What is it?"

"Are you kidding me? After this light, hang a left where that big yellow and red sign is."

I pulled over, and we ordered a bucket of fried chicken, some biscuits and honey, and large Cokes.

"This chicken's ridiculous, right?" Lenny said, tearing into a juicy thigh.

I admitted it was the best I'd ever had.

"It's all about the 'flava,' like the sign says. Mmm . . . And how about these crispy biscuits with honey?"

"I could eat ten of these things."

"Just stick with me, and I'll hip you to all the LA hot spots. Next time I'll take you to Pink's Hot Dogs. They're insane."

After we wiped our greasy hands, we drove for another ten minutes, then pulled up to his family's midcentury modern home. It perched on the top of the hill. When he told me Ray Charles was his neighbor, I nearly lost it. Moments later, we were in the kitchen, already hunting for something else to eat, when Lenny's mother came in carrying groceries. She was a tall, slim, attractive, and elegant woman with impeccable manners. Lenny introduced her as Roxie Roker, and I recognized her immediately. She played Helen Willis on *The Jeffersons*—one of the most popular sitcoms of the day. Lenny had never told me his mother was a TV star.

On the show, Roxie's character was married to a white man named Tom Willis. In real life, Roxie was married to Lenny's father, Sy Kravitz, an ABC News producer of Russian Jewish descent. Sy was a distinguished man with a strong presence. He stood about five feet seven and had a slight paunch. While I was surprised to find myself standing in the kitchen with Roxie Roker, it was clear that in this environment she was simply Lenny's mother, who called him "Leonard" and welcomed me into their home.

From there, Lenny gave me a tour of the house, leading me out to the backyard pool, where we took in the view of the mountains, the Hollywood Hills, and the Coliseum. One thing was for certain: this was nothing like the dirt yard that once circled our trailers, where my siblings and I had played in bare feet and chased chickens. I never could have imagined any kid calling a place like this home.

Later that night, Lenny asked his parents if I could stay over since it was Friday.

"They gave me the song and dance about not knowing you well enough," Lenny said, frustrated by their rigid rules. "Sorry, but you can't stay."

"Not knowing me well enough?"

"Yeah, they've never seen you before, don't know your family."

In that instant, I went from feeling welcome to excluded and unwanted, an all too familiar situation that had followed me through life like a stray.

Sensing my disappointment, Lenny had an idea. "Just sleep out here in your car," he said, standing with me in the driveway.

I pinched my brow as if he were crazy.

"For real, man. I'll bring you blankets. Pillows. You won't get too cold. Then we can head out again early in the morning."

Maybe it was the magic I had felt that day. Maybe it was Lenny's persistent pleas. Maybe it was my desperate desire to make real friends here in this new world, but for whatever reason, I agreed to his nutty idea, hoping his parents wouldn't catch on and ban me from their house for good.

Lenny came to check on me throughout the night, bringing water and extra blankets, apologizing for his parents' strictness. He didn't know I had spent many nights sleeping in a car, just never in the shadows of such a lovely neighborhood with a breathtaking view of the city lights that overlooked Los Angeles.

The next morning, we left at the crack of dawn before his mom and dad could discover that, despite their resistance, I had spent the night there after all. We were barely out of his Baldwin Hills neighborhood when Lenny said, "Let's go to Big Ben's."

"What's that?"

"A really dope record shop just on the corner of La Brea and Rodeo. I know the manager. He'll hook us up with a discount."

"I'm down. Lead the way."

Ready for adventure and eager to escape his dad's watchful eye, Lenny directed me down the hill to that busy intersection. There, we picked out a few of our favorite new albums, then headed to Hollywood, where he told me to park. "I'm taking you to another one of my favorite joints," he said.

After walking a couple of blocks, Lenny started sniffing like a bloodhound, quickening his already fast pace with long strides.

"Man, you walk fast," I said, trying to keep up with him.

"I'm from Brooklyn. That's how we roll there." Then he stopped and said, "Smell that?"

I breathed in the most scrumptious smell imaginable. "Smells like cookies," I said, taking another whiff after catching my breath.

"These ain't no ordinary cookies." He smiled and pointed to a quaint little A-frame hut on the corner of Sunset and Formosa. "Right there is the Famous Amos cookie store—the holy grail of cookies."

"Who's Famous Amos?"

"*Who* is Famous Amos?" he laughed. "They don't have one of these in Eugene?"

"They don't have a lot of things in Eugene."

"He's like the Black Willy Wonka, and this is his chocolate factory. Follow me."

Inside we ordered a batch fresh from the oven, then devoured some of the tastiest chocolate chip cookies you could ever sink your teeth into.

"You can't have cookies without milk," I said. "I'll grab us a couple of cartons."

As we sat there gorging ourselves, we rattled on about our dreams.

"I'm gonna be a rock star," Lenny said confidently, "and prove to all those chumps who make fun of me at Beverly that I've got what it takes. Most of the good musicians at school don't take me seriously because I change up my image all the time. But they'll be sorry one day when they see my name up in lights. I'm gonna show my dad too. There's just no two ways about it. I'm gonna make it big. I can see it in my mind already."

"You and I are so much alike," I said. "I'm gonna be a world-renowned drummer, and I'm gonna write books one day too."

"Great. Now that that's settled, let's have some more cookies," Lenny said, laughing with his whole soul, the way he frequently did when we hung out together. Like me, he was always ready to laugh.

Compelled by our mutual desires, Lenny and I formed a close bond and quickly became inseparable. We were both hard workers, and together we hustled to move those dreams forward in every conceivable way. We practiced together. Networked together. Chased girls together. With a much closer connection to the entertainment industry, Lenny was always trying to school me about show business. One evening he invited me to a taping of *The Jeffersons* at Metromedia in Hollywood. It was fascinating to see how they put the show together.

"Man, it's impressive to see your mom shift in and out of character so easily."

"Yeah, she's something special . . . but she's been working at it for a long time. She started her career doing theater in New York. We moved out to Santa Monica when I was eleven, right after she landed the *Jeffersons* gig."

"How does she remember all those lines?"

"I go over them with her."

"You ever want to do any acting?"

"I dabbled in it a little already . . . a play, a commercial, a few other things. Maybe one day I'll dive in. But I love music more than anything, and that's all I really want to do—write, produce, and perform music, like Prince."

Most afternoons after school, I drove us around LA while we listened to Prince; David Bowie; the Jacksons; Kiss; Led Zeppelin; Stevie Wonder; the Beatles; Earth, Wind & Fire; and our hero, Buddy Rich. Despite his family being well off, Lenny's parents seemed determined to teach their only child to have a strong work ethic. Plus, they were strict. For these reasons, Lenny didn't have his own car. But since he knew LA better than I did, I asked him to do all the driving in mine so I could practice drumming on the dashboard. He obliged, and I went to town on that dash, banging my way through the miles until the board was demolished. My dashboard may have gotten thrashed, but my drumming chops were getting into top form, and Lenny and I were forming a solid brotherhood beat by beat.

My frequent visits to the Kravitzes' household led to a close relationship with Roxie and Sy as well, and sleepovers were no longer a problem. Sy and I were both avid jazz lovers, and we talked passionately for hours about our favorite artists. This formed something of a bridge between the strong-willed father and son, who were often at odds with one another. In time, Roxie became more like a second mother to me, and on many occasions she would make us breakfast.

While eating one of her hearty meals and watching her code-switch into her native Bahamian accent and more laid-back personality as she cooked, I thought about how much my life had changed since I dared to walk into Beverly Hills High. Growing up, we could barely afford to eat cereal. Now a TV star was cooking me a full breakfast in a fabulous home on a hill.

One morning, as I reveled in the smell of scrambled eggs, French toast, and conch fritters from Roxie's kitchen, I wondered why there wasn't a television show about a single immigrant mother, like Mama, trying to survive and "raise her kids up right" in a new land. Surely there were millions just like her who couldn't find themselves represented on a prime-time network show, even though they were the backbone of this country, doing the work no one else would do. Mama could have played that true-to-life groundbreaking role just as Roxie had helped normalize interracial marriage. I thought about how my life might have turned out if Mama had become the movie star she had once dreamed of becoming. If she had been given a fair shake, I might be living Lenny's life.

I was happy for Roxie's success, which had led to the privileged life Lenny was accustomed to. But I was sad that my mother didn't have such good fortune. As I continued back down La Cienega to Patricia's apartment, I wondered why some people got all the breaks in life. Instead of feeling sorry for myself, though, I decided to take my destiny into my own hands and make something of myself. Maybe I could make up for Mama's broken dreams. *Might even be able to buy her a house like Sy and Roxie's*, I thought. Yes. I would settle for nothing less.

CHAPTER 38

Don't Stop Believin'

The courtyard area outside the swim gym was where a lot of the performers at Beverly High congregated after school—dancers, musicians, actors, all with aspirations of stardom. By showing up there daily, I got asked to play at several cast parties for the school's top-notch theater productions. Those shows featured some gifted young performers, such as Nicolas Coppola (who would later change his last name to Cage), and their dedication to the craft continued to inspire my own ambitions.

To sharpen my skills, I spent a lot of time practicing at Osama's place, listening to jazz records at Vadim's, or jamming at Donn Wyatt's pad, which I loved, because his mother Gwendolyn would usually lay out a nice spread of soul food for us to keep the funk alive. When I wasn't with one of those guys, I was usually spending time with Lenny or cruising with Kennedy on the west side.

Kennedy was one of my few friends who had a car. Plus, he liked to drive, which meant I didn't have to pay for gas all the time. Like me, he loved to clown around and get a laugh out of total strangers. But after about a month of running around together in his silver Camaro Z28, I still knew very little about him, aside from our shared love for music and laughter.

All of that changed the day he decided to take me to his house. We were heading west on Sunset toward the beach when he took a right onto Bellagio Way through the exquisitely sculpted columns of the west gate of Bel-Air.

As we ventured into this residential enclave for Hollywood celebrities and the insanely rich, the sweet fragrance of floribunda rose bushes breezed into his sports car. I was wide-eyed as I peered through massive hedges to catch a glimpse of these luxury estates.

After passing the Bel-Air Country Club and working our way up the most charming winding roads, I was eager to see which of these mansions my friend called home. A few more miles of turns up the mountain, and we arrived at a formidable, wrought iron gate that was shrouded in dense greenery. Kennedy announced his arrival on the intercom. As we waited for the gate to open, he mentioned that his house was formerly owned by comedian Red Skelton and that actor Tony Curtis lived just down the hill from him. Mama and I loved Red Skelton and had watched a lot of Tony Curtis movies together. I couldn't wait to phone her about all of this.

While driving up the long, winding driveway, I spotted two llamas grazing to my left. "I've never seen real llamas before," I blurted out.

Kennedy smiled. "That's Fernando Llama and Como Se Llama," he said, chuckling. I cracked up because Fernando Lamas was a famous actor from Argentina who Mama thought was handsome, and *Como Se Llama* meant "What's your name?" in Spanish. A good sign that Kennedy had earned his sharp wit from his family.

We continued upward toward the main residence and drove past a tennis court before pulling into a cobblestone driveway. The Tuscan-style mansion sat atop a well-maintained compound overlooking Century City. It was, by far, the most spectacular home I had ever seen, surpassing even Lenny's.

Inside, Kennedy introduced me to his father, a confident and friendly man with ultra-white teeth and scintillating hazel eyes. He stretched out his hand.

"Hi, I'm Berry," he said with a distinctive voice and the same Cheshire cat smile as Kennedy's.

"It's a pleasure to meet you, sir." I shook his hand, pretending to feel perfectly at ease in these surroundings. When they weren't looking at me, I tried to get a closer look at everything. Whether it was the elegant decor that filled the room or the stunning vistas just beyond the windows, everywhere I looked was spellbinding. It couldn't have been more obvious that Kennedy and I had come from very different worlds. And yet music made us equals. Even friends.

Upstairs in Kennedy's bedroom, I learned that his father, the man I had just met, was the legendary music icon and founder of Motown Records, Berry Gordy. *What?* I couldn't believe it! Motown was my favorite record label of all time. What little extra money I had in my youth was usually spent on Motown records by artists like the Jackson 5, Stevie Wonder, Diana Ross & the Supremes, the Temptations, Marvin Gaye, the Four Tops, the Commodores, and the rest of the hitmaking roster. I couldn't think of anyone who had done more for Black music than Berry Gordy.

Everyone in my family was a Motown fan, as were millions of other families across the world. There was only one difference between me and those millions of fans—none of them were up at the Gordy compound that day.

As the school year progressed, I spent more and more time with either Kennedy or Lenny. Hanging out with them was the equivalent of getting a college education in the entertainment industry. The best part of it all was that both of them not only wanted me to be in their lives but also in their bands. I loved building such genuine friendships, something that had been foreign to me most of my life.

Finally, I had found my tribe. With the two of them by my side, I was welcomed into many of the finest homes in the area and introduced to their esteemed owners, who were writers, directors, producers, actors, superstars, and moguls.

Occasionally the three of us jammed at Kennedy's house in Berry's music room. Whenever we were hungry, one of their chefs would whip up whatever we wanted and bring it out to us. On weekends Kennedy would usually drive me around Westwood, stopping at Westwood Village, the trendy nightspot for students attending UCLA.

Once in a while, Berry would take us out for dinner to one of the city's culinary hot spots, such as Spago, Chasen's, or the Palm. Sitting in the back seat of his Rolls-Royce on the way to these five-star eateries was beyond grand. Completely enamored, I wanted to have my picture taken in it so I could send it to Mama, but I resisted the temptation, acting as if I did this every day.

On Kennedy's seventeenth birthday, his father threw a big bash for him at Le Dome, a chic French restaurant in West Hollywood that looked like a fifteenth-century château. Seated in an elegant private room with a luxurious chandelier, we ordered from a handwritten, pastel-colored menu and were given fine linen napkins. I had never eaten French food and was unfamiliar with most of the entrées. Sitting next to me, though, was a sophisticated woman who looked like she knew what to order, so I asked her politely, "What's your favorite thing on the menu, ma'am?"

"Oh, honey, my name is Suzanne. And I love the beef bourguignon. But if you want a really special dessert, you must have the chocolate soufflé. It's to die for."

"Yes, I heard that's very good here," I said. Of course, I had no idea what I was talking about.

"Trust me, honey child. You won't be disappointed. But be sure to place your order when the waiter comes back. It takes about forty minutes to prepare."

As the Gordy family and key Motown figures sat around the enormous Brazilian walnut table, Berry gave a toast and shared the inspiration behind his son's name. "I gave Kennedy his first name in honor of President John F. Kennedy and his middle name in honor of my dear friend William "Smokey" Robinson," he said. "As you all know, he was one of the first artists I signed to Tamla Records before we formed Motown."

The scene seemed too perfect to be true. Kennedy's father made a toast to him, just like dignified people did in the movies. How special it must have felt to be named after such iconic figures, men who changed the world in their own unique ways. Even better to have a father who not only cared enough to choose your name but threw you a birthday party to celebrate your worth.

I remembered Lenny telling me his dad had served as a Green Beret in the Korean War and that the uncle he was named after had not only died saving his entire platoon in the same war at age twenty but had also received the Congressional Medal of Honor. I was just plain old Danny Donnelly, the kid with an unimportant name. Although I was named after my father, he had scammed my mother into a marriage to avoid serving in Vietnam, and he had certainly never done one thing to make me feel that I was wanted, let alone special and treasured.

As the celebrated family and distinguished guests nibbled on French baguettes and sipped expensive wine, I thought about Mama's past life. I imagined she must have had countless dinners like this in Mexico when her esteemed father was alive. I felt sad for her. Sad that such luxuries were no longer in her life. How she must have missed the grandiosity of it all. I was just beginning to understand the immensity of her loss and who she was. This was the world she had come from, and there was no way it could ever leave her heart. Now that I had seen how the other side lived, I desperately longed to be a part of that world. And I hoped that if I ever did manage that, it wouldn't all get taken from me the way it had been taken from Mama.

It was commonplace to see famous people at the Gordy compound, and I always had to subdue my excitement and be careful not to act like a fan. Berry provided a safe haven to the many stars who had signed with Motown, giving them a place to be themselves without public intrusion.

During one of my visits, the lovely Diana Ross was having a peaceful lunch on the patio. I greeted her on my way to the music room, and she was ever so sweet to me. I wanted to tell her in the worst way that her concert back in the late '60s at the Long Beach Municipal Auditorium had been my very first, at age seven, and how it had inspired me to become a drummer. Somehow, despite being completely starstruck, I managed to contain myself.

On another occasion, I was playing pinball in the front room while

Kennedy was taking a shower upstairs. Kennedy was the only kid I knew who had an actual arcade in his house. I had kept myself amused for hours with pinball, Pac-Man, Donkey Kong, and Sea Wolf. The best part was I didn't have to put money into these machines. I could play them for free to my heart's content. And so I did!

While submerged in a round of Sea Wolf, I glanced out the huge front bay windows and noticed two Rolls-Royces, black with silver and gold trim, coming up the driveway. A few minutes later, the doorbell rang. No one answered it, so I strolled over to the entrance and pulled back the heavy oak door. I gulped. *Was this a mirage?*

I was gobsmacked to find myself greeting Michael Jackson and the Jackson 5! As they entered the foyer and pulled off their shades, my heart raced. Outwardly, I tried to appear calm. Inwardly, I was trying to process the enormity of this unbelievable twist of fate. While they waited for someone in the family to officially greet them, I seized the opportunity and tried to get them to jam with me in Berry's music room. "Michael, Jermaine, Jackie, Tito, Marlon," I said brightly, "I know all your music, guys! You name it. I can play it on the drums! 'ABC,' 'The Love You Save,' 'I Want You Back.' Come on, Michael," I looked straight at him. "How about we jam together?"

In a polite and soft-spoken manner, he answered with an amused twinkle in his eyes, "Aw, kid, you got a lotta heart. What's your name?"

"Danny," I said, reaching to shake his hand.

"Thanks so much, Danny," he said, returning the handshake as I glanced down at his shiny black loafers with white socks. "We're here for an important meeting with Berry. But I look forward to hearing you play, though. Next time."

I wasn't about to give up so easily. Since no one seemed to be in a rush to greet them, I thought I would give it another try with something more specific. I knew Jermaine played the bass, so I made another impassioned plea. "Hey, Jermaine, Kennedy's got a great bass rig. You'll love the sound. We can groove together on 'Let's Get Serious.'"

This was Jermaine's first solo number one R&B hit, a single that Motown had released a little earlier that year. It was still in heavy rotation on the radio, and I knew that drum beat like the back of my hand. With a radiant smile, Jermaine said, "You like the groove on that, do you?"

"It's a wicked beat," I said. "I know it well."

"I'm glad you like it." He smiled. "We worked hard on that record."

I continued to hold court alone with the brothers while we waited.

After a bit more chatter, Berry finally made his way down the staircase. Wearing a mint-green velour robe, he greeted the Jacksons with a big smile and hugs all around. It was inspiring to see the man who had launched their careers doling out so much affection, even though they had recently left his record label. Everyone, that is, but Jermaine, who had married Berry's oldest daughter, Hazel.

Later that evening, while driving home, I kept replaying in my mind what had just happened. I couldn't believe that Michael Jackson and his brothers were all talking to me, and very kindly too. They had no idea I had once belonged to their fan club or how excited I had been each time the package with Jackson 5 paraphernalia would arrive in the mail. Or how, as a young boy, I fantasized about living next door to them and that I had made this declaration in my diary: "One day I will meet all of my musical idols."

Maybe I had the luck of the Irish after all because, aside from the Disneyland debacle, I was beginning to find myself in the right places at the right times. The night I met the Jackson brothers, I wrote another entry in my diary: "No one will believe me when I tell them I met my favorite Motown group—the Jackson 5. Man, even I can't believe it!"

I couldn't wait to tell Mama.

CHAPTER 39

Heroes

There was a higher likelihood of running into someone famous in Beverly Hills than practically anywhere in the world. I was barely a couple of blocks into my walk down Rodeo Drive one late afternoon when I saw actor Sylvester Stallone having a drink outside the Daisy, a private discotheque frequented by Hollywood celebrities. Mama and I loved how he had beaten the odds in *Rocky* and *Rocky II*. I meandered past one extravagant window display after another, wondering what it would be like to buy anything I wanted, the way movie stars like Sylvester Stallone could do.

As I continued browsing the windows of this famous street, I noticed a slender man standing under a streetlight. Catching a glimpse of a famous actor was one thing. Spotting the world's greatest drummer was quite another. It wasn't fame that impressed me as much as talent. And Buddy Rich was a drum god. Whenever he made an appearance on *The Tonight Show*, Mama would call for me, "*Dan-yell!* Hurry, hurry—Buddy Rich is going to play drums on TV with the Doc Severinsen Big Band."

She loved seeing the expression on my face as I watched him do what no other human could. His performances were jaw-dropping—whirlwinds of inspiration that whipped around and lifted me off the ground. After seeing how taken I was by his deft hand and footwork, she would say, "I know you'll meet him one day, Danny. I just know it."

I remembered Mama's words as I crossed the street, where I found Buddy standing in a cobalt-blue cashmere sweater outside Vidal Sassoon, a swanky hair salon. He had an intimidating presence, but I walked up to him anyway, stuck my hand out, and said, "Buddy Rich!"

He reached back gleefully and said, "Absolutely right," and then shook my hand.

"My mother told me I would meet you one day."

"Mothers are always right, son. Always listen to your mom."

I agreed, then asked if he was performing anywhere in town.

"*The Tonight Show* this week, and I'm recording a new album."

When he told me he had just finished tracking cover versions of "Fantasy" by Earth, Wind & Fire and "Never Can Say Goodbye" by the Jackson 5, I promised I would be at Tower Records on Sunset the day his new album was released.

With dark hair and loose jowls, he looked just like he did on the cover of my *DownBeat* magazine. While he was giving me his autograph, I studied the gold ankh pendant draped around his neck, wondering if that was the key to his supernatural powers, the way Bobby's crucifix around my neck had so often strengthened me. I thanked him and shook his hand again, hoping for some mystical transference of his virtuosity. When his wife and daughter came out of the salon with their stylish big hairdos, I knew our time together was over. As he walked down the street with his confident stride, I couldn't help but wonder how many people would walk right past him, having no idea they were within inches of one of the greatest musicians on the planet.

After my fateful encounter with the man who had once roomed with Frank Sinatra, I continued walking down Rodeo Drive with unspeakable joy in my heart. No celebrity sighting could top that experience.

A couple of weeks later, I was cruising around Hollywood listening to "Celebration" by Kool & the Gang. As the song faded, the DJ announced that members of Earth, Wind & Fire would be performing a one-time gospel concert called "Jesus at the Roxy." I immediately made a U-turn and headed to 9009 Sunset Boulevard in West Hollywood—home of the Roxy Theatre. There, I double-parked my car, flipped on my hazard lights, and jumped out to buy a ticket for the show. The cost was $7.50.

On the night of the concert, I arrived early to secure a table near the front of the stage. From my pocket, I pulled a letter I had written to Philip Bailey, the lead singer of Earth, Wind & Fire, who was known for his remarkable falsetto. Then I angled the envelope behind my glass of soda so Philip could see it when he was singing. During the concert, he looked down at me a few times. Each time he did, I pointed at his name written in big, clear print with a black marker.

The Roxy was a small venue, and I was hoping to run into him after the show, but he was nowhere to be found. I waited until the place was nearly empty. Still no luck. While the crew was breaking down the equipment, Ralph Johnson walked onstage wearing his signature wrap-around shades and midsized Afro. As one of the original drummers of Earth, Wind & Fire, he was another heroic figure to me. When he had finished talking to his roadie, I walked on stage and introduced myself, then asked if he had any advice on how to break into the business.

"Well, are you studying with someone who can help you hone your skills?"

"Not currently."

"Would you like to study with me?"

I steeled my nerves. "Are you serious? You'd really take me on as your student?"

"Why not? You look serious enough."

I could no longer contain my excitement. "Heck yeah, man! When do we start?"

He remained calm. "How does next Monday at noon sound?"

"Sounds perfect!"

That next Monday I pulled up to a lovely home on Encanto Drive in Sherman Oaks. I saw Ralph's salmon-colored Porsche 911S in one bay of his garage. It was a work of art with metallic paint that glimmered in the sun. I walked past the colorful flowerbeds to the front porch, rang the doorbell, then waited eagerly.

Ralph answered the door in a white terry cloth tennis outfit and flip-flops and graciously welcomed me into his home. As I made my way to his drum studio, I walked by walls lined with gold and platinum albums such as *Head to the Sky*; *Open Our Eyes*; *That's the Way of the World*; *Spirit*; *Gratitude*; *The Best of Earth, Wind & Fire, Vol. 1*; *All 'n All*; and *I Am*, all of which I had learned by heart. How many times had I practiced these beats, dreaming of someday meeting my favorite group? But this? This was unbelievable!

I tore into all of my best stuff on Ralph's drums, hoping his nods and smiles were good signs. When I concluded, he chuckled kindly and said, "Man, you don't need any lessons." In his cool radio DJ voice, he added, "You're gonna be one of them superstar drummers."

As much as I appreciated his affirming remarks, my heart sank. I didn't want this to be my first and last time with him. "Thanks, Ralph, but I know I still have a long way to go. I've only been playing for a couple of years."

"Two years? Well, you're a natural."

I gave him my most serious look. Unlike most of the talented musicians I had met, I hadn't had access to a lifetime of drum sets and private lessons. I knew I wasn't at the top of my game, but I was determined to do the work to get there. I just needed the right mentor to show me the way.

My unspoken message got through, and Ralph said, "Okay. I get you, my man. Whatcha think you need help with most?"

"My rudiments, reading music better, along with jazz and Latin rhythms," I replied.

"Sure, I can help you with all of that. Let's get started. But first let me preach the truth to you to set you straight. The drummer's main function is to keep solid time for the rest of the band, not to be flashy and busy all the time, so don't ever forget that. We're the engine that keeps it all going. The band is relying on us to set the tempo, keep the meter, so everything you practice has to be in time."

"How do I work on that?"

"By practicing with a metronome. This way, you are building your internal clock. Your goal is to become a human metronome and develop a sick groove or 'pocket' as we call it in the biz, to be the red carpet the other musicians walk across that shows them off. Do that, and everyone will want you as their drummer."

That day Ralph taught me a Nigerian rhythm called a Nanigo and a Latin rhythm called a Guaguancó, and he got me started on the first pages of *Progressive Steps to Syncopation* and *Advanced Techniques for the Modern Drummer*, two of the gospels in the drum canon.

When the lesson was over, I asked for a receipt for the ten dollars I paid him so I could have his autograph as proof this day had actually happened.

As he walked me out, I caught myself staring at the Grammy Awards on the mantel and again at the glistening gold albums on the wall. This time, with the sun shining through, I could see a reflection of my face in the frames. At that moment, I had an epiphany. I realized I had dreamed myself here, and if I could dream myself here, perhaps I could dream myself anywhere.

On the way home, I dreamed that one day I would have gold albums of my own—that my music would do the same thing for others that the music of Earth, Wind & Fire had done for me.

Five months later, Ralph invited my brother Bobby and me to his thirtieth birthday party on the Fourth of July. We gathered in the backyard with his wife Susie, his family, and other members of Earth, Wind & Fire, including Philip Bailey. It was hard to believe I was swimming and bouncing a beach ball across the pool with one of the greatest bands in the world, devouring succulent barbecue and shooting the breeze about life, music, and God.

Studying with Ralph proved inspiring, and I began to wonder if I might be able to connect with a few more of my drumming idols. Back at the apartment on Oakhurst, I perused my new Zildjian cymbal catalog that featured a full-page profile on the company's prominent endorsers. At the end of each bio, it mentioned where the drummer currently lived.

Since LA was the recording capital of the music industry, many of them lived in the area. I called up directory assistance to see if they had a listing for the drummers I wanted to meet the most. Harvey Mason, Jeff Porcaro, James Gadson, and John Robinson were among the top studio drummers in the world, all of whom were playing on the majority of the rock, pop, and R&B records coming out of Los Angeles. Their combined list of credits was a who's who of music industry icons. I came to know of them through my teacher Kent Clinkinbeard because they were his favorites. As luck would have it, each was in the phone book.

I called every one of them, but none answered the phone. I had saved Alphonse Mouzon for last. He had been my favorite jazz-fusion drummer since the moment I first discovered his work at Play It Again Records in Eugene. So I said a prayer, took a deep breath, and dialed the number.

"Hello," a man with a silky-smooth voice answered.

"Hi. Is this Alphonse?"

"Yes, it is."

I went into my well-rehearsed spiel and hoped for the best.

After patiently listening to me, he said, "Welcome to Los Angeles."

For the next half hour, he graciously answered all the questions I hurled at him as I flipped through his albums, amazed I was talking to the very man whose face I was staring at on the covers.

"You know, you remind me of myself," Alphonse said at the end of our conversation. "You're tenacious. Don't ever change, because the only way to make it in this business is *to be tenacious*."

To say that I reminded him of himself was the ultimate compliment.

The next day, I went to the post office and sent him a thank-you note and a demo tape of my drumming. After receiving my package, he called to invite me to his performance at Concerts by the Sea, a popular jazz club on the Redondo Beach pier. That night he was on fire, burning up his drums with a barbarous ferocity that inspired me to keep stoking the flames of my own potential. After hearing him perform, I knew how much further I had to go to reach greatness.

Meeting my heroes was a godsend, and my time with each of them was beyond inspiring. Still, I knew they wouldn't be able to help me break into the business until my drumming could command attention the way theirs had. Nothing if not determined, I sequestered myself and practiced intensely for hours on end.

Returning to California was proving to be the best thing that I could have done, and it was Patricia who had made it all possible, even handing me a wad of cash to get started until I could get back on my own feet.

The rest would be up to me.

CHAPTER 40

Dream On

Living in Beverly Hills was offering me countless opportunities of storybook grandeur. But the balance in my savings account was as thin as a communion wafer and dissolving just as rapidly. I needed to generate some cash flow in order to stay in LA, feed my Famous Amos cookie addiction, and keep my dream alive. I would eventually come clean with Lenny about not really being enrolled at Beverly, and he had covered for me, sometimes telling people I was his cousin from New York who had just transferred there. In Lenny's mind, he didn't feel it was that much of a stretch since I could have easily been one of his Jewish cousins, and people already knew he had a family with diverse ethnicity. He wanted me at school with him every day and was willing to say whatever he had to in order to keep me around.

One day at school, Lenny and I were brainstorming about how we could make money. When I told him about Disco Dan, Inc., the successful DJ business I had started in Eugene during my senior year, he perked up. "We can kick off the same business right here in LA. I've got tons of connections, you've got the equipment, and everybody wants a good DJ these days."

That day we formed GQ Productions. Soon we were deejaying all around LA, spinning the sounds for everything from house parties to high end events for celebrities and people of affluence. On the nights of our engagements, we would show up "clean" (street slang for looking sharp) as if we had jumped out of the pages of *GQ*, the hip men's monthly that had inspired the name of our company. We wanted to attract a sophisticated clientele, and our chic appearance was the key to achieving that.

For a while we were booked solid, but eventually the DJ gigs waned, and our cash flow dried up. Lenny got a job at a friend's fish fry joint called Leroy's, and I started playing with a variety of jazz and cover bands and on tons of demo recording sessions.

In the spring of 1981, I bought tickets for Lenny and me to see Buddy Rich in concert at Disneyland. When I got to Lenny's house, he was raring to go in a suit and tie like me. Out of respect for the world's greatest drummer, we wanted to look dapper. We were two teens with old souls who were eager to see our hero shred on the drums. But just as we were about to head out for our big night, Sy Kravitz confronted Lenny. "You're not going anywhere," he said. "You were out last night, and you haven't finished your chores."

"I know, but Danny already paid for two tickets."

"Tough. He can give yours to someone else."

The showdown quickly escalated into a heated head-to-head between them. I thought for sure that Sy, with his deep love for jazz, would give Lenny a pass just this once. But he wouldn't budge. Lenny was fuming. He had finally had enough of his father's rules, and he was ready to brawl.

"I'm going!" Lenny yelled. "And you can't stop me."

Sy arched one of his eyebrows, giving his son a deadly glare. Nostrils flared. Inches from each other, they had a stare-down. Lenny's breathing was hard. Sy's hands were shaking.

My stomach was in knots watching it all go down. I feared what might happen next.

Sy was built like a Rottweiler. With his military background, he could easily take Lenny down. I was hoping I wouldn't have to jump in to defend my friend, but I was willing to if necessary.

Lenny stormed off to his bedroom. I followed behind.

"Leonard," Sy said in a threatening tone, "if you walk out that door, you better plan on leaving for good."

With his eyes welling up, Lenny grabbed some of his essentials and threw them into the trunk of my Omega. Once in the car, we both took deep breaths. Exhaling, we headed down the hill on Cloverdale and off toward the 405 Freeway. My pulse finally slowed.

At age sixteen, Lenny had left his house for good and would never again live under the same roof as his fastidious father. It was a disconcerting moment to witness and a sad one. After having felt rejected by my own father all my life, I was angry at Sy for not loving his son the way he should have, for not seeing the wonderfully sweet soul Lenny had, and for not admiring his passion for music. Lenny and I weren't troublemakers. We simply wanted to see one of our musical heroes perform live. It wasn't some kind of racy nightlife that drove Lenny from his father's arms; it was the music, along with the dream, that kept pushing him forward at all costs.

At the concert, Lenny held back tears as we focused on Buddy's musical genius. With the big band slamming hard, Lenny was able to forget about his woes at home, at least for a short while. After the show, however, his dilemma became all too real.

That night, he crashed at my Beverly Hills' apartment on Oakhurst, near the corner of Doheny. Patricia's roommate, Judith, had been kind enough to allow me to stay, but she drew the line at Lenny staying for any serious length of time. We both understood, because with only two bedrooms, we were crowding her space.

From that point on, Lenny floated around from house to house, crashing wherever he could find sanctuary, a couch, or a floor. He even rented a Pinto, parking it in the driveways of rich friends late at night, the way I had slept in his driveway the first time he had invited me to his home. Occasionally he would stay overnight with me, but he was always on the run, not wanting to wear out his welcome.

I felt so bad for my friend. I kept thinking he shouldn't have to live this way since his parents were well off. Roxie was a devoted mother with a kind heart, but Sy had always ruled the home with an iron fist. Out of old-world respect, she went along with his decisions. That's when I first realized that not having a father might not be so bad after all. At least with my single mother, I always had the freedom to be myself.

While Lenny was trying to find his sound, I kept honing my chops as a drummer. That's when Vadim told me about Berklee College of Music in Boston, where he would be attending in the fall of 1981. Berklee was one of the most prestigious music schools in the country, the alma mater of producer Quincy Jones and scores of other legends of similar stature.

If I could get an education like theirs, I thought I would have a better chance of competing with the heavyweights in LA, many of whom were formally trained. I talked with Ralph Johnson, Alphonse Mouzon, Berry Gordy, and a few other mentors about it. They agreed this would be a significant next step.

The only problem was that I couldn't afford to go.

One afternoon while Patricia and I were having lunch at the Apple Pan on Pico, I shared my dilemma with her. Having made her own dreams come true, she wanted to see me make it more than anything. Without hesitation, she said, "I can cover tuition. No problem." With a heart of gold, she would have laid down her life for anyone in our family. Her generosity had once again brought renewed hope for my future.

I filled out the application, sent in a demo tape, and included recommendation letters from some of the top people in the music industry, including the Gordy family. A month later, I received my letter of acceptance from admissions. It was a day equal in excitement to the one when Mama got the letter from the Farmer's Home Administration telling her they would be building us a house. Mama was thrilled for me.

After sharing the great news with Lenny, I drove over to Sy and Roxie's and tried talking them into sending Lenny with me to study there. He had become a brother to me, and I couldn't imagine moving across the country without him. I argued that with his determination and passion for all things music, he would excel there if given the chance. But things were still tense between Lenny and Sy, and the answer was a firm no.

Meanwhile, Vadim, Osama, and I continued to help each other grow as musicians. I taught them a lot about R&B music. They exposed me to more jazz. We practiced together every chance we got. It was comforting to know Vadim would be one of my roommates out east. However, we were both apprehensive because we would have a third roommate once we got on campus. There was no telling what he would be like.

When moving day arrived, Patricia drove me to LAX. At curbside check-in, she gave me a hug and told me how proud of me she was for getting accepted. I thanked her for believing in me. "I promise I *will* pay you back one day."

"Your success will be the best way to pay me back. That's all I want."

"That I can do," I said, once again relying on her belief in me to propel me forward.

By the time I stepped out of the plane at Logan Airport in Boston, I was ready to take on the world.

On that clear day in the fall of 1981, after getting checked into my fourth-floor dorm room, I strolled along the banks of the scenic Charles River. Mesmerized by the sailboats and legions of rowing teams racing with Ivy League competitiveness, I took in every bit of the picturesque landscape, studying the architectural details of the charming brownstones and the renowned Gothic structures known as Harvard, MIT, and Boston University. More than anything, I wanted to share this wonder with the people I loved, especially the historical spires that spiked through the glorious autumn leaves of maple, honey locust, and oak trees. The pictures of New England that Mama and I used to look at in her magazines were certainly no match for the real-life vibrancy of a Boston fall.

At Berklee, I played regularly with topflight musicians while gaining invaluable recording experience. I doused myself in this contagious creative spirit and was stretched on all sides by my fellow students and teachers alike.

Shortly after the semester started, Ralph Johnson invited me to see Earth, Wind & Fire in Providence, Rhode Island, as part of their Raise tour. Vadim had a recital that night, so I took our third roommate, Dan Donifrio, a stocky Italian from Connecticut with a sidesplitting wit.

Dan played trumpet and shared my affinity for Frank Sinatra, which bonded us immediately. We got spiffed up, like Lenny and I had done the night we had gone to see Buddy Rich. After a two-hour bus ride, we arrived at the Civic Center, where we picked up our tickets and passes.

The show was thumping with kaleidoscopic bursts of energy. Their new hit single, "Let's Groove," which had been burning up the charts, was whipping the crowd into a frenzy. As the stage pulsated, the feeling rushing through my body was one of total euphoria.

Just like my childhood concert experiences, every atom inside me was being awakened by the memorable melodies, enigmatic arrangements, and cosmic costumes. Verdine White's hypnotic bass lines pierced my spine with an unrelenting fervor that drew me fully into the groove. Philip Bailey's angelic falsetto soared over the rush of sound, and Ralph was on point too, juggling the vocals, percussion, and intricate choreography with ease.

After the show, the lobby of the Biltmore Hotel was a madhouse, swarming with fans. Smooshed in the crowd behind the velvet ropes, Dan and I couldn't have looked more out of place, all decked out and so young.

We spotted Ralph hopping into the elevator. As the door was closing, he pointed to us and said to the hotel security, "Those two gentlemen are with the band."

The crowd parted, and jaws dropped as Dan and I joined Ralph in the elevator. In their penthouse suite, Ralph played us a cassette tape of their new album, *Raise*, from first to last. It was a sonic groove masterpiece, and I felt part of the inner sanctum hearing it a month before the release date. We hung out with the band so late that we missed our bus back to Boston. Ralph paid for us to have a room at the Biltmore on the same private floor. It was one of the greatest nights of my life, and the closer I got to the inner courts, the more I could see myself being there one day. After showing everyone our all-access backstage passes the next day, Dan and I were the envy of the school.

I studied at Berklee for two semesters and then returned to LA because I didn't have enough money for the following academic year. I wasn't about to ask Patricia for more since she had already done so much to help me. It was time for me to hold my own. Her generosity had already been life changing. In Boston I had found my proving ground. When I walked off the plane from my return flight to LAX, I felt the same kind of confidence that I had once seen on Ricardo's face at the Medford airport, the Christmas he had come home from boot camp. I had arrived at Berklee as a boy. I was now a man.

Back in Los Angeles, with my newly acquired pedigree, I felt a sense of self-respect rise within me. I was excited to show the world what I had learned and proudly wore my Berklee College of Music T-shirt to every audition and rehearsal.

By this time, Bobby had finished high school and gotten married, so with a little coaxing from me, Mama and Lisa moved back to Los Angeles. The three of us lived together in a house she purchased in Chatsworth, a suburb in the San Fernando Valley, where I was eager to reconnect with Lenny, Kennedy, and my other friends from Beverly High. As our relationships deepened, I felt more comfortable sharing my backstory. Despite the gulf between me and them, they proved to be true friends. They never judged me for my family's struggles and never once hesitated to hang out at our humble house.

In fact, they welcomed it more than I had expected. Though Lenny and Kennedy had these incredibly charmed lives, in many ways they were lonely souls, each hurting in their own way. I may have been many things growing up, but lonely was not one of them. I always had someone to talk with, sing with, dance with, dream with, and be crazy with. My family was a spirited brood, full of fun, love, and laughter.

Our house wasn't filled with famous people. I didn't have impressive views, an arcade, a pool, private chefs, or a Rolls-Royce. But I had something that could not be purchased with fame or fortune. I had the unconditional love and support of my family, and that was more valuable than anything in the world.

Until this point, I had envied my wealthy friends, wishing I had grown up with the same opportunities and privileges. It took seeing their response to our atmosphere of love and acceptance for me to realize what I truly had. In my family's home, they could let their guard down and be themselves. Something as simple as that proved to be more of a blessing to them than I could have imagined.

They came to love Mama, Lisa, and Patricia like family, and—finally realizing the irreplaceable value in what we had—I was happy for them to learn more about my life. Lenny's mother, Roxie, even invited Mama, Bobby, and Lisa to her Christmas party that December, where they met the cast of *The Jeffersons* and other A-list celebrities. And if that weren't already enough, during the party, Lenny, Vadim, and I performed for the crowd.

Mama wasn't living the Hollywood life she had dreamed of, but at least she got to be around it through Patricia and me, which was so much fun for her.

Lisa was now attending Chatsworth High School, and during this season, she became my pal, happily tagging along with me around Los Angeles with her sweet smile. My twelve-year-old niece Lydia came down often and spent the summers with us too, and together we had a blast. I could count on hearty laughs from both of them anytime I cracked jokes, which was most of the time.

After spending months refining my skills in various clubs in the Crenshaw district and all-night jam sessions with my growing group of musician friends, I landed my first real tour. I couldn't have been more excited. But as I was getting ready to head to the airport for the first concert date, I received a last-minute call informing me that the tour had been canceled. Shortly after that, Lenny asked me to join a band he was forming called Wave. The music was up-tempo and hard driving, with hints of New Wave, rock and roll, and R&B. With the financial assistance of a classmate and the help of Mr. Farmer from the music department, he was able to secure the Beverly Hills High School auditorium for our debut concert. With our fourteen-piece ensemble that included horns and background singers, Lenny went all out, even inviting record executives to attend. A true visionary, he always had his eye on the prize—a record deal.

We had elaborate lights, flashy costumes, professional sound men, and a fog machine. To put some glitz and glam on the whole event, Lenny printed silver embossed tickets and rented a limo for our after-party at actor Martin Landau's house.

The concert took place on Friday, December 3, 1982. Lenny shared the spotlight with me by giving me a full-blown drum solo. Mama, Lisa, Lydia, Roxie, and Sy were in the audience, which meant the world to both of us.

With the success of our showcase and a feature in the Beverly Hills High newspaper, Lenny managed to convince Sy to use his college fund to record some tracks in hopes of securing a record deal for Wave. Even though Lenny was no longer living with his parents, Sy showed his support by paying for recording time in Studio C at the A&M Records lot in Hollywood, a landmark facility where many a legend had recorded: the Carpenters, Frank Sinatra, the Police, just to name a few.

Lenny insisted that Sy pay me union scale for my work on all the tracks. Sy grimaced and mumbled something incoherent under his breath as he wrote out the largest check I had ever received for my drumming services. Five thousand dollars! Cashing it sent a surge of confidence through my bloodstream.

By the time 1983 had arrived, things were looking up. I landed a national tour. A week before the first concert, though, I was replaced with a more experienced touring drummer. This time I was shattered because I had already told my friends I was going on the road. I felt like an idiot.

I decided then and there I would never tell anyone I was on a big gig until I was well into the tour. Along with being sacked for a lack of touring experience, which of course I couldn't get unless someone gave me the chance to tour, I was told that I didn't play loud enough. That I could fix, and I vowed it would be the last time anyone ever made such a complaint.

The unexpected rebuff filled me with more self-doubt. I wanted to be a drummer. I had worked hard to be a drummer. And I refused to give up on being a drummer. But did I really have what it took to be a successful drummer?

I was beginning to wonder.

"It's just a matter of time," Mama kept saying. "God has the right time for you in his hands. Believe."

While my confidence was fading, I followed the advice of Buddy Rich and listened to Mama. I also continued to broaden my musical scope by playing every local gig I could land with a stable of fellow unknown artists. It was called "paying your dues," and I did a lot of paying for the next couple of years, hoping that one day it would all be worth it.

It was January 25, 1985, a time when the LA air was crisp and the trees on Marilla Street were reduced to stick figures. I had just shut my front door on my way to a club gig with a Top 40 band called Nu Breeze when the phone rang. I jammed my key in the door and ran to answer it. It was Lenny.

"I need you to come to my house," he said in a firm voice.

"I'm on my way to a gig. Can I swing by when I'm done?"

"Yeah, but come over afterward. It's important."

"I'll shoot right over, but why the urgency? Are you back up at the Cloverdale house now?"

"Only for a few days. Mom's letting me crash here while Dad's out of town. Look, I was going to surprise you, but . . . I just hooked you up with an audition with . . . get ready for this . . . New Edition."

"Are you kidding me?! You mean . . . *the* New Edition, as in that popular R&B group that's like the new Jackson 5?"

"Yep, that's right, my brother. They need a drummer for their upcoming tour."

"How the heck did you pull that off?"

"I was up at MCA Records, and I told Jheryl Busby and Bill Dern to stop all their calls, because I've got the perfect guy."

"Who are they?"

"Who *are* they?" Lenny responded sarcastically. "Well, Busby is only the president of MCA Records, and Dern happens to be New Edition's manager. *That's* who they are."

"Man, this is wild. New Edition . . . I can't believe it."

"That's right. And the audition is tomorrow morning," he said, "so hurry and get over here." Then he hung up.

On the way to my gig, I made a quick stop at Tower Records to pick up the latest New Edition cassette tape. Time was of the essence, and I wanted to familiarize myself with their music as much as possible before the big audition.

I didn't get to Lenny's place until 3:00 a.m., and I wasn't even sure if he would still be up. He left the front door unlocked for me, so I tip-toed across the dark hardwood floor, passing his parents' room. Then I made my way to Lenny's bedroom at the end of the house. Seeing light under his doorway, I slowly opened his door to find him hunched over his record player with his headphones on. We locked eyes, then passed a smile to one another. He took his headphones off.

"You made it," he whispered.

I whispered back, "Yeah, finally. Sorry it took so long, but the band played overtime, and we had to pack up our gear. What are you listening to?"

"New Edition. I'm trying to figure out the guitar parts from their new record."

"Why?"

With a gleam in his eye, he answered, "I didn't want to tell you over the phone, but New Edition is also looking for a guitar player. I'm trying out for the spot. We're going down there tomorrow to lock down that gig for the both of us."

I couldn't have imagined anything better. We talked quietly for a while, then Lenny set his blue alarm clock so we could get a few hours of rest before having to leave for the audition. With my mind racing, I kept going on about how great it would be for us to go on tour together, but Lenny fell asleep while I was still talking.

Except for the glow-in-the-dark hands from his clock, the room was pitch black. I tossed and turned, dreaming about what it would be like for us to take the stage with one of the hottest bands in America. When the alarm went off, we jumped up and got ready in record time. After

Roxie made us a quick breakfast and wished us well, we headed out in my car for the thirty-minute drive to Audible Rehearsal Studios in Burbank. On the way, we hyped each other up about how we were the right guys for the gig—the *only* guys for the gig! Then we talked about all the girls who would give us attention. The girls we had met as DJs were one thing, but joining a big act on tour? We figured that might bring us to a whole new level. We were pumping ourselves up, mile by mile.

By the time we pulled in front of the studio, we were surprised to discover there were no parking spots. Every street adjacent to the facility was lined with wall-to-wall clunkers. Turns out this was not a private audition after all. Word had gotten out, and the studio's hallway was filled with hungry musicians. Walking past them was more than intimidating, especially after I recognized some of the most revered drummers in the business waiting their turn to try out. When I saw how confident they appeared, I began to doubt I could beat out any of them. Lenny saw the fear on my face and took me aside. "Come on, dude, you've got this."

"I'm not sure, Lenny. Some of those guys are legends."

"So what."

"And they all have experience touring. The one thing that keeps getting in my way."

"Look, New Edition needs a funky drummer, and you are the funkiest drummer I know. Would I have recommended you unless I thought you were the best man for the job?"

"I guess not."

"Don't guess. *Know* it," he said with conviction. "These cats all look like typical studio musicians with no sense of style. They're too old. It's showbiz, baby, and your 'Zorro' brim makes you stand out. You've got energy, charisma, and a positive aura the group will dig. All you have to do is go in there, be yourself, and take care of business." Then he quietly sang the hook from "Eye of the Tiger" from *Rocky III*, and we both cracked up.

It was do or die, but I wasn't sure if I would be the one doing or dying. Turns out, the members of New Edition weren't even there. Instead, their backup band and musical director, Carl Smith, a New Yorker with a hardcore Bronx attitude and eyes like a shark, would be conducting the first round of auditions to narrow the field down to the best candidates. To accentuate his muscular frame, Carl wore a tight red New Edition T-shirt, and his neck was adorned with an array of thick gold chains.

He counted off the first tune without the slightest expression. I was so nervous I could feel my hands shaking. This, of course, had an adverse effect on my timing. Sweating profusely, I missed a simple turnaround at the end of a medley that led into their first hit song, "Candy Girl." The percussionist, a hairy guy they called Suave Bob, glared at me disapprovingly. The little confidence I had took a nosedive.

All I kept thinking about was how the other famous drummers were going to nail this stuff and make me look like a novice. Previous criticisms—*too young, not enough tour experience*—echoed in my mind as I played for twenty humbling minutes, giving what felt like one of my worst performances. Under the intense pressure, I just couldn't seem to pull myself together. I felt horrible about how I had played but even worse for letting Lenny down, especially after he had bragged about me to Bill Dern and Jheryl Busby, telling them I was the best man for the job.

On the way out, Carl remained stoic as he asked for my résumé. I knew it was merely a formality and that he had no intention of ever calling me back. Nonetheless, I left him a copy and waited in the hall for Lenny to finish his audition.

When Lenny walked into the hallway with his shoulders slumped, I knew he must not have done so well either. With our heads hanging low and neither of us uttering a word, we got into my car and headed back toward Baldwin Hills.

A few miles down the road, we ran out of gas.

I suddenly realized that if the studio had been just a few miles farther, we would have never made the audition in time. At this point, though, that didn't seem like such a terrible thing. At least I wouldn't be feeling like a huge disappointment to my friend who had stuck his neck out for me.

"I can't believe that right after getting our butts kicked, we run out of gas," Lenny sighed as we stood stranded on the side of Victory Boulevard.

"Sorry, Lenny. After I bought the New Edition cassette tape last night, I was only able to put a few bucks in. I thought it would get us there and back."

"Well, you thought wrong." By this time, Lenny was pacing the side of the road, fuming.

I opened my wallet and pulled out my card. "Don't worry. I'm a member of Triple-A."

Instantly, he shouted, "Ah, heck yeah!" and slapped me a high five so hard my palm stung.

While we headed down the boulevard in search of a pay phone, I asked him, "What went wrong at your audition?"

"I was nailing it, man. Burned up the guitar. But the backup musicians snubbed me because all the other cats came in with their professional amplifiers and what not, and here I come waltzing in with my cheap, toylike Rockman X100 headphone amp. After I pulled that out, they practically laughed me out of there. I just think they didn't dig my vibe. I was too edgy looking, too New Wave for them with the green dye in my hair."

"Maybe we're both too LA for them. They're as New York as it gets."

"You got that right. They remind me of the type of cats that roamed the streets of Brooklyn when I was a kid."

"Well, at least you played great," I said. "There's no way they can dispute your funky guitar playing. That's for sure. I, on the other hand, crumbled under the pressure."

"Well, I guess neither of us is going on tour with New Edition," Lenny said. There was a pause. After a few seconds, we were cracking up again.

"Look at us two fools, stranded on the side of the road. My green hair. Your Mexican hat." Lenny laughed again. "But hey, at least we have each other. We'll catch another break. Just wait and see. Then one day when we're rich and famous, we'll tell this story of us being so broke we couldn't afford to put gas in the car."

CHAPTER 41

Eye of the Tiger

After so many failed auditions, I wanted to forget about my tryout with New Edition, but that wouldn't be easy. I kept wondering what they thought of me, hoping I hadn't sounded as bad as I feared and hoping the other drummers hadn't sounded as good as I had imagined. I didn't want to take the chance of missing a call from Carl Smith, so I stayed close to the phone—just in case. Every time it rang, I ran to answer it, hoping for good news, *any* news. Limbo was a horrible place to be, and I hated every minute I spent there.

The days that followed were long and disappointing. Eventually I quit sprinting to the phone. Then, on a day when I was no longer eager, Carl called.

"Are you playing anywhere in town where we can take a closer look at your live performance skills?" he asked.

"Tonight, at the El Gato Club in Pacoima," I said, "I'll be playing with a Top 40 band called Nu Breeze."

Still with no emotion, he said, "We'll try to swing by."

During my first set, I kept looking around to see if Carl was there. Midway through the second set, I spotted him at the back of the club, along with the entire New Edition backup band—all the same tough guys from the Bronx I had played with at the audition. I was pumped. Nu Breeze was a stellar band, and their gig showcased what I could do well. This was a great way for Carl and the gang to see me in action.

Bruce Soto, the leader of our group, randomly asked us to play New Edition's new hit single, "Cool It Now." He had no idea I had just auditioned for New Edition and that members of their backup band were in the audience, scoping me out for further consideration. When Carl heard us go into "Cool It Now," he raised his eyebrows and glanced at the rest of his bandmates. The look on his face was, *Let's see how well these cats play our song.* There was no better way to display my ability, and I had the drumbeat down pat. In contrast to the botched audition, I felt confident about my performance.

When I walked off stage for our break, Carl made his way to me straight away. I was certain that after playing so well, he would offer me the gig right on the spot. But without so much as cracking a smile, he said, "We'll call if we want you back for the next round of auditions."

I was bummed.

After not hearing back for another long week, I finally hit a wall of despair. I lost my appetite and soon looked gaunt, with dark circles under my eyes from not sleeping well. The light had gone out of my eyes, the life out of my voice. And now I was becoming cynical, doubting myself and feeling down on the music business as a whole.

Seeing me like this broke Mama's heart. That bummed me out even more because I didn't want to hurt her. Still, I couldn't help how I felt. I was tired of being so optimistic, so "up" all the time. Wanting something so badly yet being powerless to attain it had become too painful. I couldn't do it anymore. I just couldn't. After two decades of being the resilient kid who never gave up, the hard worker who was getting after it, the tenacious drummer who took huge risks . . . I was done.

Just when I hit bottom, Carl phoned, asking me to come down for the final callbacks the following day. This time I would be playing for the singers of New Edition—the stars themselves. Only five other drummers remained in the running. I didn't want to know the names of my competition because that would only make me more nervous.

The fact that I was one step closer should have lifted my spirits and put me back in the game. But it also meant the letdown would be bigger if I bombed. I wasn't sure I could handle that.

The truth is, I was overcome with fear. The fear of not performing well. The fear of failure. The fear of never getting out of professional limbo. I sat on the living room couch to tell Mama my decision. "I'm not going to the callback. It's been five long years, and I still haven't scored the big gig. I've been on countless auditions, and they've led to nothing but heartache. One letdown after another. I can't handle it anymore. I'm not good enough. It's time I faced the truth and got a day job. Pursued something realistic."

Mama was livid. "My father never wanted me to go into show business. He wanted me to be a diplomat like him. But I refused. I wanted to pursue acting. I studied hard, made contacts, and was getting bit parts here and there. I was making it happen. Then life got in the way. I was never able to live out my dream and make my father proud. I failed him. I failed myself. So I can't let you give up. You see? I *won't* let you give up!"

She rose to her feet. Her Latin temper flared as she paced the floor. She worked herself into a frenzy, then sternly pointed her arthritic finger at me. "You listen to me, *Dan-yell*, and listen good. Ever since you were a little boy, you've been banging on things. You know why? Because God gave you a gift—the gift of rhythm. What you need right now is the courage to face your fears, and believe me, I know a thing or two about courage. If you only knew how much courage it took to raise all seven of you, to keep on rolling with the punches, you wouldn't give up so quickly. So stop your sulking, and give it one more try. If you don't, you'll live with that regret for the rest of your life. Like I have. Trust me—that's a load you don't want to carry."

"I'm just not as good as I thought I was, Mama, and I don't want to disappoint you anymore. Or myself."

"Remember, my father was a great man. Greatness runs in your blood, Danny. It's time to restore our family name back to its former glory. It's time to show your father, yourself, and the rest of the world who you really are—a winner. Now I want you to get off that couch and muster up all the backbone you can. Then go back to that audition and take what rightfully belongs to you. I know you can do it, *mijo*. I *know* you can!"

After Mama's impassioned speech, I was inspired to go to that last round of auditions. Only now I would return with a greater sense of determination. I wanted to make up for her disappointments, for how unfairly life had treated her. I wanted to make my brothers and sisters proud, especially Patricia, who had invested so much in me. I wanted to show my father that I was able to succeed without his love and support. I wanted to prove to all those who had berated and doubted me. I wanted them to know that I *was* a winner.

I followed Mama's directives and marched back into battle with a flame of generational vengeance burning in my soul, ready to unleash my fury. But first I had to wait my turn. While I sat patiently in the hallway, I listened to a few of the other drummers through the door. This helped prepare me mentally for what was about to go down.

Finally, it was my turn to play. The members of New Edition entered like soldiers. Their choreographer, Brooke Payne, a stern Bostonian with a well-chiseled jaw, was there to direct the auditions. With his Boston accent and low voice, he instructed me to accentuate the group's key dance moves with rhythmic embellishments on my hi-hat cymbals and snare drum.

Since total synchronicity between the drummer and the group's choreography was the key to their live show, Brooke wanted me to mirror every little step they were doing, just as Ronnie Tutt had done with Elvis. Yet at the same time, I was expected to continue playing the drumbeats exactly like the record. Never before had such onerous tasks been demanded of me musically, technically, and emotionally.

After a rigorous face-off, it was time for a dinner break. I was so wound up I couldn't think about food. Instead, I sat in my car and tried to calm my nerves. I was tempted to drive home so I wouldn't have to go through the next segment of the audition. But I knew I couldn't look Mama in the eye if I didn't at least see it through to the end. Alone in the quiet, I said a little prayer.

While my legs were sticking out of my car window, a lanky guitar player with a thin mustache and an olive complexion walked up to the car door. It was Louis Metoyer. I had met him earlier that year at a city park when we were playing at a Battle of the Bands contest for KACE radio station. Although we were in competing bands, Louis had come up to me after my performance to tell me how much he had dug my drumming. I was equally impressed with his fiery guitar work, and we hit it off right away. He and I hadn't spoken since then, so it was a nice surprise to run into him at the audition.

"What are *you* doing here?" I asked him, delighted to see another LA musician. Like Lenny and me, he shared our happy-go-lucky attitude, a nice break from the tense New York atmosphere in the audition room. With his spandex tights and one-of-a-kind mullet Afro, his presence made me feel more relaxed.

"I just landed the gig playing guitar for New Edition," he said with a glint of pride in his eyes.

"Awesome. Totally awesome," I replied. While I was happy for Louis, that meant Lenny was no longer a candidate. My heart sank. Gone was our dream of touring together with this big act.

Louis went on to explain that he was there so they could audition the remaining drummers with the entire rhythm section. I felt better knowing he had been impressed with my drumming that day at the park. He knew what I was capable of, and knowing one person in the backup band helped to subdue my nerves a little.

He leaned down and looked me straight in the eye. "You'd kill this gig, man." As he strutted off to get his equipment set up in the studio, he turned around and said, "I'll be rooting for you in there."

Like Lenny, Louis tried to convince me I was the perfect guy for the gig. Suddenly I felt full of hope, full of positivity—so full, in fact, it felt as if I was radiating starlight from the heavens. It felt as if God had answered my prayer by sending Louis my way. That gave me the fortitude to go back and fight for what I wanted and, if what Mama said was true, for my birthright.

While walking back into the studio, I began reciting affirmations to myself:

You're the man.

This gig is yours.

Your name is written all over it.

This is your time.

Mama is counting on you, your brothers and sisters are counting on you, and all of your ancestors in heaven are rooting for you. This is what you were born to do. Now go in there and take what's yours, Danny Donnelly!

A discernible change had taken place in me. I could feel it.

After the dinner break, I joined Louis and the other musicians for another round, including keyboard player John Steiner, who seemed to have earned the name "Johnny 80s" for his New Wave look, and T-Bone, a funky bass player who was straight-up Bronx.

With a cigarette dangling languorously from his lower lip and a white Kangol hat pulled down tight over his Jheri curl, Brooke Payne tried to break me down. "Yo, yo, yo, give me an accent right here," he yelled, sliding his arm down in a sweeping motion, making the sound of *bzzzt!*

He called out cues like an imperious Hollywood choreographer, but I held my own, catching everything he threw at me with a tempestuous conviction. Each time I met the challenge, he slowly whisked his hands down his goatee while exhaling a cloud of smoke, pondering what else he might do to stump me. I wasn't having it. With laser-sharp focus, I nailed every toilsome thing he asked me to do as the showdown continued. Whatever the final outcome, I would leave that audition knowing I had conquered my fears and delivered my A game.

As I left the room, I overheard T-Bone's deep voice say, "That Zorro cat's got it. He's got the groove, man! I'm locking in with that brother, and it feels great."

I went home that night exhausted. When I awoke the next morning, I was hoping to get a call before the day was over. Minutes turned into hours. The call never came. Days passed. Nothing. I grew increasingly frustrated and was growing despondent.

One afternoon later in the week, I was lying on my bed, depressed, staring at the posters of my favorite bands on the wall. The phone rang in the other room, but I didn't run to answer it. Mama, however, did. I couldn't make out who she was talking to. I knew it couldn't have been very important since the call was such a short one.

After hanging up, she gently knocked on my door. "Come in," I said reluctantly. The last thing I wanted from Mama was another pep talk. Or worse, her telling me how sorry she felt for me.

She walked in, tears streaming down her face, moving slowly toward my bed. And as she did, my heart began to race. I had a flashback to the time she had received the news her mother had died. I wondered if something horrific had happened, and I immediately thought of my siblings. I was nervous about what would come out of her mouth.

"What's wrong, Mama? Tell me. Tell me, please!"

"Nothing is wrong, *mijo*—nothing at all. That phone call," she stammered, "that—that phone call was from Carl Smith—with New Edition. He said—he said . . ." She took a long pause, and suddenly her countenance changed. "You got the job with New Edition!" she blurted out. "Rehearsals start tomorrow morning!" She broke into a happy dance.

I popped out of bed and hugged her so hard I thought I might have cracked her ribs.

Whenever words failed to express the depth of her emotions, Mama always spoke with her hands, then she'd make a sigh that sounded like bacon sizzling in a pan. She ran her fingers through my hair for the longest time while we held each other and cried rapturous tears. When she finally spoke, she said, "You did it, *mijo*. You did it. I always knew you would."

CHAPTER 42

When You Wish Upon a Star

After two weeks of grueling rehearsals, we had a few days off to pack and get ready for the road. Despite their tough appearance, the New Yorkers in the band turned out to be teddy bears and embraced me with brotherly love. I was looking forward to hanging with them every day. But the first order of business was a trip to Western Costume—a legendary boutique that supplied wardrobes for film and television—where I paid a hefty sum for one of their premier hat makers to make me a Spanish gaucho-style hat. I had loved hats since I was a young boy from watching old movies with Mama.

The gaucho-style hat I had worn to the audition was a cheaply made souvenir from Olvera Street, and I had worn it so much it was starting to separate at the crown. New Edition really liked it, and they had already started referring to me as Zorro, even if their Boston accents did make it sound more like *Zarrow*. Who could have known I would carry my drugstore-bandit spirit onto the world's biggest stages? One thing was certain. I had come a long way from that Zorro-mask-wearing little boy who was trying to survive the streets of Compton.

Two days later I picked up the most lustrous black hat I had ever seen. It fit me perfectly and was made of the finest materials available.

This would be my new identity. While the other musicians had each found their look, I was proud to represent Mama's heritage and to celebrate what made me unique.

Ready to step into stardom, I legally changed my name to Zoro, following Mama's suggestion to spell it with one "r" to set myself apart. She loved the new image and affirmed that I shared traits with Zorro, who, like her father, had a heart for the underdog. I no longer wanted to carry on the Donnelly name since I meant nothing to my father. Making my new name legal was my way of wiping the slate clean. So with Mama's blessing, I let go of the only remaining trace of my father. And just like that, Danny Donnelly became Zoro.

There was no turning back.

Later that week, I was scheduled to fly with the band to Hollywood, Florida, for a week of production rehearsals to incorporate lights, sound, and staging into our performance. Before I left the house for the airport, Mama handed me a small, laminated picture of Saint Christopher. "Keep this with you," she insisted. "He'll protect you." According to a legend rooted in Catholicism, a small child asked Saint Christopher to carry him across a river. As he was carrying the child, the river rose, and the child became unbearably heavy. When he asked the child why he was so heavy, the child told him he had "borne upon his back the world and he who created it," revealing he was Christ himself. For centuries Saint Christopher has been the patron saint of safe travels for those who trust in him. Mama was counting on him to keep me safe as well.

I thanked her for the keepsake as I stared into her careworn face, etched with wrinkles from the harsh journey life had taken her on. Though she tried to conceal it, I could see the concern in her eyes. I could feel something of the worry in her spirit. Despite her apparent fears, I knew she was elated for the sojourn I was about to take. Determined to keep the mood upbeat, she put her acting skills to work once again. "Now, don't forget to get me a ceramic mug from all the important places you visit," she said, chuckling.

"Okay, Mama. I will," I said as I kissed her on her cheek.

On the plane, I pulled out the small, laminated card from my wallet, turned it over, and recited the petition to Saint Christopher. I pondered it for a moment, realizing what a saint Mama had always been. I thought about how hard she had fought for me, how she encouraged me, and how often I saw her on her knees sending up prayers. Prayers for protection. Prayers for healing. Prayers for guidance. Prayers that carried me safely across all the rivers along the way to *this* river. As those memories of Mama's love flashed before me, my heart filled with gratitude for her, for the answered prayers, and for the exciting season that was upon me.

Traveling to Florida wasn't just my introduction to the South, it was the first time anyone had flown me somewhere to perform, and it served as a reminder that the sky was the limit from this moment on. At the airport, our road manager handed me a thick manila envelope. "Welcome to the band," he said in a monotone voice. "Your laminate and per diem for the week are inside." I had no idea what either of those things was, and for fear of looking green, I didn't ask. While he continued handing out packets to the other band members, I slipped into the adjacent gift shop to pick up a ceramic mug for Mama. I chose a bright red one with "Hollywood, Florida" etched on it in black.

When I got to my hotel room, I opened the package to find an assortment of five-, ten-, and twenty-dollar bills. The total came to a whopping $245. Next was a yellow, laminated, all-access tour pass labeled "New Edition: No Hang Ups Tour." Seeing my new name, Zoro, printed on the back brought both a smile and tears. I had finally become somebody. The pass made it official.

Eagerly, I flipped through the tour booklet to see all the places we would travel to. The detailed itinerary listed the cities, dates, venues, departure times, hotels, flights, and contact information for the entire organization. Later that evening, Carl told me the money inside the envelope was to pay for my food.

"I thought that was my pay," I said.

He laughed. "No, that's your per diem."

I was so ecstatic to be on the gig that I never thought to ask what the job paid. I couldn't believe that on top of getting a salary for doing something I loved, they gave me extra money for food.

The first meal I used my per diem for was the "All-Star Special" at Waffle House. I wolfed down three fried eggs, two pork sausage patties, and an order of hash browns so big they hung over the side of the plate. For dessert, I ordered one of their famous waffles slathered in butter and syrup. Oh, how I wished Lenny could have been there to share the experience with me.

The management rented the biggest concert venue in the city for the week so we could rehearse with our complete stage set and instrument risers. Hearing my drums pumping at full volume through the massive sound system in the arena felt empowering. Watching the light show come together was electrifying. They also hired the "magicians' magician," Doug Henning, to bring his mojo to the show. Shaggy-haired Doug was a bona fide celebrity in his own right as a result of his annual NBC prime-time television special, *Doug Henning's World of Magic*. Doug, along with his young protégé, David Copperfield, had previously created illusions for Earth, Wind & Fire and Michael Jackson.

For us, they designed a spaceship that landed on stage. One by one, New Edition would climb inside to head for outer space. The ship would rise to the highest point in the venue and then suddenly open, and the guys would no longer be in it. Instead, they would magically appear on different parts of the stage. It was mind-blowing. I could never figure out how they did it. The fellas were sworn to secrecy by a legally binding contract and wouldn't divulge the mystifying feat to anyone, even though I repeatedly tried to pry it out of them.

At the end of the week, a forty-five-foot Eagle tour bus pulled up to our hotel, where I was waiting in the lobby. Eager to climb aboard, I ran out and stood by the side of the bus. Just after the pressurized door opened, our driver slowly walked down the stairs in his Wranglers and cowboy boots. With a deep, gravelly voice, he greeted me while adjusting his oversized western belt buckle.

"Howdy! I'm Larry Cole. Are you one of my band members?"

"I sure am," I said, trying to make my way up the stairs with my two suitcases.

"Now, hold on a minute there, partner. This must be your first rodeo. The big bags go in the bay."

"Where's that?"

"Follow me, and I'll show you, kid."

The silver-haired man knelt by the side of the bus, took out a leather wallet that was fettered to him by a chain, flipped through a large collection of keys, and opened the lever to a storage area. "Here's where your bags go."

"Thanks, Larry."

"Now go on up and git yourself a bunk right quick before the other guys get here. You'll want to pick you out a nice middle bunk."

I ran up the stairs and chucked the burgundy briefcase that Patricia had bought me for the tour onto the first middle bunk that I came to. For safe measure, I threw my jacket across it too, because I knew whatever bunk I placed dibs on would be mine for the duration of the tour.

I went back up front to check out the plush lounge area. There was a kitchen with a refrigerator, microwave, and dining area, plus a bathroom and a full entertainment center. Just past the sleeping quarters, there was another lounge. Like the front, it was outfitted with a TV, a cassette deck, a VHS machine, and an array of the latest movies.

After gawking over the interior furnishings, I went back down the stairs to scope out the exterior. Both sides had been masterfully airbrushed with a western-looking mural that ran halfway across the length of the bus. Directly on the back was another beautifully crafted image, this one of a stagecoach with horses that continued the theme.

Above the windshield were the words "Private Coach," and on the bottom grill, an emblem of an American bald eagle. Along with the hotels listed in my itinerary, this would be my home for the next year. It far surpassed the trailer homes of my childhood, and I was jazzed about traveling in high style.

After our final run-through at the end of that exhausting week, we headed to central Florida for our first show. On a Saturday afternoon in

February, our caravan of buses pulled into the back entrance of Disney World. Upon arrival, we were given a behind-the-scenes look at the cavernous maze of tunnels called the Utilidors, a well-orchestrated network of machine works that made all the splendor above possible.

As we drove around in golf carts through these seemingly endless corridors, I was stunned at the expanse of it all. Thousands of employees worked in tandem in this underworld city to create a memorable experience for each and every visitor to the park. At the end of our sound check, we were given special passes that allowed us to skip to the front of the line on all the rides. For the next few hours, I rode more rides than most people did in three days, with multiple visits to Pirates of the Caribbean. I just couldn't seem to get enough splashing and swashbuckling.

Nightfall came with sparkly lights that gave off an enchanting ambiance. That evening was not only magical because we were playing at the "Magic Kingdom," but also because it was the biggest gig I had ever played in my life. In fact, New Edition set an attendance record with more than eighty thousand fans showing up for the concert.

Being there triggered a flashback of my failed audition at Disneyland in Anaheim with the Romano Brothers back in 1980. It had taken me five years to storm the gates of Cinderella's castle. Now, I was performing with one of the most popular headlining acts in the country!

Just before I hit the stage, I tucked my drumsticks in the back pocket of my black satin pants and called Mama from my dressing room. I told her about the enormous crowd and reminded her how it had all started with that $9.99 Disney Rocktet drum set she bought me for Christmas when I was a boy.

I could picture her dressed in her chenille robe, sitting next to her cluttered mahogany nightstand with the avocado-green dial-up phone in her hand.

"I'm sorry I can't be there tonight, *mijo*, but I know you'll be fantastic."

I performed for her that night as if she *were* there. I imagined her, my siblings, and my long-gone ancestors all in the front row, cheering me on. As I gazed down Main Street, USA, with a bird's-eye view of the rambunctious crowd, I was overcome with emotion. It felt as if all the stars had aligned for me that night, as if God himself had especially prepared this moment for me. Even the fabric of the skirting attached to my drum riser matched my blue jacket perfectly.

That night, my impossible dream came to life. As the stars twinkled across the cold winter sky, I remembered watching *Pinocchio* as a little boy and singing along with Jiminy Cricket about the power of believing in magic.

CHAPTER 43

It Was a Very Good Year

That night at Disney World was beyond belief. But it lacked one thing—one very important thing. No one who was dear to me was in the audience, and my best friend, Lenny, wasn't on stage with me. I wanted someone there who understood my arduous journey. Someone who could appreciate the magnitude of it all and celebrate along with me.

Before boarding our bus after the show, en route to Miami, someone asked me for my autograph. It was another milestone moment, one I would never forget. Thinking back to how the security guard had shunned Mama after she asked for Sinatra's autograph, I gave the fan my full attention by sharing a conversation and taking a photo with her before boarding the bus. When I climbed into my bunk, I was wiped out. I had put so much energy into the rehearsals, along with an equal amount of reflection on the wonder of it all. Before I conked out, I couldn't help thinking what might have been if our stray Saint Bernard, Manny, hadn't developed a sudden appetite for chicken catch-iatore, which tragically ended D&B Poultry Produce Co. If it weren't for that one dog's killing spree, I might have become a chicken farmer rather than a professional drummer. "Thank you, Manny," I said before closing my eyes. "Thank you very much."

For the next four months, New Edition and I toured across the United States with back-to-back sellout shows at all the famed venues, including a double-show day at Madison Square Garden in New York City. Each day, I took in another part of the country I had only seen in history books. In Memphis I visited Graceland, the home of one of my first heroes, Elvis Presley. In Saint Louis I made it to the top of the Gateway Arch, where Louis Metoyer and I stood in awe, watching the stage crew set up our show in the distance. In upstate New York, with the thunderous sound of Niagara Falls surrounding me, I leaned so close to a rainbow I could practically grab it. On one of our days off, we made a detour to visit the Grand Canyon. Mile by mile, America was coming to life for me. I was grateful that Mama had immigrated to this wonderful country, and I made sure to pick up a ceramic mug for her from each place I visited.

The best part was taking in the local cuisine that each region was known for. It was beignets in New Orleans, cheesesteak sandwiches in Philadelphia, a slice of pie and a hot dog in Manhattan, seafood gumbo in Baton Rouge, lobster rolls in Maine, and dry-rub ribs in Nashville. This was a far cry from the Rice-A-Roni and Kraft macaroni and cheese I had grown up on.

Day by day, my palate was expanding from all these dishes, but fortunately, since I was burning so many calories at the show each night, my twenty-two-year-old body remained toned. Our dressing room was stocked with every kind of soda imaginable, reminding me how much I had wanted to buy a can of Coke at Sparks' corner store back in Compton when I didn't have any money. Now, with Coca-Cola sponsoring the tour, the drinks were free, and I was bent on making up for the deprivation of my childhood. I guzzled all the Coca-Cola I could get my hands on.

I took full advantage of the unlimited access to soda and food, but booze and drugs didn't interest me for a couple of reasons. First, I was so happy playing drums for a living that I didn't need an artificial high to satisfy me. Being a top-tier drummer was all I had ever wanted. That was more than enough to keep me satisfied. Second, money had been so hard to come by growing up that I wasn't about to blow it on something I drank, smoked, snorted, or shot up. For a young man working hard to make something of himself, those vices seemed foolish.

I was hungry to grow as a musician and expand my knowledge, so I spent my money buying records, studying the liner notes from top to bottom to see which musicians played on them. I also continued taking lessons with the best drummers in each major city we visited. The rest I saved to buy a new car and to help Mama pay her mortgage.

But that didn't mean I didn't have my weaknesses too. While I had dated a couple of girls by then, I had spent a lot of time dealing with painful rejection from them in my youth. This, compounded with the shame I had long carried about our family's poverty and the core wound of my father's abandonment, still left me longing for approval. I hadn't yet realized that all my high achievement was not just about my desire to play music, although that was certainly the lion's share of it. It was also an attempt to prove my worth and gain the acceptance of others—especially women. I may not have succumbed to the temptation of drugs, alcohol, or other vices, but women were another story. I was no fool. I knew they were only interested in me because I was on stage, touring with one of the hottest bands in the nation, and because I was featured in fan magazines every month. But I took their amorous offerings, trying desperately to fill a void that I had carried all my life.

It took eight tour buses and fourteen semitrailers to transport our show. We had riggers, soundmen, stagehands, managers, accountants, carpenters, lighting directors, wardrobe valets, roadies, instrument techs, caterers, drivers, personal assistants, and a host of others to pull it all together. With a crew of more than fifty caravanning from town to town, it felt as if I were a part of the Barnum & Bailey Circus. I was now doing what Elvis's drummer Ronnie Tutt and Beverly and Bill's son Jeff had done for so long, and what a feeling it was.

Every night we improved. I was pleased we were perfecting the show before we were scheduled to play LA because I wanted our performance to be tight by the time we got back to California in the middle of June. The LA show was special to me for a variety of reasons. First, I would be playing in my hometown two days after my twenty-third birthday. That meant I would get to town early enough to celebrate it with Mama. Second, I would be playing at the Universal Amphitheatre, a prestigious venue next door to Universal Studios. The concert hall was known for its superb acoustics and wonderful sight lines. And, of course, the hottest groups of the era played there.

My closest friends were coming to see me, and most importantly, Mama, Bobby, Lisa, and my niece Lydia and nephew Anthony would be there too. I was sad that Patricia, Mary, Armando, and Ricardo would not be able to attend. But my heart was bursting with excitement, knowing Mama would be watching me live, especially since it was she who had convinced me to go back for the last round of auditions. None of this would have happened if not for her unfailing belief in me, plus the support of Patricia and the rest of my siblings.

Before the show, I triple-checked with the road manager to make sure Mama's tickets and backstage passes were at will call. I also set up tickets and backstage passes for Lenny and Kennedy, who were coming to the show together.

A year earlier, Kennedy had changed his name to Rockwell and released a hit record on Motown called "Somebody's Watching Me." He had enlisted Michael Jackson for the lead vocals on the chorus and his brother Jermaine for some backups. At that point, he was the first of us three to hit the big time.

Lenny and Kennedy had been so instrumental in opening doors for me that I wanted to make them proud by playing my best for them that night. Of course, having Lenny in the audience was bittersweet because we had imagined doing the New Edition gig together. I was sad it hadn't worked out the way we had wanted, but I thanked him repeatedly for getting me this shot, and he was genuinely happy to see me succeed. Kennedy and I both knew his time would come too. We never doubted it for a second.

In the meantime, Lenny was about to find success of another kind. Downstairs by our dressing rooms, I noticed him locking eyes with Lisa Bonet, a gorgeous young actress who played Denise Huxtable on the megahit television sitcom, *The Cosby Show*. Like Lenny, she was half Black and half Jewish, so they could relate to each other culturally. Every guy there wanted to get next to Lisa, but it was clear that she and Lenny hit it off right away, and if he had ever felt down about the gig, he was certainly feeling happy now.

Along with an intimate group of people who meant the world to me, the concert was also attended by a number of celebrities, including members of the Jackson 5. They had even brought their kids, who were huge New Edition fans, just as I had been a huge fan of the Jacksons around that same age. I was told by our management that Michael Jackson himself was at the show in disguise. Life was coming full circle.

After the house lights came down, I counted off "Kinda Girls We Like," our opening number. Immediately, I spotted Mama wearing one of her favorite scarves. When she looked up on the stage, much to her surprise she saw her baby boy wearing the orange silk scarf she had tied around my neck for picture day in elementary school. She didn't know I still had it. I had worn it just for her.

Six thousand one hundred and eighty-nine people filled every seat in the auditorium that auspicious evening. But I played for only one. Tears of joy streamed down Mama's trembling cheeks as I glanced out at her. In her bright face I saw a reflection of sacrifice—all the dreams she had given up to make mine come true. Behind her brown eyes were years of suffering. Streaming out of them now was so much happiness and maternal pride, all of which inspired me to play my heart out. And, boy, how I played for her that night! My whole soul was in every note. The band was on fire, charging the air with a fervent glow as we took command of the stage, a Broadway-level set with a medieval castle built especially for the show.

As an accoutrement to the extravaganza, I wore a rhinestone band around my hat that sparkled in the light. Kicking it up a notch was our state-of-the-art laser show, which gave our audience their money's worth.

As I laid down the funky beat and thousands bobbed their heads to the rhythm, my heart was filled with a sense of divine purpose.

After the show, Mama, Bobby, Lisa, Lydia, and Anthony came backstage to the green room. Mama had gotten her hair done at a salon, special for the occasion, and she looked lovely. When she saw me at the other end of the room, her eyes lit up.

"I am so proud of you, *mijo*. You were phenomenal up there!" Dressed in her white pantsuit and red blouse, she giggled in her uniquely rhythmic way. "I can't believe you still have this scarf."

"What can I say? I'm sentimental, like you."

She laughed.

"That scarf means so much to me," I said, "because it reminds me of the words you spoke over me when I was a little boy. Do you remember what you said?"

"Yes, of course," she answered proudly. "I said you would do something fantazmical with your life. And now you are!"

"I really am, Mama. And it's all because of you. And Patricia, of course."

She started crying again, this time in front of everyone, but the room was so chaotic I doubt anyone noticed. After holding her close for a minute, I asked her to untie my scarf and take it home with her. I didn't want it to get lost backstage.

That night, the scarf made its one and only appearance. But it was a monumental one. It represented so much more than that present moment. It epitomized the power of a mother's words and their ability to transform a child's future. I was that child. And that day, I was living in a future my mother had seen by faith years earlier. That orange silk scarf would tie our hearts together and remain a symbol of the unbreakable bond of love between us—one mother and one son, bound by unending devotion to one another and a mutual love for music and the stage.

I would have many extraordinary experiences to follow, but very few nights would feel more special than this one.

Later in the year, I invited my father to a New Edition concert in San Diego. He brought my half sister, Megan, and a bunch of his friends. I was taken aback to see him proudly leading his guests into my dressing room as if he had played a part in getting me to this point in life. They seemed to have no idea that this was only the third time I had ever seen him.

My emotions were all over the place when I left the show. I had wanted him to be proud, but I also wanted his friends to know the truth—that he had never been there for me. And that I had found success in spite of all he had done to hurt me and the people I loved.

Knowing how important this night was for me, Lenny had ridden his motorcycle from LA to meet my dad. After the concert, the two of us stayed up, talking for hours at the Queen Mary hotel. We talked about music, girls, and life, but mostly we talked about our fathers. Mine was a deserter who had shown no interest in me whatsoever. Lenny's was an ever-present domineering force of discipline who didn't understand his son. Yet, in a way, I was still envious of Lenny for having a dad who cared at all. Sy had done many things to hurt Lenny, which hurt me too, but he had also taken him to concerts, bought him instruments, paid for his first demos, bailed him out of trouble when he needed it, and granted him culturally enriching experiences that I could only have dreamed of having throughout my youth. Lenny and I came from opposite ends of the spectrum, no doubt, but we had both spent time living in our cars as homeless kids longing for our father's love. That made us brothers. For life.

By the end of that unbelievable year, I had performed live before hundreds of thousands of people in stadiums from coast to coast, plus millions more on television. I was finally able to join Local 47, the prestigious musician's union in Hollywood, where I had made a promise to myself to make it in this industry. My first recording session as a member of that union was at Cherokee Studios in Hollywood for New Edition's *Christmas All Over the World* album. I had even secured endorsement deals with my favorite drum, cymbal, percussion, drumstick, and drumhead companies—DW drums, Sabian cymbals, Latin Percussion, Vic

Firth sticks, and Evans drumheads. The craziest thing of all was that I became a pinup in a wide variety of fan magazines. Still unable to fit into any box, I was named Black teen centerfold of the month, white teen heartthrob of the month, and Latin teen sensation of the month. There was even a national "Win a Date with Zoro Contest" in one of the major fan mags.

Each demographic accepted me as their own, which thrilled me, especially since I was half Irish and half Mexican and, because of my early South-Central upbringing, Black at heart. After struggling all my life to fit in, it felt rewarding to be blessed with a new identity that transcended the confines of race.

The dream continued to deliver one surreal moment after the next. I met welterweight boxing champion of the world "Sugar" Ray Leonard. I was featured in a music video with Magic Johnson of the Lakers. I hung out at parties with Cyndi Lauper, Kool & the Gang, Bryan Adams, the Beach Boys, Janet Jackson, and Jimmy Page, just to name a few. I was now living in a world so far removed from that of my childhood that I sometimes wondered if it really was still a dream.

The best part was when my drumming idols Steve Gadd, Harvey Mason, Jeff Porcaro, and Bernard Purdie came to see me play. These gifted timekeepers were legendary studio drummers who played on classic records with everyone in the business. Steve and Bernard reigned supreme in New York City. Jeff and Harvey were the drum gods of the LA studio scene and had been on the short list of drummers I tried to call when I first arrived in Los Angeles. They were the most recorded drummers in the world. My heroes, whom I loved and admired, were now cheering for *me*. When Jeff told me he "loved my hi-hat work," and Steve, Harvey, and Bernard said they "loved my groove," I knew no other words would mean more to me as a drummer. My mentors Ralph Johnson and Al McKay of Earth, Wind & Fire drove two hours to see me perform at Disneyland, which touched my heart more than they would ever know. Even my old North Eugene High School crushes, Korin Hughes and Misty Gattis, showed up at the concert in Portland, Oregon.

By October, I had a feature interview in *Modern Drummer*, the premier drum magazine in the industry. Then, during our break in December, I dropped by the Pro Drum Shop in Hollywood. When I saw a promotional picture of me hanging on the wall of fame, I thought I had died and gone to heaven. It was as I imagined it would be. Only better!

Back in 1975, I was just trying to stay alive. In 1985, I had *come* alive. Ten years had passed since I had attended the Frank Sinatra concert, where I left dreaming about being on stage. And just the way Sinatra reminisced in his nostalgic song, I was having a very good year.

A very good year, indeed.

CHAPTER 44

Life in the Fast Lane

The year 1985 turned out to be an extraordinary kickoff to a decade of sheer elation as I circled the globe, doing what I was born to do. I continued touring with New Edition at the height of their popularity for the next couple of years, relishing every moment of the fantazmical journey. As their momentum grew, so did my reputation as a drummer, which earned me worldwide respect and created a greater demand for my services.

One of the lead singers of New Edition was Bobby Brown. With his incomparable sense of humor and an energy that could keep up with mine, Bobby and I had become best of friends, so when he left the group in 1987, he asked me to go on tour with him.

I loved Bobby, but there was no guarantee he wouldn't flop like countless other lead singers who had tried to go solo. I would be taking a big chance leaving the security of New Edition. But Bobby shared the limelight with me both on and off stage, and that had always made me feel honored. On top of that, we always had fun together. He was one of the funniest people I had ever met. We made each other laugh. A lot. Though the risks were many, I followed my heart and chose friendship.

While I was touring with Bobby on the King of Stage tour in 1987,

Lenny married Lisa Bonet, and a year later they gave birth to their daughter, Zoë. Though he hadn't found himself musically yet, he *had* found love. I was proud of playing a part in that. I continued to invite Lenny to all my Bobby Brown concerts in LA and New York, as he was traveling back and forth between both cities by then. Backstage I always talked Lenny up, as he had so faithfully done for me. Without him, I would have never gotten the New Edition gig in the first place. Without me, he would have never scooped up a Hollywood starlet as his wife and become a father. Our destinies were intertwined from the start, but neither of us knew where life would take us from there.

As usual, following my heart paid off. By 1988, Bobby Brown was on fire, and I was fanning those flames with the sound of my funky beat. His second solo album, *Don't Be Cruel*, exploded and spawned five top-ten hits on the *Billboard* Hot 100.

With megahits like "Don't Be Cruel," "Every Little Step," "Roni," "Rock Wit'cha," and the number one "My Prerogative," Bobby had become one of the most popular artists in pop music and the first teenager since Stevie Wonder to hit number one on the *Billboard* chart. Through it all, I added more gold and platinum albums to the ones I had earned while playing with New Edition a few years earlier.

"My Prerogative" became one of the most played music videos on MTV for years. For the shoot, I played a cherry rose drum set with my Zoro logo on the bass drum and wore my sister Patricia's red and black suede Claude Montana jacket. Bobby told the director to make sure I got some close-ups, which helped boost my profile immensely.

Months later, while rehearsing for the Soul Train Awards at the Shrine Auditorium, I was having an in-depth conversation with producer Quincy Jones about the incredible arrangements he wrote for Frank Sinatra and what it was like working for him. Whitney Houston stood beside me with a big smile on her face. She was eyeing Bobby, who was still on stage, working out some moves with his dancers. As soon as Quincy took his leave, Whitney said, "Zoro, Zoro. You gotta introduce me to Bobby! I just love the way that boy dances!"

Even though Whitney was a huge star herself, at that moment she was like any other starstruck fan. After introducing them, I never imagined they would marry a few years later in 1992.

Don't Be Cruel became the top-selling album of 1989, selling over five million copies and leading Bobby to win a Grammy in 1990 for best male R&B vocal performance. We toured relentlessly, selling out the largest venues, while playing on television shows and hobnobbing with the rich and famous in between.

On one of my breaks from Bobby's tour, I visited Lenny and Lisa at their vibey little place in Venice, California, near the beach. That evening, Lenny played me a demo of some tracks he had been working on. A respite from the gaudily overproduced music that dominated the airwaves at the time, his sound was raw and unpretentious, soulful and pure.

"You've done it, man. You've found your sound!" I was so happy for him.

Lenny credited Lisa for being instrumental in his arrival as an artist. She was his flower child soulmate, and he drew inspiration from her.

"I just signed with Virgin Records," he said, telling me all about his new record deal.

"Virgin? They're on the rise. You'll do well there." I gave him a big hug and said, "I always knew this day would come."

"There's only one catch." He paused. "You have to be my drummer for this to make sense." I sat in pensive silence. "Look, I know you're riding high and all with Bobby. But you're still a backup musician. My thing is a rock and roll band, and you'll be at the center of it. How about it, Z?" When Lenny believed in something strongly, he had an infectious enthusiasm that was nearly impossible to resist. On my way out, he said to me, "And by the way, my first concert will be watched by two billion people."

"Come on, now. How the heck are you gonna make a debut like that?" I asked. Lenny's visions and dreams were always bigger than anyone I knew, but *this*?

"It's a global broadcast called 'Our Common Future' from the producer of Live Aid to raise environmental awareness. Elton John, Stevie Wonder, Sting . . . all the biggest names will be on the gig."

"How'd you get on the roster when your record isn't even out yet?"

"The producers loved my song 'Does Anybody Out There Even Care.' Thought it was the perfect theme for the whole event. Jeff Ayeroff, one of the label heads at Virgin, went to bat for me."

And so a few months later, after finishing up with Bobby Brown, I moved into a loft with Lenny and Lisa in SoHo, an artsy district near Greenwich Village in Manhattan, not far from the World Trade Center. Once again, I had followed friendship and wanted to be there for the friend who had first believed in me. Like hippies from the '60s, Lenny, Lisa, and the entire band lived together with the peace-and-love ethos of a bygone era. The flow of cheerful, creative energy recharged my soul during the otherwise cold and corporate world of the late '80s. Having always been surrounded by a big, loud family with lots of children, I also liked being around their baby girl, Zoë, who was a bright bundle of joyfulness for all of us (a bright bundle who had a promising future ahead of her as an actor, singer, director, and model.)

True to Lenny's word, our first concert on June 3, 1989, was televised to more than a hundred countries around the world. We played the once-in-a-lifetime event at Avery Fisher Hall in Lincoln Center, where we rolled onstage with the tribal attitude, "We're gonna tear the roof off this mother." We were hungry to win the crowd and hungry for the approval of our idols. After giving an electrifying performance of "Does Anybody Out There Even Care" and "Let Love Rule," we earned both!

Lenny's debut album, *Let Love Rule*, was released a few months later in the first week of September. In support of it, we did a short US club tour, then headed to Europe, where the album was really taking off, eventually selling more than two million copies. Night after night we rocked out for audiences that were steadily growing. Lenny tore up every show. After our breakthrough performances in Amsterdam, Hamburg, and Paris, he pummeled his way to superstardom. I couldn't have been happier to see him finally have his day in the spotlight. Through it all, he stayed grounded thanks to his mother, Roxie, who had never let Hollywood inflate her ego. Lenny and I referred to the kind of humility our mothers taught us as "good brought-upsy."

In between concert dates, we shot our first music video for the single

"Let Love Rule." Wearing her groovy sunglasses and loosely fitting bo-hemian attire, Lisa directed it, shooting it all on Super 8 film. The result captured our retro vibe. We loved it.

I was living *la dolce vita* as I spent the next three years touring the world with Lenny. Some of the highlights from this period included playing *The Tonight Show* in the same sacred space where Buddy Rich had played when Mama and I watched him on TV. The other was per-forming on *Soul Train*, a show I had watched every Saturday morning with my brothers and sisters, dancing in the living room and practicing our moves. Those shows had played such an integral part of our lives, and my family was just as thrilled for me as I was.

We even played the Prince's Trust Concert at Hyde Park in London with Prince Charles in attendance. Mama used to recite a proverb to me after I had finished a long practicing session. "Do you see a man who excels in his work?" she would say. "He will stand before kings; he will not stand before obscure men." Now I was living out those very words as I played my drums before royalty.

Lenny and I were in musical heaven as we shared the stage with Bob Dylan, Mick Jagger, Steven Tyler, Bruce Springsteen, Tom Petty, and more. We even played three concerts around the world in a twenty-four-hour period. The first was in London, then Tokyo, then off to LA to play at Dodger Stadium with David Bowie. Being a huge Elvis fan, I was excited to meet Lisa Marie Presley, which led to our friendship and to my recording her very first tracks. The pace was relentless. But I was too amped up to be tired. All that stamina I had developed as a child was finally paying off, and I thrived on the whirlwind of exhilaration.

In 1993 I embarked on the Natural High tour with French super-star Vanessa Paradis in support of her self-titled album that Lenny had just produced. He had put her band together and secured my spot in the drum chair. We performed extensively throughout France, England, and Canada, even traveling way down to the exotic Mauritius Island. I spent the better part of that year living in Paris and loving the European *joie de vivre*. We also recorded her first live album, *Vanessa Paradis Live*, at the famed Olympia Theater in Paris.

My gift continued to connect me with a slew of international artists on stage and in the studio, including some of my childhood idols.
One of those was Philip Bailey, the lead vocalist of Earth, Wind & Fire,
whose celebrated voice was only surpassed by how wonderful he was to
work with. I also worked on solo projects with some of the other band
members, as well as playing live with the Earth, Wind & Fire All Stars.
A standout memory was playing behind one of the lead singers of the
Temptations. This was another full-circle moment since they were the
first group I saw in concert. The hardest part of this period was all the
great gigs, many of them from other idols, that I had to turn down because I could only be in one place at a time.

Nevertheless, the most surprising thing of all was making it down
to the fifty-yard line in the NFL, but not as the quarterback I had imagined being as a kid. Instead, I took center field as the timekeeper of the
band, and together Lenny Kravitz and I ignited a furnace of groove that
brought sixty-five thousand screaming fans to their feet at a game between the Patriots and the Colts.

Those days were fast, furious, and fierce. Every now and then, I
would step back and think about those long, cold, hungry nights of my
childhood, and I would feel overwhelmed with gratitude. I never took
one of those moments for granted.

I had no idea what was around the corner and was about to learn
that you can be expecting one thing and instead fall headfirst into your
destiny.

CHAPTER 45

Can't Take My Eyes off You

Throughout the 1980s, I never forgot how Mama had scrimped and saved to surprise us with Frank Sinatra tickets back in 1975. The concert had served as one of those pivotal turning points in my life, filling my heart with wild imaginings of musical grandeur. Ever since then, I had longed for a way to repay her. I finally thought of the perfect plan.

In January 1995, I flew Mama and Bobby to Las Vegas for a weekend at the legendary Sands Hotel and Casino. The Sands had been home to the Rat Pack during their heyday, and Frank Sinatra had recorded *Sinatra at the Sands* with the Count Basie Orchestra in its world-renowned Copa Room. Since that was one of Mama's favorite records, I thought she would be pleased by the nostalgia of staying there.

After driving them past the iconic "Welcome to Fabulous Las Vegas Nevada" sign, I held up a sealed envelope. "I bought tickets for a very special show," I said, "but you have to guess which one."

They called out the big-name entertainers from the marquees as we drove past the neon signs for the Aladdin, Caesar's Palace, the Flamingo, and the MGM Grand. I reveled in the charade until I pulled over and pointed up to a big sign with cursive letters, set against the expansive desert skyline.

"Frankie Valli and the Four Seasons!" Mama shouted.

"I know how much you've always loved their music, so I bought you and Bobby the best seats in the house."

Despite her excitement, Mama was disappointed to learn I had a gig and wouldn't be joining them. "Can't you get someone else to sub for you tonight?" she pleaded.

"We'll spend all day tomorrow together, I promise," I replied, but little did she know I had another trick up my sleeve.

While Bobby and Mama took their seats in the Copa Room, I went over the set list in my dressing room to make sure I had memorized the musical transitions for my show.

Minutes later the burgundy velvet curtains drew back as the orchestra played an overture of the Four Seasons' hit songs. The dimly lit drummer (guess who?) went into a locomotive groove that segued into the unmistakable Four Seasons' signature harmony on "Who Loves You."

The crowd roared when Frankie Valli strolled on stage with his perfectly coiffed hair, belting out the falsetto for which he was famous. The crimson lights cast an elegant ambiance over the room.

Midway through the song, the dazzling, bright white lights exploded. Mama's eyes practically jumped out of her head when she realized I was the one playing the drums. She screamed so loudly the entire venue heard her. From behind my drums, I saw her bouncing up and down like a little kid, looking back and forth at Bobby to see his reaction. He was glowing with pride. The look on her face was priceless, the same look I had seen when she had gazed at Ol' Blue Eyes back in '75.

When the song concluded, Frankie announced, "I haven't heard a woman scream that loud for me since the '60s."

The audience howled.

Mama proudly pointed at me and hollered, "That's my son on the drums! That's my son!"

Frankie swung his head back at me, smiled, and said into his microphone, "Apparently, your mother is very excited to see you up here, Zorelli." Zorelli was the Italian nickname Frankie had given me. "Ladies and gentlemen, give it up for Zoro on the drums!" The audience clapped.

"And how about a big round of applause for his mother, who is with us tonight?" The crowd cheered and whistled. Frankie winked at Mama and said, "Maria, this next song is for you." After the horns softly crept into the intro, he looked directly at her and sang the opening words from "Can't Take My Eyes off You."

Right away, Mama was grabbing tissues out of her purse, dabbing them across her face. We continued with a two-hour set of back-to-back hits that included "Grease" (one of the first songs I had ever learned to play on the drums). Afterward, Tiger, our bristly-haired head of security, went to Mama's table and brought her and Bobby backstage to the green room. Mama's eyes sparkled as she entered, then she patted me on my shoulder. "You really fooled me. How did you manage to keep this a secret?"

"Bobby was in on it."

She gave him a look as if to say, I can't believe you two.

"We wanted to make tonight as special as when you surprised us with Frank Sinatra tickets twenty years ago," I said.

In the meantime, Frankie was making his away across the room. Although she hid her nerves, my mother was flustered when her idol greeted her by name and said, "You're even more beautiful than Zoro described." Frankie made quite an impression in his bespoke slate-gray suit and alligator loafers. "He's told me so much about you that I feel like I know you already." He gave her a big hug and a kiss on the cheek before handing her a bouquet of fresh pink and persimmon roses. "Thanks for raising a great son. The best drummer I've ever worked with."

Mama blushed. My becoming the drummer for Frankie Valli and the Four Seasons was a source of jubilation for her. My heart was full as I watched him make my mother feel like a queen.

That night was the gift of a lifetime—for both of us.

Shortly after that, I made good on my promise to Ms. Pearl from the Music Shop. I surprised her with front-row tickets to see me with Frankie when we played at the Seven Feathers Casino, just north of Grants Pass. Frankie rolled out the red carpet for her just as he had done for Mama. Ms. Pearl was beside herself. What a feeling it was to fulfill a promise I had made twenty-five years earlier.

A few months later, another surprise was waiting to unfold.

A recent acquaintance set up a blind date with her younger friend. I had been on blind dates before and was skeptical. Amid all my dreams coming true, I quickly learned that a string of flings was not for me. After a series of these and one short-lived marriage, I was still hurt and cautious about relationships. But I still hoped the right person might be out there for me, one I could connect with on the deepest level. With a little coaxing from my niece Lydia, I decided to give love another try.

I made reservations at a cozy Greek restaurant in Malibu. I anticipated her arrival but was not ready for what would happen. In walks this absolute vision of beauty with the kindest smile and most hypnotic eyes I'd ever seen. My heart must have known what my mind didn't yet realize. She was going to be the love of my life.

We talked for hours. She was warm, vibrant, and down to earth. No airs, no pretense. She was grounded and humble, even though I could tell she was extraordinary. I had met many women in my life, but no one like her.

After dinner, we sat in my car and talked for another few hours. She was the daughter of a pastor, the eldest of three children, and from a solid family. I'll never forget the look of love in her eyes when she shared her dream of someday having her own family. I still remember her laugh—our laughter—the way she looked at me when she listened, the way I felt listening to her. I couldn't wait to see her again.

A couple of days later, I asked her out on an official date. I took her to dinner at Kevin Costner's Twin Palms restaurant in Old Town Pasadena. We shared frozen yogurt at Humphrey Yogart, and as we strolled Colorado Boulevard, it felt like we had known each other all our lives. When I was with her, it felt like I was *home*. She seemed so familiar to me. In her presence, I was suddenly alive, hopeful, even wide-eyed. I didn't want that feeling to ever go away.

But time was ticking. I had a concert with Frankie out of town the following week. Renée and I had only known each other a week, but with the feelings we had for each other already, it felt like we'd packed a year into that week. Renée drove me to the airport. Outside the jet bridge, she hugged me and gave me a kiss. I shuffled onto the plane light headed and spent the entire flight thinking of her. I couldn't wait to get back home.

I had been looking to be loved and accepted for who I was all my life. I wanted someone to see the good in me without having to perform to prove it. Renée saw it. She made me feel loved and accepted in a way no other woman had, except Mama. In her presence, I felt known, and I wanted to be more known by her. I couldn't get her out of my mind.

I called Mama and told her Renée was the one. She was overjoyed and said it was the answer to her many prayers for the right woman to come into my life. It had only been two weeks, but I had zero doubt. Renée and I were soulmates, meant to spend the rest of our lives together. I wasn't an eighteen-year-old kid anymore. I was a thirty-two-year-old man who had seen it all, done it all, and I knew there was nobody on earth like Renée.

Then on Sunday after church, we went back to my house. While we were cuddling on the couch watching *Coming to America*, it just rolled out of my mouth. "Would you marry me?" I didn't even have a ring. That would come later. I felt a wave of relief when she said yes. It felt so incredible to be chosen by her too. I didn't plan that moment. It just happened. But while I was at her father's church listening to his sermon, I gazed at her and felt God whisper, "She is the one I have chosen for you." So I followed that voice and my heart, as I always had.

Four months later, we exchanged vows at the Odyssey in Granada Hills, a venue overlooking the San Fernando Valley. It was a gorgeous Friday night, and the room was packed with our closest friends. My siblings and Mama were there. So was Frankie Valli! At the reception, I got up and made a toast to my bride. "If I were a singer of songs, I would sing to you, but since I am the minister of groove, a bishop of the beat, I will serenade you with my drums instead." Then I poured my already bursting-at-the-seams heart into that drum solo, every rousing rhythm and clashing cymbal crash a testament to my love for her.

Finally, every piece of my dream had come to fruition. I was now in love and happily married, loving every moment of my life. Four years later, Renée gave birth to our beloved son, Jarod. Two-and-a-half years afterward, she brought our precious daughter, Jordan, into the world.

While Renée was pregnant, I made a ninety-minute cassette tape telling each of our children how much I loved them, how excited I was for them to come into our lives, and how they were destined for greatness. I read poems I had written for them. Then I placed the headphones on Renée's belly and played the tape for them every night. The one thing I wanted was for my children to know they were loved—even before they arrived.

As a young boy, I promised myself that when I became a father, I would never allow my children to feel how my father made me feel. I was determined to break the cycle of fatherlessness, be the patriarch of a new generation, and pass on the blessing of love to my children.

Even with my boundless imagination as a kid, I still couldn't have envisioned what it would feel like to become the kind of husband Mama never had. Or the kind of father *I* never had. The feeling brought me more pride than anything else I had accomplished. Yes, it did feel like an "accomplishment." Not in the same way as any of my professional achievements. Sure, I had worked long and hard to be the drummer I became. But in contrast, with Renée it felt like I had been graced with this remarkable woman and beautiful family *and* like I had never stopped believing it was possible. Maybe that's part of the feeling of accomplishment. Holding onto the faith and hope Mama had instilled, despite all the uncertainties, heartache, and pain along the way.

Love found a way to us. We found our way to love.

Seeing Renée so happy being a mom filled me with pride and admiration. She had always told me how it was one of her greatest dreams to have children, and watching her with Jarod and Jordan, I was in awe. She has always brought a spirit of excellence to everything she does, whether it is simple day-to-day activities, whipping up incredible meals inspired by the Food Network, or navigating storms with valor.

It's safe to say that I wouldn't be where I am today without Renée. That may sound like the beginning of every acceptance speech, but it's true. And here's why:

I thought I was strong, but Renée has a quiet determination that I took years to develop.

I thought I was patient, but Renée's patience has taught me more about timing and trust than I could have ever learned without her.

I thought I pretty much had it together, but nobody else I know can hold things firmly in place when complete chaos is swirling around us.

Not like Renée.

She's the dream weaver of our family and turned our home into a fortress of fun with her playful spirit, filling it with love, laughter, safety, and comfort. She made it possible for me to grow into the man I have become, enabling me to perform, speak, teach, write, dream, and reach new heights. She always believed in me and encouraged me through some of the toughest times, never dismissing my wild ideas or big visions. And she has done the same with our children. As they venture off to pursue their dreams, they are going to succeed, serve, and change the world largely because of her.

When I look back, I marvel at where we started and where we are now. I think of all the hardships and transitions we've weathered. I'm thankful that our faith and laughter have always kept us strong, connected, and hopeful. Often these days, we love to spend evenings watching old episodes of *Seinfeld* and *I Love Lucy*, laughing out loud together as the rest of the world slips away.

Renée is my rock, my confidante, my best friend. She is the person I never knew I'd find, but the one I knew I'd found when she walked into my life nearly three decades ago on that fateful night in Malibu.

CHAPTER 46

Mama Liked the Roses

Maria loved her native Mexico, but her heart belonged to the United States. From early childhood she had been lovesick for American culture. The movies, the music, the fashion, the language, and the people had always enamored her.

She had also imagined herself on the big screen, especially after she had a snippet of screen time in *Salón México*. In the fall of 2020, I purchased the DVD and sat in my favorite brown leather chair as the 1949 film played on my television. My heart raced. I didn't dare fast forward for fear of missing her scene.

Suddenly there she was, a mere teenager, sitting at a table and talking with a man who would soon become her husband. There were no Super 8 cameras in those days. This would be the only moving footage I would have of her life in Mexico. The moment I saw her, I wept profusely. For the first time in my life, I didn't see her as my mother. I stared through my reading glasses at a vibrant, young, beautiful Maria—before the world had done its best to break her.

I could feel her sense of hope at that age, as she was making great strides toward her dream of becoming a leading actress. A flood of emotions flowed over me as I watched the film. I wanted to jump into the screen and hug the young Maria, tell her how proud I was of her for trying so hard, how sorry I was that things hadn't worked out as she had hoped. Though she would never become the movie star she could have been or find the loving husband she should have had, some thirty-eight years after immigrating, at age sixty-nine Mama was determined to fulfill her dream of becoming a United States citizen.

She filled out the lengthy application, and then, after checking the mail for weeks, she ripped open the package containing the *US Citizenship and Naturalization Handbook* when it finally arrived. For months she immersed herself in every page, committing the facts to memory as she prepared for the test. Determined not to make a single mistake, she even took classes and asked us to quiz her daily with flash cards. By the time she appeared before the US district court in Portland, Oregon, in 1999, she knew more about the history of the United States, its government, and its constitution than any of her children who were born here.

I was never prouder to be her son than the moment she raised her right hand, was sworn in, and became an official citizen. As I took it all in, I thought about what America meant to my mother. Then I realized what it meant to me. I thought about the price she had paid to call this country home and how hard she had fought to make this land our own. Our lives were made better because she had been a fearless warrior who, like so many other immigrant parents, sacrificed her own dreams so her children could realize theirs.

Growing up, I had never understood how my mother could carry herself with such dignity, despite enduring so many circumstances that could have destroyed her self-worth. How was she able to look beyond the poverty and the hardship to keep moving forward with a smile?

Sometime later in my life, I realized that the secret to my mother's strength lay in her identity. She knew who she was and where she came from, and she had carried that dignity with her across the border. Though many people tried to strip that truth from her, she refused to let anyone—or anything—break her spirit or undermine her worth. Now watching her being officially welcomed into the country as one of its own meant even more to me than it did to her, even though she was clearly reveling in the pomp and circumstance.

As we took photos to commemorate the momentous occasion, Mama proudly waved the American flag in her right hand while holding her Certificate of Naturalization in her left. The cycle was complete. All the members of our family were now citizens.

When the next presidential election took place on November 7, 2000, Bobby drove Mama to the local elementary school, where she was first in line to cast her vote. My mother's biggest contribution to her new country, though, would be more than just casting her vote. It was the seven children she had reared as a single mother. We were a complex bunch, fractured yet formidable, but each of us would make a positive difference in the land that became her home. Standing in that courtroom, we celebrated a long journey that had seen each of us fulfill our dreams, all because Mama had convinced us we could. At that moment, it seemed nothing could ever break us.

But that moment would not last . . .

It was an unforgettably bone-chilling night in Cologne, Germany, that November in 2004, colder than usual for that time of year. But the most memorable part of the evening was not the weather. It was an event taking place five thousand miles away, something that would change my life forever.

I was having dinner with Lenny at Ristorante Etrusca, a divine Italian bistro with old-world Tuscan charm. We had been on a promotional tour of Europe for his new album, *Baptism*, and had just finished recording a television show earlier that evening. As we were eating a savory meal, Lenny randomly started talking about my mother. "Your mom's amazing, ya know?"

With a mouthful of pasta, I nodded.

"Man, what she went through for you kids. All seven of you. And without a husband, no relatives, nothing. Just love. And faith."

"Yeah, man. I don't know where I'd be without her," I said, taking another bite, and through the pasta added, "prison, probably."

Lenny laughed. "All the times I've been around her, she's never complained. Not once."

"She doesn't complain much," I said. "She's the most grateful person I've ever known."

"And she's hilarious too."

"I don't think she tries to be. The things she says, they just come out funny."

He loved my mother, and I had loved his. Lenny's mother, Roxie, had died of breast cancer in 1995 at the young age of sixty-six. After her passing, he wrote "Thinking of You," a touching tribute to her that moved me every time I heard it. Lenny continued talking about my mother throughout dinner. Together we laughed as we shared more hilarious stories about her.

At one point he started to take out his cell phone, but then put it back. "What is it?" I asked.

"Nothing." He checked his watch. "It's getting late. We'd better go."

We rushed back to the hotel to grab our luggage. Then we were driven to the airport, where we boarded a private 737 to Los Angeles. After a long flight, three black SUVs transported us directly from the LAX tarmac to the Shrine Auditorium, where we were scheduled to do a run-through for the American Music Awards. From the SUV, I called home to check in with Renée.

Her voice was shaky. "Have you talked to anyone in your family?"

"No. Why? What's wrong?"

Renée started crying. Through her tears, she said, "Your mother . . . she died last night."

"Noooooooooooooooooo! Nooooooooooooo! Nooooooo!" I wailed. "Oh, no. Oh, God, nooooooooo!" When I finally contained my emotions enough to catch my breath, I asked, "How?"

"She had an endoscopy late in the day. Sometime in the middle of the night, Bobby woke up, checked on her, and she . . . she wasn't breathing. He administered CPR until the paramedics arrived, but it was too late."

The band's road manager, Eric Barrett, was riding with me and heard fragments of my conversation with Renée. He looked to me for an explanation. I lowered the phone, told him, and he immediately called Lenny, who was in the vehicle right behind us. When I got off the phone, I slumped in shock. Eric put his hand on my shoulder, trying to console me.

When we arrived at the Shrine Auditorium, I got out of the car, and Lenny ran over and hugged me. "I'm so sorry," he said. "This is crazy, man. We were just talking about her last night. I can't believe it. I almost called her from the restaurant. Man, if only I—"

I realized that for some reason God had put Maria in our hearts at about the time she was leaving this world. *If only we had made that call.*

We were on a tight schedule, so I had no choice but to head straight to our rehearsal slot. Bobby called during our sound check, but I knew that if I heard the sound of his voice, I would fall apart. I needed to keep it together until I made it through the song, so I switched my phone to vibrate.

It took all the strength I had to greet the other musicians backstage. All I could think of was the lyric from Nat King Cole's recording of "Smile" that Mama always sang to me when she was trying to soothe my broken heart.

After our practice run of "Lady," the hit song we would be performing on the show the next night, I looked for a private area backstage to return Bobby's call. As soon as he heard my voice, he burst into tears. "Mama's dead, Mama's dead, Mama's dead."

Through my tears, I tried to console him. "You were a great son to her. She loved you so much." He was crying so hard I couldn't tell if he could hear me. I was a mess. Tears ran down my cheeks, my chin, my neck.

After I said goodbye, I wiped my face with my shirt and hurried to the SUV. While I was asking the driver to take me to my house in Chatsworth, I heard Lenny tell his manager, Craig Fruin, "Cancel my press engagements. I want to be here for Zoro." At that moment, we were united by the loss of our mothers. I had gone to his mother's funeral and mourned with him. Now he was mourning with me. We climbed into the SUV, and Lenny did his best to console me. For a long time, I just cried and cried. Along the way, I called Renée to tell her Lenny would be spending the night. My wife and children ran to the car as we pulled up, and then there was another round of tears.

Shortly afterward, I walked past my desk and saw a five-by-seven manila envelope addressed to me in my mother's handwriting. I picked it up and looked at the postmark: October 29, 2004. She had mailed it ten days earlier while I was in Europe. I hardly had the strength to hold it, let alone read it. I slowly opened the envelope and pulled out a greeting card. My hands trembled; my whole body shook. After wiping my tears with my shirt, I closed my eyes, took a deep breath, and opened the card.

October 10, 2004

Dear Danny,

    You are really a great son. I am praying to God that everything will be okay so I can come and visit you and your family next year sometime. Thank you for everything you have done for me today and always. Good luck in your career. Call me when you have the time. God bless you.

Love,
Your Mother

We had planned to fly her down to visit us in October, right before she mailed the card, but due to her health, the doctor had said she shouldn't fly.

Or had he said she *couldn't* fly? I couldn't remember. I couldn't think. My brain felt as if it were pushing against the inside of my skull, keeping me from holding a coherent thought. My head was throbbing. I thought it was going to explode. There was such a terrible lump in my throat. The muscles in my face were so taut it felt like they were going to tear. My jaw was sore at the joints, and my eyes were hot and gritty. My mouth was so dry, so very, very dry. I dropped the card onto the desk and rubbed my face, my eyes.

Lenny hung out all night, playing with my kids, talking to Renée, help-ing out wherever he could. When my family went to bed, he stayed up a while to talk with me. After he turned in, I went to the living room and stretched out face down in front of the fireplace. I cried for hours, groaning from the depths of my soul. I tried to remember the last time I talked with Mama. It was a call I had made from the airport the night before I had left for Europe. As usual, our final words to one another were, "I love you."

The next afternoon, another black SUV picked us up. Lenny had the car stop at Roscoe's Chicken and Waffles in Inglewood, one of our favor-ite soul food joints, where he tried to cheer me up with a big plate of fried chicken and waffles. Afterward, the driver took us to the Shrine Auditorium.

Later that night, with the curtains ready to open for our performance, Lenny turned to the band and said, "This one's for Maria. Let's do it!"

It meant the world to me that he honored my mother that way. When the curtains went up, we rocked the house. I gave it my all for Mama. I wondered if she could see me from heaven and if she knew how heavy my heart was as I played . . . for her.

A couple of days later, Renée and I flew to Oregon for the funeral. I was sad that it was a typical gloomy Eugene day as my siblings and I gathered around Mama's casket to say our final goodbyes. It would be the last time we would ever see her face. The weight of that, the fi-nality of that, was too much for us to bear alone. So we did what she had taught us to do. We leaned on each other. We each had a private moment to say goodbye to the woman who had fought so hard so that we could have a better life.

While standing over my mother's casket, a lifetime of memories flooded over me. I reached for her hands and gently rubbed them the way I had done as a little boy. That had always been my way of show-ing Mama how much I loved her.

Then I pulled out the orange silk scarf she had tied around my neck when I was seven years old. I wrapped the scarf around a pair of my drumsticks and placed them together across her heart. "Hold these for me, Mama," I whispered, "until I see you in heaven."

Along with family and a few close friends, the ceremony was attended by a fair number of strangers, each eager to share their testimony of how Mama had touched their lives. Doctors, pharmacists, nurses, bank tellers, supermarket checkers, and a host of others told how Mama had encouraged them to smile through all the pain and heartache and how she had made them laugh. It warmed our hearts to know what a profound impact our mother had in the small circle that was her life.

All seven of us eulogized her. As I read the letter I had written to her, I played Glenn Miller's "Moonlight Serenade" in the background. It was one of her favorite songs and the one we had danced to the most when I was a boy. As the sentimental ballad played, I had to stop several times to gain my composure. I directed these words to my sweet Maria:

> *My warmest memory will always be of you dancing with me when I was a little boy and how you held me close to you, where I could feel the warmth of your love, the security of your arms, the beat of your heart. I was truly blessed from the moment I entered the world and saw those affectionate brown eyes staring at me with such wonder and expectation.*
>
> *Yours will be the first face I seek when I get to heaven. And though I may not recognize you, I will look for the woman with the brightest smile, which I am certain will be yours. At that moment I will jump into your arms as the little boy you loved so earnestly.*
>
> *Goodbye, my love. Goodbye, my laughter. Goodbye, Mama. I thank God with all my heart that he chose you as my mother, because in you I found the greatest love of all.*
>
> *Your loving son,*
> *Danny*

Ricardo then shared how much our mother loved roses and that she had planted them at our very first home in Grants Pass. Then he played Elvis Presley's melancholy song, "Mama Liked the Roses." By the time the church bells rang in the second verse, tears were gushing down my face, and sniffles could be heard throughout the chapel.

It was true that Maria loved roses, but the roses that had made her most proud were her seven children—in whom she had lovingly planted her seeds of kindness, resilience, faith, and love. How Mama loved *these* roses!

After the tear-filled ceremony, we proceeded outside for the burial, my three brothers and I serving as pallbearers. From the corner of my eye, I noticed the heartache on Ricardo's face. Bobby looked like a vacant building. Armando's eyes were the saddest I had ever seen. My sisters were to the side, sobbing.

But then, just as we were about to lay our precious mother to rest, the grass started to shimmer. A shaft of sunlight shone through the clouds, bringing warmth and color to everything around us. Maybe it was the starry-eyed boy in me, but I believed it was God's assurance (or "sign") that Mama was with him in a home beyond her wildest dreams. For the first time that day, all seven of her children looked up to the heavens . . . and smiled.

As we placed roses on her grave, I imagined passing over the rainbow to join her.

I arrive as a little boy again. After a long hug, Mama says, "I've missed you so much, mijo. And I've missed your music too." She wraps her scarf around my neck and hands me the drumsticks I'd placed in her coffin. "Play for me, won't you, Danny?"

I take the sticks and turn to a set of drums gleaming golden in the light. As I take my seat, an audience of angels surrounds me, waiting to hear me play. I smile at Mama and announce:

"This one's for Maria!"

Epilogue

On June 13, 2019, I arranged to take my two kids to a taping of *The Tonight Show Starring Jimmy Fallon*. It was a beautiful, clear summer day in New York City, and I was in town with my family for my fifty-seventh birthday. My kids, Jarod and Jordan, had pestered me to attend *The Tonight Show* for years, but you had to be at least sixteen. Jarod was now twenty, and Jordan seventeen. Luckily, I knew the music supervisor of the show, Keith McPhee, a stand-up guy, and after a quick phone call, he was gracious enough to arrange for tickets.

It's been over twenty years since Mama's passing. Hardly a day has gone by since that the tender memory of our journey together doesn't find a way into my heart. I feel her passion in my daughter's love for the arts and her concern for others in the sympathetic heart of my son.

Even now, I remember the day clearly. We arrived at the NBC studios in Rockefeller Center at 3:10 p.m. The NBC page called up to the sixth floor, and we were given special passes after each of us showed our ID. We rode up in an exclusive elevator that would only stop at the floor for which you had clearance. We passed the Seth Meyers floor and then the SNL floor, finally stopping at the sixth-floor home of *The Tonight Show*. The elevator door opened, where we were welcomed by Keith and several members of the Roots. Renée and the kids were thrilled. James, the keyboard player for the Roots, who is best known for doing "Thank You Notes," told us that Questlove wanted to say hello, and he shuffled us into his dressing room.

Music has been the heartbeat of my family's life ever since I can remember. It pulsed throughout our home, wherever that may have been at the time. More than any other art form, music has a mystical power that can seemingly transport us back in time to feel the presence of those we have lost. Whenever I want a good cry and to feel her strong spirit, I'll put on a song Mama loved. One of her favorites was "You're the Best Thing That Ever Happened to Me" by Gladys Knight & the Pips. She would often repeat this refrain to each of her children, but really it was Maria Islas-Bravo who was the best thing that ever happened to *us*.

Questlove could not have been kinder. We took pictures together, and he gave my daughter two pairs of drumsticks she had wanted for two of her drummer friends. He also signed a pair of mine. We talked music for about half an hour. I could see the joy in my kids' eyes. Right in front of them, on the same playing field, were Zoro and Questlove talking shop. It was game meeting game. Perhaps Questlove had a similar upbringing. I didn't know. I only know that his musicianship reflects the same heart and soul I try to bring to my craft every time I sit in front of a set of drums, starting with that cardboard set Ricardo helped me put together for the fourth-grade talent show.

There have been other *fantazmical* times I've had in the intervening years. How I wish I could have told Mama about the time I was invited by Paul Allen, the cofounder of Microsoft, to record music aboard his private yacht, the *Octopus*. I had been welcomed aboard by the director James Cameron, and we traveled the South Pacific, sharing one exquisite meal after another. As I sat listening to Paul's stories about Bill Gates and Steve Jobs, it felt as if I were in the company of Thomas Edison or Alexander Graham Bell, men who had changed the world. Mama would have loved to hear all about it.

Another surreal moment happened on June 13, 2012, when I was invited to the White House for the Fatherhood Champions of Change celebration. What a way to commemorate my fiftieth birthday! There I was, the son of an immigrant who had once lived in a car I had dubbed "the White House," being acknowledged by our nation's leaders for making a difference in the lives of young men by teaching them the lessons my *mother* had taught me.

Many such events have catapulted me far from the boyhood I had known, including being voted the number one R&B drummer in the world. Though I've never stopped drumming and continue to play with various artists around the world, today I am also a motivational speaker with a passion for helping others reach their potential and succeed. Like my mother, I guess, I find great rewards in helping people discover their own paths and encouraging them to explore roads they may only encounter in their dreams.

Once the taping started, I was thrilled to hear, live, the music from the Roots. The sound in the studio was incredible. I should have known. They were a hundred times better in person than on television. I wish my childhood friend, Lenny, could have been there with me at that very moment.

Midway through the show, Jimmy came into the audience to chitchat while the production crew was getting ready for the musical guest. He kept glancing over at me. The audience was asking him all kinds of questions. Finally, he looked over and said, "Hey, man, how come you're not sitting in with the Roots?" I said, "I would love to, but no one asked." He introduced me to the audience and said, "Ladies and gentlemen, we have a legendary drummer in the audience with us tonight, Zoro. He's played with some of the greats, like Lenny Kravitz, Frankie Valli, and New Edition." Jimmy looked over at Questlove for approval. Questlove nodded. Then Jimmy asked, "Zoro, would you mind getting up there and playing for all of us?" Feeling like a kid again, I looked over at Renée to see if it was okay. She nodded her head as if to say, "Sure why not." That's all I needed to hear. I jumped up, and I was ready.

I grabbed a pair of my signature Vic Firth sticks and walked toward Questlove's drum set. Jimmy shook my hand on the way down, and I said to him, "I prayed to God for this." Jimmy looked shaken. I saw a tear come to his eye. In that moment, I felt the spirit of my mother course through me.

Maria was part gentry, part gypsy. A part of her was broken by life;

a part was brimming with it. She was, in one sense, the tragic character in a fairy tale. In another sense, she was the hero. My hero.

Knowing I'm still close with all my siblings and their families, along with my mentors and heroes, would have pleased her. She'd also be happy to know I've remained faithfully married to my precious bride for more than twenty-nine years and have lavished our two children with unconditional love.

When my father deserted me at six months old, leaving me only his bongos, he could never have guessed how prophetic they would become. But life is full of irony, and when you least expect it, the shadow of poetic justice jumps from behind a corner and surprises you.

Following Mama's example, I have forgiven everyone who hurt us along the way, including my father. My relationship with him never grew into what I had hoped for, and I eventually became tired of doing all the pursuing. I finally realized I couldn't make him love or value me the way I wanted and needed him to do. Maybe he was unwilling to love me. Or perhaps some childhood trauma prevented him from opening his heart. Whatever his reason, I'll never know. But I learned to accept that I could never do enough or be enough to earn his love, no matter how much I achieved.

I sat down at the throne of drums on the *Tonight Show* stage and gave the audience a three-minute solo that rocked the roof off the studio. My funkiest grooves were followed by others that were even funkier. I ended it with a parade of cymbals that echoed throughout the sixth floor. I made sure that even Seth Meyers could hear me. Immediately, the audience jumped up and gave me a standing ovation. Jimmy and Questlove ran over and gave me big hugs. To top it all off, Jimmy turned around to the audience and led them in a rendition of "Happy Birthday." Jarod and Jordan couldn't believe it. I was their father? For so long, I had felt forgotten and that no one cared about me anymore as a musician. It was overwhelming. I didn't even feel like Zoro in that moment. I felt like Danny Donnelly.

Although my cowlick is long gone and age has taken its toll, that audacious boy still lives in me. I've fought hard to protect his childlike spirit. Most importantly though, I've done my best to help that tender-hearted kid grow into the kind of man who would make his Mama proud.

Looking back now, I still love little Danny. I applaud his spunk, fervor, and resiliency, even if he was a little rascal at times. I keep him close to my heart. Whenever he summons me, I lean in to listen closely and follow his whimsical directives with the same determined spirit that guided my early steps. And he never fails to lead me to a magical place that only he can see—a place of pure imagination that helps me to look past seemingly insurmountable circumstances to keep dreaming big and believing in the impossible.

At the conclusion of the taping, Jimmy walked up to me and continued to gush. He said, "You were amazing!" He even shook my son's hand and said, "Thanks for coming." Not realizing we were still on the air, I tried to wrangle my family to take a photo with him. It was all broadcast around the country for everyone to see. The most famous talk show host in the world was a fan of mine. I was walking on air. As we exited 30 Rock and continued down Fifth Avenue, I thanked the Lord. And Mama. My wife yelled out for everyone to hear, "Well, I don't think anything else will top that today!"

As I look back, my story was over the rainbow—the dreams that I dared to dream really did come true. It is as much my mother's story as it is mine and my family's. In many ways, it is also a story of America and the hardships that each generation of immigrants has encountered. I hope it will encourage you to follow your own dreams, wherever they may lead, however impossible they may seem. Or if you, like my mother, have to leave your dream behind, I hope you can be to someone what my mother was to me.

Today, I still wear scarves in her honor. Every time I do, I feel closer to that spirited woman with the soulful eyes. She taught me to write my story the way I wanted it to be written, and what a fantazmical story it became.

Thanks so much for sharing this journey with me! If you enjoyed this book, I would be grateful if you would post a review, share it on social media, and tell your friends. Remember, dreams are important, so never give up on yours.

Zoro

Acknowledgments

There is no such thing as a self-made man. We are made up of thousands of others. Everyone who has ever done a kind deed for us, or spoken one word of encouragement to us, has entered into the makeup of our character and our thoughts, as well as our success.

—Commonly attributed to
George Matthew Adams

Bringing this book to fruition has been an incredibly heart-wrenching, cathartic, and rewarding experience similar to a long-distance marathon. What began as diary entries over fifty years ago morphed into vignettes. Those became the skeletal chapters that turned into this book. Along the way, numerous people have made this book possible in one way or another. They are the guiding lights and earthly angels who've traveled alongside me. They are the friends who have loved, supported, encouraged, equipped, and taught me. Each has played a pivotal role in my life.

With all the gratitude a mere mortal can muster, I thank my friend Jesus for loving, forgiving, protecting, guiding, and giving me favor all the days of my life!!!

Next, I owe a huge debt of gratitude to my brother Bobby for bringing these stories to life more than anyone else and to my older brother,

Ricardo, and eldest sister, Mary, for their help in shaping the accuracy of these events. No words can adequately express my gratitude to my beloved friend, Ken Gire. You were the first to champion my story with your amazing heart and countless hours of your time. Your soul is a big part of this manuscript. My mother would have loved you, Ken!

To my sweet friend, Julie Cantrell, a gem of a human being. Thank you for generously pouring your heart into shaping this manuscript in its latter stages. Your light-filled words got me through the dark days.

For helping me churn out an early draft of the proposal and editorial counsel along the way, I offer a bow of gratitude to my friend, Lu Hanessian. Our brainstorming sessions were a whirlwind of creative wonder.

Thanks to Marcus Brotherton for your critical insight, your friendship, and for introducing me to Julie Cantrell. You're one of the most generous, patient, and talented writers I know.

A fervent thanks to my amazing screenwriter friend, Tony Abrams, for your help in revisioning and recrafting the epilogue with such power and punch!

And, forever and ever, I thank my dear friend Eric Rhodes for listening to every chapter as it developed. Your creative input helped shape many scenes, and I remain grateful for how you steadily cheered me on. We did it, my brother!

My deep appreciation goes to Amy Hagberg for her indispensable help through the years. You are a great writer, and I remain grateful for all you did to help shape the original proposal and early chapters and for the numerous ways you instructed, guided, and encouraged me. You have been a great friend and an asset to my life.

To Lisa Cieslewicz, thanks for your never-ending faith in me and all you have so generously sown into my life's purpose. Your pitch-perfect editorial wisdom, honesty, and many prayers have helped shape me into the writer and man I am today, and I value your friendship more than you know.

Georgia Varozza, you are a kind and generous soul who always made me look like a better writer than I am, and you assured me that this memoir would be published. Whenever I needed your help, you were ready with your editorial intelligence and encouraging words. What a blessing you are.

Thanks to my friend Greg Johnson for believing in my writing potential and introducing me to Ken Gire and Marcus Brotherton. Heather Huether, thank you for your stellar design work over the years and for always being such a pleasure to work with.

For being fountains of encouragement and feedback, a heartfelt thanks to Michael, Janelle, Austin, Adriana, and Alesia Bahn, Jerry Hammack, Michelle Salvatore, Johnny and Christine Loos, Michael Hauge, Christina Boys, John Badalament, Bob Kilpatrick, Cliff Castle, Chuck Pennington, Rick Joyner, Robert Jolly, Dan Donifrio, Louis Metoyer, Jusden Aumand, Kevin and Jackie Yttrup, Jon and Shari Godley, Haji Shearer, John Sloan, Sarah Kim, Sheri Luevano, Liam Brewster, and Melanie Mercer.

To Senior Acquisitions Editor Marilyn Kretzer at Blackstone Publishing, you are an angel, a great shepherd, and the answer to many prayers. Thank you for believing in the power of my story and its purpose and rallying an army of literary activists behind it.

Thank you to developmental editor Holly Rubino for your discernment, acuity, and sage edits, which vastly improved the final manuscript. Working with you has been too fun to be legal, and I will miss our times of collaboration. Thanks to Michael Krohn and Courtney Vatis for their astute copy edits, which further improved the manuscript.

Thank you to Rick Bleiweiss, Greg Boguslawski, Josh Stanton, Anthony Goff, Josie Woodbridge, Lysa Williams, Anne Fonteneau, Stephanie Stanton, Rachel Sanders, Rebecca Malzahn, Sarah Bonamino, Nicole Sklitsis, Tatiana Radujkovic, Francie Crawford, Isabella Bedoya, Azalea Micketti, Nathan Torrance, Laura Skulman, Nikkie Carrero, Coral Robinson, and everyone at Blackstone Publishing for being the dream team and throwing your overwhelming support behind me and this book. From editing to production to sales and marketing, I could not find myself in more talented and passionate hands. Also, special thanks to Alenka Linaschke for her beautiful design work and exquisite layout from cover to cover and to Larissa Ezell for her stunning chapter illustrations which helped bring the book to life in a most magical way! Another round of cheers to senior producer Jesse Bickford and engineer Josh Bierly for their outstanding work in producing the audio version of the book. What a joy it was to work with and be directed by the two of you! Also, a hat tip to Jason Daniel, Jeff Davidson, and Benjamin Blue Abben for the post-production and mastering of the audiobook. Thank you, Sean Thomas, for your most excellent video footage.

I thank my agent, John Talbot, for getting behind this book confidently, which put me at ease. You're a diamond. Thanks to my soul brothers, Andrew Rogers and Phil Fernandez at IAG, for your love and for connecting me with John. To my brother from another mother, Remi Adeleke: thanks for going to bat for me with John. Thank you, Rick Eldridge, for believing in me and my story and introducing me to Andrew Rogers. Thanks to Linda Biagi, my foreign rights agent, for getting my story out to the world.

To my lifelong friend, Lenny Kravitz: Thanks for being an advocate from the onset. You paved the way for my gift to be used before the nations of the world and were the catalyst for all that would happen in my career. What a thrill it has been to realize our dreams together. I'm so proud of the man you've become. A shout-out also goes to Frankie Valli; New Edition; Bobby Brown; Philip Baily of Earth, Wind & Fire; Lisa Marie Presley; Lincoln Brewster; and the many recording artists I've had the privilege of working with for the past forty years. What a joy it has been making music with all of you!

My sincerest thanks go to the following individuals who hold a special place in my heart for their love and unwavering support: Patricia Bravo Weiss and George Weiss, Wil and Sandy Strong, Jay and Pamela Sekulow, Mark and Gia Kramer, Andrew and Ulara Rogers, Dyan Cannon, Jim and Marlece Watson, Edgar Cabrera Cozza, Bob and Jenifer Cashier, Bill and Robin Siren, Marty and Tracy Layton, Gary and Fay Asher, Bryan and Nancy Heath, Ken and Sandy Ristuben, Mike and Debbie Griego, Dan and Tania Chrystal, Greg and Debbie MaGill, Lindsey Crow, Keith and Heidi Hershey, Patty Gilstrap, Anthony and Rosanne Albanese, Frank DaMatto, Dennis and Anita Tinerino, Mark and Jeanne Bryers, Ted Baehr, Karen Covell, Cheryl Benedick, Jules Follet, Jim Alexander, Steve Trudell, Holt Vaughn, Mike Loomis, Laura Munson, Susie Stangland, Jon Jon Wilkins, Danny Meyer, Osama Afifi, Donn Wyatt, Joyce Donnelly, Megan Donnelly, Chris Reed, Kim Clement, Tom Turpin, Eva Hill, Curt and Kelly Harlow, Phil and Carin Bodine, Vic Comstock, Gabriel Thomas, Andrew Collins, Robby Robinson, Karen Wulff, Jackie Monaghan, Scott Jette, Roland Beigler, Ken Christie, Doug Zachary, Josh D'Aubin, Jamie Warren, Eric Cieslewicz, Blake Thompson, Ana Gonzalez, Eddie Luisi, Steve and Carol Gadd, Brian Carpenter, Dale Williams, Bryan Hardwick, and Kathy Mitchell. Special thanks to Ray and Carol Johnston, Scott Shaull, John Harris, John Volinsky, Johnny and Julie Shroyer, Jim Holst, Michael Metcalf, Peter Burton, Brandon Yip, Drew Seawright, Joy Miller, Andrew and Isabelle McCourt, and the entire staff and congregation at Bayside Church in Roseville, California.

Thanks to all book retailers, media outlets, and indie bookstores who have helped my story find its way into the world. Also, thanks to all my social media followers worldwide who have blessed me with their affirming comments and continued interest over the decades. You are more important to me than you know. Thanks to Jo Mignano and Nancy Schuster at J Migs PR for their hard work in getting me and my story before the masses.

Thanks to all the other bestselling and award-winning authors and accomplished individuals who were gracious enough to write an endorsement for my book. What an honor to have your great names associated with my work.

Eternal thanks to my amazing wife, Renée, and incredible children, Jarod and Jordan, for being the best part of my life and encouraging me through the lengthy process of writing this memoir. You are everything, and I'm beyond blessed to be the recipient of your love, laughter, patience, grace, and forgiveness. The deepest thanks go to each of my siblings. Along with our mother, Maria, you've enabled me to live the impossible dream. Armando, for a time, you filled the role our fathers should have, serving as protector over all of us. You were always ready to stand up to the tyranny of evildoers with righteous indignation. Mary, your stout-heartedness helped our family thrive in the face of great adversity. You gave up much of your youth to help raise us and made it possible for us to survive against all odds and have a better life. Ricardo, your natural talent for drafting and carpentry improved the quality of our lives in many practical ways, as did your strategic thinking skills. As the custodian of family memories, you were the first to chronicle our family history. You gave me a diary when I was ten, and I've been writing ever since. Patricia, you have always put our family first and in times of crisis have never wavered. Your valor, steadfast love, and generosity have changed the trajectory of our lives, and your incomparable sense of humor brought much-needed laughter to our often weary souls. My life would not be what it is without you. Bobby, you always did whatever was necessary to help bring the family goals to fruition. It was nothing for you to part with something if you knew someone wanted or needed it more. You remain my best friend and one of God's greatest gifts. Lisa, as the baby of the family, you brought us happiness with your perpetual bright smile and cheery disposition. You gave us something to protect and fight for, an innocence that was stolen from the rest of us. I could always count on you to laugh at my jokes and outlandish pranks, no matter how ridiculous. To all six of you: I am so proud of all you have endured, who you have become, and what you have accomplished. I am blessed to be your brother and couldn't have survived this life without your love, support, and forgiveness. It took all of you to hoist me onto the world stage, and I will forever be grateful for the indispensable role you each played.

To my very special niece, Lydia, one of the purest souls I know. Thanks for the myriad ways you have loved, supported, and encouraged me from the moment you arrived. I also want to recognize my other nieces and nephews and their children, who've been an important part of my life: Anna, Corina, Linda, Armando Jr., Anthony, Gina, Travis, Stephanie, Andrey, Angelina, Jordyn, Calvyn, Haymanot, Yonas, Cristina, Katrina, Sabrina, Esai, Mosi, Antonio, Jadon, Sienna, Priseis, Isabella, Eysiah, Leon, Roman, and all my relatives in Mexico.

There have been countless mentors who have touched my life in meaningful ways. Here are just a few: Eric Christianson, James

Worthington, Ed Williamson, Bill and Beverly Large, Joe Kantola, Kent Clinkinbeard, Donn Essig, Ralph Johnson, Al McKay, Alphonse Mouzon, Steve Gadd, Bob Robertson, and Mark Arnold. I hold you all in my heart. There have also been important organizations that had a huge impact on my life: Head Start, the Shilohs, the Jaycees, 4-H, Big Brothers Big Sisters of America, the Boys & Girls Clubs of America, the Boy Scouts of America, the Salvation Army, the Marine Corps Toys for Tots Program, Refuge Foundation, Compassion International, Canby Grove Christian Center, St. Anne's Church, Faith Baptist Church, and Wilderness Trails. Thanks to Berklee College of Music for my training as a young musician. To Belmont University: thanks for the privilege of being an adjunct professor there. Thanks to Jamie Robben and Matt Kovacs at Youtheory products, as well as Rob Chemaly and the Life Time Fitness crew for keeping me healthy! Also, thanks to the Josephine County Historical Society, the Josephine County Library System, and Rogue Community College in Grants Pass, Oregon, for providing invaluable historical research and archival material.

Thank you to the following musical instrument manufacturers for contributing to my life's work as a musician: DW drums, Sabian cymbals, Latin Percussion, Evans drumheads, Vic Firth sticks, Audix microphones, Audio 64 In-Ear monitors, PreSonus mixing consoles, Big Bang Distribution, and SKB cases. It is an honor to represent you and to perform with your incomparable equipment.

Reading Group Guide

Make your friends your teachers and mingle the pleasures of conversation with the advantages of instruction.
—Baltasar Gracián

Like food, clothing, and shelter, stories are an essential part of our
survival—our emotional survival. Stories are what makes us human,
how we preserve history, and where we find timeless wisdom. Only by
sharing our stories can we make sense of life and learn how to better
navigate it. I hope mine will prompt you to reflect and ponder deeply
about things in your life in a way that sparks hope, healing, and imagination. We tend to thrive better when we are part of a community, and
life becomes bearable when we have people to journey with. So, gather
your friends or reading group, sit down for a cup of coffee or a meal, and
discuss the issues that my story brings to the forefront. Here are some
questions I hope will provoke meaningful conversation and reflection:

1. The title of this book is *Maria's Scarf.* What does it mean in
   the context of the memoir?

2. What prompts Dan Donnelly to change his name to Zoro?

3. The theme of home is present for both Maria and Zoro
   throughout the book. How is the concept of home

experienced by them as both a physical space and an emotional one?

4, How does Maria's experience as an immigrant contribute to her appreciation of life and her approach to it? How was she able to stay positive and march forward with vision and tenacity in the face of constant adversity and disappointment?

5. What parts of Maria's character and personality made you grow to love her?

6. How do you think Zoro's story would have been different had his father never left and instead remained as a loving father and husband?

7. What part of Zoro's story do you think was the biggest character builder for him? Was it a choice he had to make? A specific act of courage? Was it an event or something that happened to him? Why do you think that moment was pivotal in forming his character?

8. Much of Zoro's understanding of himself comes from what he believes to be his lineage. How does Zoro's understanding of lineage and identity change over the course of the book?

9. What importance do you see in the role of Zoro's friendships throughout the story?

10. What did you find most inspiring about Zoro's memoir? Most relatable? Most moving? Most memorable? Most humorous? How has your thinking changed because of what you read?

11. Zoro's life has been deeply affected by his mother's stories.

How have memories in your own family passed from one generation to the next? In what ways have those stories shaped or influenced how you relate to the world and the choices you make?

12. Zoro shares that Maria was helped in many ways by the kindness of strangers and community members. What examples of this kind of altruism and care do you see in the world today? Who is the biggest encourager in your life? What specifically does this person do or say that makes you feel encouraged?

13. Do you recall a time when you were discriminated against or bullied or teased? Take a moment to remember how you felt. Have you done the same thing to other people? What practical things can you do to bring about unity and to encourage and cheer on those who are different from you? Is there someone in your life now that you can start treating better today? Do you need to apologize to someone for how you've treated them?

14. What social realities did Zoro face? How was his life different from those around the same age, and how was it similar? Consider your own economic background. How did economic opportunities, or the lack of them, shape your experience as a child?

15. Throughout his story, Zoro wrestles with trying to understand his father's indifference toward him. A major theme running through the book is the question, How do we come to terms with what we will never know about our own families?

16. Who in your life has given you good and wise counsel? Do you have someone in your life that you trust to speak the

truth to you even if it's something you don't want to hear? Would you listen to them? If you don't have these people in your life, what is your plan to find them?

17. Zoro's family faced several challenges and hardships and yet always remained close to each other. How important is family to you? Why? Maria sacrificed much to give her children the life she had always wanted. Who has sacrificed for you? Have you made sacrifices to help someone else?

18. Music is a common thread throughout Zoro's story. What is a common thread in your own life? Do you see significance or value in it?

19. Zoro faced many obstacles—growing up without a father, having very little money, feeling the weight of responsibility for his family, facing rejection. Which of these, or any others you can name, did you relate to most? What disappointments have you had to face in your own life (for example, failed dreams, rejection, not being accepted, feeling unloved)? How did you overcome them, or how are you currently working through them?

20. Zoro surrounded himself with others who shared his passion. Think of his relationship with Lenny Kravitz. Who in your life have you surrounded yourself with? Who shares a similar dream? Who is sharpening you and picking you up and cheering you on toward success? How are you helping someone pursue their dreams?

Zoro loves his fans! And he would love to Zoom with you at your next book club gathering. To find out more, visit MariasScarf.com or email Lydia@ZoroTheDrummer.com.

Subscribe and SOAR!

Subscribe to Zoro's newsletter for inspiration, special offers, and a **FREE** copy of his impactful book, *SOAR! 9 Proven Keys for Unlocking Your Limitless Potential.*

ZoroTheDrummer.com/Subscribe

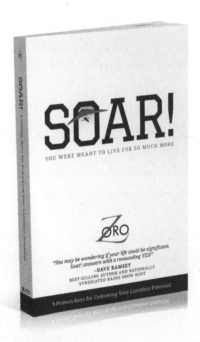

"Zoro's heart, discipline, and passion are what propelled him to greatness . . . His music and life lessons are about using your God-given talents to the maximum."

—Lenny Kravitz, Grammy Award–winning
recording artist and actor

Bring Zoro to Your Event!

Zoro is a real, relevant, and relatable voice for the generations. He speaks on a wide variety of topics, but every message touches hearts and leaves audiences with renewed hope, vision, and energy. The world-renowned drummer opens with an unforgettable drum performance, then delivers his inspirational message with his signature style, sense of humor, and contagious conviction.

Some popular messages from Zoro:

How to Unlock Your Limitless Potential and SOAR!
The Power of Words
Seven Roles of a Father
The Impact of a Mother's Love
Five Keys for Thriving through Adversity in Marriage
Navigating the Storms of Life
The Power of Passion, Patience & Perseverance

To inquire, contact Lydia@ZoroTheDrummer.com
or visit **ZoroTheDrummer.com/Speaking**

"Zoro shows there's more to the man than just his music."
—Dave Ramsey, *New York Times*
bestselling author and radio show host

"Your speech inspired all of us!"
—Judy Vredenburgh, President,
Big Brothers Big Sisters of America

Connect with Zoro

@ZoroTheDrummer

@SuperFunkyFan

@ZoroTheDrummermusic

ZoroTheDrummer.com

MariasScarf.com

ZoroTheDrummer.com/Subscribe

Photo by Rick Van Horn

Other Zoro Books & Products

Enjoy some of Zoro's other award-winning books and drum products. Available at your favorite bookstore, music store, and online retailers.

Sabian HHX Groove Hats   Sabian HHX Groove Ride

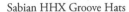

Vic Firth Zoro Signature Drumsticks (SZ)